AMERICAN COBRA
PILOT

A MARINE REMEMBERS A DOG AND PONY SHOW

CAPTAIN J.L. "BIGSBY" GROOM

Copyright © 2016 by Jeffrey Groom.

Library of Congress Control Number: 2016902241
ISBN: Hardcover 978-1-5144-5942-3
Softcover 978-1-5144-5941-6
eBook 978-1-5144-5940-9

All rights reserved. No part of this book may be reproduced or transmitted in any form or by any means, electronic or mechanical, including photocopying, recording, or by any information storage and retrieval system, without permission in writing from the copyright owner.

Any people depicted in stock imagery provided by Thinkstock are models, and such images are being used for illustrative purposes only.
Certain stock imagery © Thinkstock.

Print information available on the last page.

Rev. date: 05/18/2018

To order additional copies of this book, contact:
Xlibris
1-888-795-4274
www.Xlibris.com
Orders@Xlibris.com
728896

AMERICAN COBRA
PILOT

This book is a work of satire that blends fiction and non-fiction. Some of the characters depicted by name in the book are real public and military figures. In order to delineate the line between satire and libel or defamation, the following distinction needs to be made. If a public or military figure's statements in the book are followed with a citation that matches their name to a public statement they have made, those statements are attributable to the respective individual. All other statements by actual public and military figures in the book that do not have citations corresponding to that respective individual are the opinions of the author alone and do not reflect the opinions or views of those presenting them in the book.

This book is dedicated to Senator Kirsten Gillibrand (D-NY) for her outstanding contributions to the institution of the military while serving on the Senate Armed Services Committee. She has worked tirelessly to remove the adjudication authority from military commanders in cases of alleged sexual misconduct and has courageously fought to ensure equality, fairness, inclusion, and diversity in the armed forces. My hope is that this corpus will accelerate her noble efforts.

If humanism were right in declaring that man is born only to be happy, he would not be born to die. Since his body is doomed to die, his task on earth evidently must be of a more spiritual nature. It cannot be unrestrained enjoyment of everyday life. It cannot be the search for the best ways to obtain material goods and then cheerfully get the most of them. It has to be the fulfillment of a permanent, earnest duty so that one's life journey may become an experience of moral growth, so that one may leave life a better human being than one started it.
- Excerpt from Aleksander Solzhenitsyn's
1978 Harvard commencement speech

A Dog and Pony Show: Origins

27 March 2014.

In my stateroom aboard the USS *Bonhomme Richard*, languishing off the coast of South Korea, several dozen nautical miles from Pohang, an industrial city on the southeastern coast of the peninsula. The waters in this part of the world have a blue-green tinge. Not the green of the Atlantic or the deep mysterious blue of the Pacific, but a mix of the two. As the proximity of the ship to the shore shortens, I begin to notice a higher density of large cargo container vessels—the typical rectangular box-shaped metal containers stacked high on the deck of the long and narrow ships. I've been told Pohang is the heart of South Korea's steel production. Makes sense that they are exporting a lot of materials and products. Maybe there are Kias in those containers.

I've got some pre-exercise nerves. Operation Ssang Young 2014 is only a few days away. I hope it all goes well. I'm just stressed out and struggling to plan for the role our Cobra helicopters have been given. I dig into my Naval Tactics Techniques and Procedures or NTTP for the Cobra, Chapter 1 Mission Planning. Just to get motivated and fire me up, I re-read our squadron type's mission statement.

"The mission of the HMLA (Light Attack Helicopter Squadron) is to support the MAGTF (Marine Air Ground Task Force) commander by providing offensive air support, utility support, armed escort, and airborne supporting arms coordination day or night under all weather conditions during expeditionary, joint, or combined operations."[1]

A healthy, motivating chill runs through my body. It doesn't get better than this. We have a Marine Expeditionary Unit, or MEU, the 31st to be exact, with over 2,000 bloodthirsty Marines ready and waiting to slap our trump card on the table: the amphibious assault. Pioneered by the Marines in the 1920s and '30s and perfected during the legendary landings of World War II, the amphibious assault always surprised its enemies with its audacity and shock factor. The last actual amphibious assault was in the same neighborhood of Korea in September of 1950 at Incheon.

I read on. I scroll a few pages down and find my starting point. Problem framing adapted from the Marine Corps Warfighting Publication 1 Marine Corps Planning Process.

"Problem framing enhances understanding of the environment and the nature of the problem. It identifies what the command must accomplish, when and where it must be done, and most importantly, why—the purpose of the operation."[2]

Good stuff, I think. The next paragraph breaks down the steps to executing the planning process. I'm familiar with most of these, but it's always good to review. Determine the specified tasks, or what is explicitly given to you. Destroy (my favorite), disrupt, delay, neutralize, etc. Determine the implied tasks. Not spelled out but still necessary to complete the mission. Essential tasks, what is that we *have* to do to be successful.

Gather facts, make assumptions only if you have to in order to stay on track with planning. Determine constraints, what I *must* do. Determine restraints, what I *must not* do. Know the mission of higher headquarters, know the commander's intent. The last bullet is probably most important, as hidden in the commander's intent is the previously mentioned *why*, the purpose of the operation. After every mission statement is an "in order to." Destroy the bridge in order to delay the advance of the enemy armor column, for example.

I'm about ready to dig into my notes, but I'm so captivated by re-reading this literature that I read a few more paragraphs.

The NTTP directs that once you get the abovementioned planning accomplished, the next thing to focus on is the enemy, followed by weather and terrain. Weather will be what it will be. We can plan but rarely forecast accurately. For terrain we have Google Earth. The enemy is another story. In the real world the majority of our time would be spent wrapping our heads around their capabilities, disposition, size, morale, training proficiency and the list goes on. Since this is training, we have to play make-believe to a degree. The operation planners come up with all those things and try to make it as realistic as possible based on the hypothetical enemy.

Before heading to my stateroom, I attended a preliminary briefing for the exercise and as I scan my notes it dawns on me that I haven't taken anything down on the enemy situation. I understand we were going to be doing some shooting at one of the southern ranges in the vicinity of Pohang. But there is no mention of the enemy. Nothing, the word "enemy" isn't even written. Did I just zone out? Unsat, I think to myself. I decide to ask my neighbor one door down in the officer berthing what he has. He is just as surprised that he hasn't taken anything down about the enemy.

I get desperate and knock on several more doors. Same answer. When I return back to my stateroom, I decide to check my email to take my mind off of it for a few minutes. My last course of action will be to question our detachment Officer in Charge or OIC. I shy away from just the thought of the smashing I will receive if I dare ask what should be obvious. Luckily, as if almost from heaven above, my inbox populates and I read the words of my salvation from our executive officer or XO.

From: XO
Sent: Thursday, March 27, 2014 6:54 PM
To: 31MEUACE_BHROFFICERS; 31MEUACE_BHRSNCOS
Subject: XO meeting passdown

All,

--Select officer spaces will also be inspected by the MEU XO . . . not because he wants to. On a related note, if you have spoons or coffee mugs from the ward room please return them ASAP.

--Haircuts and uniform wear. BGen Kennedy has already pulled several Marines aside for non-reg haircuts. Make sure everyone has a fade of some kind and are properly blousing their trousers.

--Vending machines . . . jamming your cash card in harder until the reader breaks does not make the items free, it just breaks the machine. No way to fix them. Do the math.

-- Bulk laundry room. Someone is taking all the knobs off the washer and dryers. While this is an ingenious way to ensure you have a machine available, it is not the right thing to do. Stop it if it is us.

--Broken door in berthing is getting higher level attention and should be getting fixed . . . sooner or later.

This last one is the most important. Everyone needs to realize this is NOT a tactical exercise. This is a political exercise to show that even in fiscally constrained times we (Uncle Sam) can still throw together a dozen ships and do a beach assault with all of our toys. What actually makes it to the beach is mostly irrelevant. So don't get bent out of shape when we do not execute like we have been for the last three weeks. It also illustrates that nothing we are doing is so important that you need to take ANY risk (airspace, routing, altitude deconfliction, etc.). If the hair on the back of your neck is standing up slow down, take a spin in holding like the CO said and work it out.

Thanks,

XO
VMM-265 (REIN) XO
31st MEU
USS BONHOMME RICHARD

I breathe a sigh of relief as I comprehend the last paragraph. I wasn't fucked up after all. There just isn't an enemy situation. None. My life is so much easier now. I re-read the last paragraph a few times, focusing on the key words. Political not tactical, fiscal constraint, toys, irrelevant. I'm not out of the woods yet, I think.

I was told another brief would be held at 2000, about three hours away. I understand that some very high-level VIPs and officers will be giving us a speech in the ready room concerning the exercise. I was sweating bullets over getting the planning done, but now that it's political instead of tactical I just kick my boots off, jump in my rack, and listen to indie music for 20 minutes before the meeting.

At 0600 on 30 March 2014 the first amphibious assault vehicles splash off the ramp of the ship, slowly making their way through early-morning fog to the uncertain beaches of Pohang. The shift to the Pacific was on.

Joining the Marines

> The army trained men for unconditional responsibility at a time when this quality had grown rare and evasion of it was becoming more and more the order of the day. It trained men in personal courage in an age when cowardice threatened to become a raging disease and the spirit of sacrifice, the willingness to give oneself for the general welfare, was looked on almost as stupidity, and the only man regarded as intelligent was the one who best knew how to indulge and advance his own ego.[1]
> -Adolf Hitler, *Mein Kampf*, 1925

For my readers it is important that I lay the groundwork for how I ended up on a ship in the Pacific off the coast of Korea. I will keep it brief and to the point. The entire story encompasses about a year and a half of time from the spring of 2013 through the fall of 2014. In the next few pages I'll cover from the time I attended officer training in May of 2008 up until the story really begins in earnest in the spring of 2013.

Born and raised in Columbus, Ohio, I had an interest in the military from a young age. My upbringing was conservative and Catholic. Being born a millennial, I acted the part even in grade school. When I was in first grade my teacher conducted an experiment to see how long we could delay gratification. She said she would give each of us a marshmallow and said we could eat it right then or wait for a few hours and we may or may not be given more. However, if we ate the marshmallow immediately, we would not have a chance for more. She excused herself to use the restroom and I immediately raided her desk drawers and ate the entire package of marshmallows along with the rest of my classmates.

I decided to attend college first and then attended Officer Candidate School (OCS) in Quantico, Virginia, for ten weeks in the summer of 2008 to become a Marine Officer. To be an officer you have to have a college degree. I still had one quarter of school left before commissioning and officially joining the Marines. I was considering full-time job employment opportunities as well as joining the military. While in college I tested the waters of the civilian world by working two non-consecutive internships with Caterpillar in Peoria, Illinois. It was a generally good experience and I enjoyed my days there. I interviewed for a full-time position with the company after returning from OCS. The company flew prospective employees out to Peoria for the interview and put us up in a hotel. I was not offered a full-time position. But I nonetheless was still torn.

As I was thinking things through, I stumbled across a video online of a motivational speech given by war hero Jessica Lynch. She was part of a "Get Motivated" speaking tour led by Zig Ziglar.[2] She spoke eloquently and at length of how her weapon had jammed due to lack of simple maintenance. When the Iraqis came, she just curled up into a ball. Her book went on to critical acclaim. Something about her speech just lit something in me. I wanted to join.

And so against the wishes and opinion of my college buddies, parents, and close friends, I joined. Surely serving the nation is something all able-bodied young men should consider after all. I had what is known as an air contract. Meaning I was given a chance to become a pilot if I could hack it. I had a seat reserved in flight school. The rest was up to me. The only people who supported it were veterans, my grandfathers. They were making the logical assumption that the leaders of the nation were nationalists like when they served in World War II. I made the same assumption.

After a paperwork error that delayed my commissioning by six months I was a boot lieutenant on my way to The Basic School in Quantico. I would like to write about my time there, but Nate Fick already has that covered. For a good firsthand account of The Basic

School that doesn't contain exaggeration or fallacy, I would refer you to Nate's book *One Bullet Away*. After finishing up there, the wait began again.

This time the wait was in Pensacola, Florida. Waiting for flight school to start. The Marine Corps is known for only being a black-and-white organization. Not with respect to race but to how we handle our business. We either do things full throttle, max effort or not at all. So when the word came down from higher that the corps needed more pilots, the recruiting efforts overloaded the training pipeline. It was in Pensacola that I was exposed to my first true glimpse of how the military chain of command works.

The wait for pilots to begin training was approximately six months. Some guys were given what was known as "stash" jobs to keep them busy in the meantime. These jobs were very menial in nature. I tutored some navy personnel in math who had trouble dividing fractions. At any one time there were about 100 lieutenants in the pool of guys waiting to start.

Most lieutenants just had to show up in the morning around 0700 to show they were alive, then we were released for the day. Released meaning go to the beach, fish, or get drunk immediately. This could only go on for so long before higher took notice. After about two months of jackassery and drunkenness, the hammer came down.

Word spread through the office one morning that any lieutenant that had four or more months to wait for flight school to start would be sent on a billet or job in the operating forces. The rumor was while the commandant of the Marine Corps, General Conway, was visiting The Basic School, one of the senior instructors told him he was worried that his lieutenants wouldn't develop as leaders while waiting six months in Pensacola for flight school. The commandant said something to the effect of, "Lieutenants are waiting for six months on the beach for flight school to start?"

Of course the fat was in the fire then and while I do not know how things progressed from there, I experienced firsthand the result of the actions that were taken. Using the end state and inductive reasoning, I will assume the sequence of events went like this.

The commandant learns lieutenants are having fun and getting paid to drink beers in Florida. On his way back to Washington, he uses his outdated Blackberry and sends a furious text to the Deputy Commandant for Aviation who also works in Washington at the Pentagon. He follows the text up with a righteous ass-chewing for not informing him of the status of the aviation pipeline. He tells the deputy commandant to fix it now. From here the shit rolls downhill.

The deputy commandant pokes the commanding general of Training and Education Command, TECOM, in the chest and says fix the problem now and report back when done. TECOM runs all the schools that train Marines in their Military Occupational Specialty or MOS.

No prescriptions are given, just find a solution. The commanding general of TECOM pokes the commanding officer of our unit in Florida, Marine Air Training Support Group (MATSG) 21, in the chest and says fix it now and report back. The colonel of MATSG-21 says "aye, aye" and pokes his operations officer in the chest and says fix it now and report back. The operations officer frantically puts together a plan to send the lieutenants to different commands on the East and West Coast, and Okinawa, Japan. All the while the commander officer is breathing down his throat for results.

The commands selected vary from active duty squadrons to logistics battalions and even the school of infantry. The operations officer gathers the lieutenants that are eligible for stashing and hands out the jobs. I somehow draw Okinawa, Japan. The party ends and we are scattered.

When I arrive in Okinawa, along with about twelve other "Lost Pilots" as we begin calling ourselves, most of the units did not even know we were inbound. One female lieutenant, whose call sign is Progerian because she looks like she has the aging disease, is almost sent home because they don't have anything for her to do. I somehow end up in a C-130 Squadron called VMGR-152. Just like my friends they had no idea I was coming. They tell me to relax, enjoy Okinawa, and get on some flights to Guam to see strippers. I oblige and essentially do nothing productive for two months. The stint was supposed to be four months, but the pipeline unexpectedly sped up. So after two months of partying, getting jacked in the weight room, snorkeling, and seeing Okinawa, I return to the States.

No sooner was the last job handed out in Florida than the operations officer reports mission accomplished to his commanding officer. Well done, says our commanding officer. The commanding officer reports mission accomplished to the commanding general of TECOM. Very well, says the TECOM general. He then reports the good news to the deputy commandant of Marine Aviation. The deputy commandant feels a weight being lifted off his chest and promptly texts the commandant the good news on his outdated Blackberry and follows up with an in-person ass-kissing session to apologize and prove he did a good job. The commandant says "very well" and nothing more is ever heard of the miserable affair.

The above vignette goes a long way to describe how the present-day military works. The main operating principle is a technique known as CYA, or Cover Your Ass. No consideration is given to training, efficiency, relevancy, or cost.

Upon my return I finally begin flight training. This is where I met my friends Dash and GYCO, as well as the Creeper. Those names are all call signs that I am retroactively assigning because at this time in training we didn't have call signs. Flight school was fun and my days in Florida were happy. I had an amazing sponsor family and they counted me as one of their own along with dozens of herons. I joined a militia known as Chumuckla.

The Creeper unfortunately didn't make it through flight school. On his first solo flight, he flew his T-34B trainer in a split-S maneuver under Pensacola Bridge with the windscreen open to honor our forefathers that fought the Japs in the Pacific. He was immediately kicked out of training. He became a painter and a night stalker and continues to excel in those efforts to this very day.

Flight school is best described as a factory. You are a number that enters the assembly line and higher always wants to know when you exit a finished product. We were told that the true training comes when you hit "the fleet," this mythical place where actual weapons are fired and the aircraft are tactical grey instead of hazard orange like in Training Command. In the meantime just get through and get those wings as quick as possible. In due time I earned those wings of gold of naval aviation. I was to become an AH-1W Cobra attack helicopter gunship pilot and be stationed in Hawaii. Before that, however, I had to spend a few months in California to learn the basics of flying the Cobra. In May of 2012 I headed west for California.

I drove across the nation with a decent amount of my belongings in my truck. I stayed at military bases along the way for security reasons. Didn't feel safe parking in a random Motel 6 with thousands of rounds of 5.56mm and multiple weapons. The first stop was Fort Sam Houston in San Antonio. As I left my room to head out for the night, I was joined in the elevator by a man in a wheelchair who did not have legs above the knee. He was with a woman helping him. I wasn't sure if it was his wife. As I made it to the street to call a cab, there were several dozen more amputees hanging out in a gazebo-type area having a cookout. Turns out Fort Sam Houston opened an Amputee Care Center in 2005, hence the concentration of wounded warriors.

I decided to dine in the Tower of the Americas. As I sat at the bar drinking multiple dirty Hendrick's gin martinis, I felt sickened by the jovial atmosphere of the restaurant because I couldn't stop thinking of the amputees having a cookout. This is a nation at war? To make myself feel better I headed to the River Walk and bought some Blue Bell salted caramel ice cream then headed back to my room.

The second day I made it to Davis Monthan Air Force Base. And finally the third day to the coast of southern California.

GYCO and Dash both selected Cobras Hawaii. I lived with GYCO in Oceanside, California, in a fairly new condo. Despite my high expectations for California, I soon realized, being a Midwest

Catholic, I was a stranger in a strange land. The girl I took to the Marine Birthday Ball refused to do a silly picture and instead only wanted to pose and look hot. It was then I knew I was in deep shit with California girls.

Toward the end of my time in California, I had an interesting encounter with a local man that had an uncanny resemblance to a sheep. He approached me in the parking lot at the 24 Hour Fitness near my condo.

I'm leaving the gym around 0630 and the guy is trailing me. He had taken an interest in the back of my shirt. Now I rarely, if ever, wear Marines gear out in town. No stickers on the truck, no moto shirts, no assault pack in public.

However, today I am sporting one of GYCO's Purdue Marines shirt. We had a joke about making fun of each other's colleges. I gave him an Ohio State shirt and he gave me a Purdue Marines shirt. We gave each other enough knowledge about the opposite school's college experience to fake the funk in a bar environment. As Purdue fans were usually drinking their sorrow away during football season at O'Henry's in San Diego, they would readily believe my stories.

The man spots my shirt and says, "Are you in the Marines?"

He must just be a red-blooded American looking to support our military. I answer, "Yes, I am."

He immediately and heartily responds, "Well, welcome home!"

With war continuous since 2001, he is rational by assuming I have been deployed somewhere. I decide to give him the benefit of the doubt of a well-wisher who just wants to genuinely thank a service member.

"Well, I'm learning how to fly helicopters and actually haven't deployed yet."

I can tell by the look on his face he doesn't quite comprehend. I think he was expecting a typical response of "yes, I just got back." He goes internal for a second. His eyes shift up and left to engage the logical part of his brain. The entire sequence of confusion, searching, correlating, and outputting takes only one to two seconds.

He confidently replies, "Well, you still stood on a wall *with a gun*, didn't you?"

It dawns on me that this man will stop at nothing to support the troops. I realize he has no idea what he is talking about but feels the need to patronize me for voluntarily joining the military. The truth will not satisfy him. I decide to just extract myself from the awkward situation entirely before he starts bashing the unpatriotic people who don't support the war effort. I force a nervous chuckle and begin running back to my condo so my well-wisher can return to watching Fox News.

I depart California on 2 January 2013, bound for the island of Oahu and my first squadron, Helicopter Medium Light Attack Squadron 367 (HMLA-367), otherwise known as Scarface.

General Glueck and the Command General's Readiness Inspection

"Can I have one of these Meals Ready-to-Eat?"- Me
"Sir, you are gonna have to talk to staff
sergeant about that."- First Sergeant

1 April 2013

I've established myself on the island. Myself, Dash, and GYCO are renting a sick pad in Kaneohe a few miles from base.

HMLA-367 was stationed in Camp Pendleton, California, for many years before the decision was made to move the squadron to Hawaii in July of 2012.

No sooner had the squadron finished unpacking the last of our boxes from our move from California when we were notified of an upcoming Command General's Readiness Inspection (CGRI) visit. Every unit in the Marine Corps that is a battalion- or squadron-sized equivalent and higher must maintain several dozen programs that pertain to running their unit. The conduct and organization of each program is delineated in Marine Corps and Navy orders. Each program has its own checklist. The checklists items are really questions that need to be answered.

For example, under the physical security program, "Does your unit maintain a lost-and-found program?"

Or, for the command historical program, "Has your command historian been designated in writing by the commanding officer?"

Each question rates its own sheet protector sleeve along with an answer. The next sheet should be the documentation that proves your answer. So for the above question about being designated by the commanding officer, you would put your designation letter. So help you God if it is not in a specific format known as the naval letter format.

If you want to see these programs, just Google "Marine Corps CGRI Inspection Checklist" and click on the first link for "Functional Area Checklists" and read up on some of the checklists.

There are inspections for our maintenance department as well that are pretty critical. They ensure we follow the letter of the law to operate the aircraft safely.

There is not an inspection for combat readiness, however. Why concern yourself with shooting enough rockets and popping enough life-saving flares when our equal opportunity binder looks like shit? Or what good does it do us to master Hellfire employment if we can't maintain a lost-and-found or convince Marines not to kill themselves?

Each program gets a binder usually. Most of our programs were in shambles due to the high turnover rate of personnel when we moved from California. Not only that, the III Marine Expeditionary Force Commanding General, Lieutenant General Glueck, was due to visit us the same week we had our inspection. Copies of the inspectable programs were distributed. Here is a list of the programs:

- Request Mast
- Career Planning
- Marine Corps Forms Management Program
- Marine Corps Records Management
- General Administration
- Performance Evaluation System
- Privacy Act

- Promotion
- Marine Corps Printing Publications Management Program
- Personnel Administration
- Military Awards
- Defense Travel System
- Marine Corps Total Forces System
- Legal Administration
- Victim and Witness Assistance Program
- Postal Affairs
- Casualty Affairs
- Separation and Retirement
- Limited Duty
- Safety (Non-Aviation)
- Equal Opportunity Program
- Substance Abuse Program
- Voter Registration Program
- Oversight, Intel
- Information Personnel Security Program
- Physical Fitness
- Body Composition and Military Appearance
- Combat Marksmanship Program
- Marine Corps Martial Arts Program
- Unit Training Management
- Marine Combat Water Survival Training
- Distance Professional Military Education
- MCI Program
- Information Systems
- Information and Personnel Security Program
- Combat Marksmanship Program
- Color Guard
- Historical Program (I volunteered this one for my love of writing and historical context)
- Physical Security
- Anti-Terrorism
- Operation Security
- Health Services Support
- Dental
- Bachelor Housing Management

- Environmental Program Management
- Aviation Logistics Information Management
- Aircrew Training
- Aviation Safety
- NATOPS (military aircraft owners' manual) Review
- Aviation Operations Administration
- CBRN Defense
- Exceptional Family Member Program
- Sexual Assault Prevention and Response Program (quite a few people fought to do this one since doing well would be noticed by Senator Gillibrand)
- Single Marine Program
- Marine Corps Unit Personal and Family Readiness Program
- Unit Readiness
- Combat and Operational Stress Control Program
- Government Travel Charge Card Program
- Suicide Prevention Program
- Marine Corps Sponsorship Program

After the binders were either found or created from scratch by their assigned responsible person we dove into the orders to ensure the programs were up to speed. The day of the inspection came quickly.

The CGRI in brief began with an extremely awkward meeting. The inspectors were on one side of the room, an eclectic crowd indeed. There were several overweight, heinous civilians, many older officer types that didn't make rank. And of course there were many senior enlisted. They were mostly squared away and jovial, nothing left to prove. Our XO call sign Squib began by explaining that our unit was new to the island and the vast majority of functional area managers had no historical documentation.

Anyways, as each functional area came up, the inspector stood up and their counterpart in our squadron did an awkward half raise out of their chair. During this time it came to light that S-6 or communications was not going to be inspected. A little aside here, there is this program called JMPS for Joint Mission Planning Software. It is basically a complex flight-planning tool that pilots use to prepare for missions. S-6 is responsible for JMPS.

So to summarize, we are an aviation unit, our goal is to provide combat-ready aviation forces to the Marine Air Ground Task Force. Rather than inspect a program like JMPS that gives an idea for how well we are ready to fight a war, the inspectors wanted to make sure we knew how to run drug tests, tape fat bodies, and maintain grounds and crypts. We dodged a bullet. If they inspected how well our flight-planning computers worked, we would be in trouble. Our suicide prevention binder got an exemplary though.

Later that week we had a midpoint brief to see how things were going. It started off with the senior inspector addressing us as HMLA-167, which isn't even our unit. A fat man in a little coat named Mr. Hay was very excited about our Family Readiness Officer program. From there each inspector stood up and told us how we were progressing. We ended up doing fairly well due to the fact that our XO was adamant about getting our binders looking good.

The III MEF commander Lieutenant General Glueck eventually made the trek to Hawaii and flew with our squadron a few times. He gave the squadron a speech afterward before our CO gave the weekend liberty brief. He invigorated our sense of patriotism by talking about how much American blood had been spilled in the Pacific Theater. He talked about this country called Nepal and how it lies along a major fault line. Every hundred years or so there is a large earthquake along this fault line. Directly along this fault line is the capital city of Kathmandu. This city is home to approximately 2 to 3 million people. If and when this earthquake happens, they estimate there will be 200,000 to 300,000 deaths and upward of one million displaced. And he then said, and I remember these words exactly, "For the first time in history we have a plan in place to execute disaster relief operations in Kathmandu."

I think he chose to let us in on this plan because he mentioned earlier in his speech that some people think attack helicopters are irrelevant on modern battlefields. Letting us in on the Kathmandu plan gives us hope we can use our sensors to locate survivors. I took a sigh of relief when I realized I would be flying to support disaster victims in a foreign country.

Immediately following his brief, we had an all-officers meeting or AOM in our ready room. I sat next to my buddy GYCO. After the meeting GYCO left his notebook behind. I assumed he was taking notes from the meeting but upon closer examination I realize all his writing was channeled into creating a poem. It went like this:

Oh, good God, what would be the point if I flew
to the destroyed city of Kathmandu
I thought my Cobra was designed to kill
Instead I'm supposed to spread goodwill?
I say we put it up for a vote
And see if this is how the average American wants to offer their bank note
Tell the plan to any simple American bloke
And he says, "This has got to be a joke"
I thought the focus was on warfare and killing
Now the taxpayer has found a new billing
How can our government pay for another country's infrastructure?
We can't even balance our own budget
Starting to feel like a mercenary at this juncture
I say let the Nepalese built their own country back and fudge it.

I considered reporting him for being insubordinate, but since he's my friend, I just returned his notebook without saying anything.

A few days later I was busy with my ground job in the squadron pecking away a flight schedule. I was not very good at it and got yelled at a lot. In addition to the flight events, I also was responsible for entering any applicable ground events like meetings or a physical fitness test. Usually these things are scheduled a good week or two in advance, but quite often we have to fit meetings in the schedule at the last second.

Our XO walked in operations and requested a training session be added to the schedule. Our operations officer, my boss, was sitting at his desk a few feet behind me. As mentioned earlier the call sign of our XO is Squib. The operations officer's call sign is Bleeder.

"Bleeder, we need to put some classes on the schedule for duty standers to carry weapons."

The squadron duty officer or SDO in the squadron is a post that is stood 24 hours a day. They essentially keep an eye on the premises after working hours and on weekends field the inevitable calls concerning Marines getting in fights or drinking and driving. Sometimes they are armed with the M9 service pistol. Per the Marine commandant's guidance in a propaganda campaign known as "The Awakening," all duty standers will be armed.

One of our pilot training officers, call sign SWUD, interjected with a logical question, "Isn't qualifying with the pistol on the range good enough? You have to prove you know how to load, unload, and fire the weapon or you aren't even allowed to carry it on duty. No one can check the pistol out if they haven't qualified."

Squib pressed the issue.

"It doesn't have to be a long class. I'm thinking like a school circle of here is how to transfer the weapon from duty stander to duty stander."

He then paused and continued, "Because we aren't going to be the squadron who writes an accident report when a lieutenant shoots himself in the foot."

Bleeder chuckled briefly and added, "Well, as long as they had the training before they shoot themselves, our asses are covered."

Bleeder ordered me to find a time, place, and instructor for the desired training.

Our ground training Marines ensured a roster was passed around the training and all attendees signed. Once we had the rosters, our asses were covered and we could produce it if something ever happened.

I learned a lesson that day. As a leader, it is acceptable for your men to fail as long as the appropriate boxes are checked, the requisite training is accomplished, and you have a paper record of it.

That paper record is what is actually important. It can be produced immediately upon an incident of any kind then forwarded to higher commands when they demand to know how such and such happened.

A good example is motorcycle riding. Everyone who wants to ride has to either complete a basic rider course or an advanced rider course. They even have motorcycle reps in the units that have tabs on all the riders. When someone is involved in an accident the first question the command asks is not "Is he okay?" The first question asked is, "Was the rider course complete?" If the answer is yes, the command can breathe a sigh of relief, no repercussions will be brought upon them. If no then that Marine will be destroyed and the command will have its ass chewed.

Some might even say we live not in the Marine Corps but the metrics corps. We love to quantify the levels of our readiness and substantiate our positions with data of all kinds.

The FROlough

There are two basic military functions. Waging war and preparing for war. Any military activities that do not contribute to the conduct of the present war are justifiable only if they contribute to preparedness for a possible one. Clearly, we cannot afford to separate conduct and preparation. They must be intimately related because failure in preparation leads to disaster on the battlefield.

- Marine Corps Doctrinal Publication 1: Warfighting

1 October 2013.

Our squadron had spent most of the summer in California training in Twentynine Palms. Things were settling back down into a predictable rhythm. That is until the government ran out of money again.

The threat of a government shutdown had been looming over the nation's head for several weeks, if not months. The Republican Congress that came to power in 2010 was serious about the deficit. Quantitative easing wasn't working, even with a 400 percent increase in Fed bond purchases. Congress had tried to shut the government down a few years back in the summer of 2011, but that was just a bluff. This time they meant business.

Almost everyone, including myself, thought it was another chest-thumping session for all constituents to see. The usual tactics were heard from both sides. People would become cannibals and eat their aborted children's fetuses if we cut off food stamps, and the North Koreans would use wooden boats with muskets and lay siege, capture, and rape and pillage San Francisco if we cut defense one penny under 600 billion a year. But this time the shutdown happened.

That particular day I was on the flight schedule as a co-pilot. Maybe it was because we tend to associate the unfamiliar with the impossible, no one was prepared and no prior orders had been issued in the event the shutdown occurred. When word spread that it shut down, a few men were recalled by their wives on base to calm them down about the prices at the commissary and base housing costs.

Would it go up? Is my dependent card still valid? Do we have to pay rent now? Will the temperature in our home rise above 60 degrees without air-conditioning? Will I have to drive more than a mile for my basic necessities? Some of us panicked. Would the United States be instantly invaded by the wolves just lurking at our doors? I tried to calm some guys down, "Be logical. Things would work themselves out," I reasoned.

I happened to be in the ready room of our squadron preparing for my flight when the bomb dropped. They actually shut the government down. One of the other guys in the ready room was Trashbag, a Huey pilot. Within five minutes of the shutdown, his wife called him. I was talking to him about mission planning when he had to take the call.

"Hey, honey. Everything okay? I heard they just shut the government down."

He gently nodded as his wife spoke on the other side of the line. After listening for about a minute, he responded.

"No, honey, they are going to keep the commissary open, I think. I still get paid though. It will be okay. It's October. It isn't as hot as it used to be. The highs are only around 70 degrees. If they cut off air-conditioning, I think we could turn on the fans and it would be okay. The dog may have to get his own air-conditioned room though."

He said his goodbyes and we continued planning because we still assumed we will be flying.

The first orders came logically from higher at the Marine Aircraft Group 24 headquarters across the street from our hangar. All flights except those for maintenance to fix broken aircraft were cancelled until further notice. I'm not sure where they got that order, surely someone way up at the wing level and maybe even headquarters Marine Corps had determined that was our way of fighting back.

"You shut us down, elected leaders, okay, well, we just won't fly," was our response.

We pouted and rightfully so.

I loitered around the ready room for a few minutes just to soak up emotions and gauge people's reactions as I detailed above. About half an hour later, I saw our family readiness officer or FRO walking down the hall. The FRO is a position in the military that, up until the wars in Afghanistan and Iraq, was filled by an officer. Their job is to keep all the families plugged into the operational and training plans for the unit. They make sure spouses and dependents are made aware ahead of time for deployments and times when their loved ones will be away.

They also plan family-type events like cookouts and meet-and-greets and help push troubled marriages in the right direction for counseling. Once the deployment tempo began to heat up during the height of the Iraq war and guys were gone every six months, they decided to place a civilian in the FRO position. But with the wind down of those wars, the opposite didn't happen. They kept the position filled by civilians drawing an extra paycheck from the government.

Our FRO is married to a retired Navy chief. She was carrying a symmetrical square box with the top open to the air. A few knickknacks were protruding from the top. This could only be one thing: a bona fide FROlough.

The FROlough is a furlough but applied to the FRO. The fun and games officer, jokingly known as the FAGO, later told me a MARADMIN was released ordering all the FROs to be released. A MARADMIN is an administrative document released by higher Marine Corps to provide guidance on a particular subject. Who rates a medal for a specific deployment, what ranks are eligible for early out, and the like. Obviously this MARADMIN was spring loaded for the shutdown that canned all the FROs.

My eyes met hers and she was hurt. I can tell. The pathos of her predicament just shredded into my heart and I had to duck back into our ready room. I held back some tears but barely. I thought of all the stuff she has done for me as a single Marine officer aviator with no dependents. She was in the process of updating our unit's equivalent of a Facebook page so spouses and parents could get updated information about family functions, deployments, and the like. I never saw a completed page while she worked for our squadron, but I'm sure she was getting close. I could usually snag her parking spot like clockwork when she left at 1500 every day.

Now what, are they gonna give her spot away or make it general parking? What will she do when her paychecks stop and her health insurance is no longer covered by Uncle Sam? The FAGO and I chatted for a bit and I learned she was earning $60,000 dollars a year, not to mention healthcare and housing allowances.

That Friday I got a reprieve from my grief. I overheard a conversation between the recently fired FRO and one of our majors during a field day picnic on base, that there was going to be some relief for the civilians working in the military. The picnic had been planned well before the shutdown and was already paid for. Inwardly I praise the DoD for seeing what really matters. Personally I would have gladly given up some 2.75-inch rockets or flying time to see her back. Sure,

I had not shot any ordnance since July, but I really wanted to see that Facebook page get going so my mom could "like" it.

Sure enough, as I scroll through online news the next day, I found out what the secretary of defense did. He used the Pay Our Military Act to order over 90 percent of DoD's 350,000 civilian employees back to work. A little background: the Pay Our Military Act was passed by Congress shortly before the shutdown to ensure the military was paid regardless of the government shutdown. The reason drew on the context of the close-call shutdown in 2011.

With this act in hand, ole Chucky Hagel's attorneys interpreted the law to mean the Pentagon could recall workers to eliminate furloughs for "employees whose responsibilities contribute to the morale, well-being, capabilities and readiness of service members."

Chucky claimed he had told Pentagon officials to "identify all employees whose activities fall under these categories." Robert Hale, the Pentagon's budget chief, added, "We've seriously harmed civilian morale; this (recall) will be a start back."[1]

Note the order of how Chucky lists responsibilities. First is morale and well-being, *followed* by capabilities and readiness. If it was the other way around, the FRO would have been at a soup kitchen within a week. Sure enough, Monday morning the FRO was back. Chucky was right.

What good are Marines if they aren't happy? What good are we if we aren't coming home to a happy family and an air-conditioned dependent sow creature ready to incubate more kids? If I recall from Marine Officer Candidate School, the purpose of military leadership is troop welfare, *then* mission accomplishment.

Chucky's objectives are in line with this and to back up his decision, I decided to research the programs available to our Marines today. I take the course of describing it to a potential Marine recruit or officer candidate. I didn't have to dig hard for this information.

If you prospective devil dogs out there have any doubt at all about whether the corps cares about you and your families' welfare, I promise they will be dispelled after reading this chapter. So many of these programs, nonprofits, and sub-DoD organizations have sprung up in the past couple years that it really does make the head spin. My goal here is to lay it out Barney-style.

I'm going to cover all the major programs, what makes them different, the same, and when you should seek out each one. If you have a large wife who doesn't feel the need to work or contribute in any appreciable way to society, please ensure she reads this too. She needs that warm and fuzzy before her hubby becomes a Marine.

Broadly speaking, there are three categories of programs available to the average Marine. There are the large DoD-sponsored ones like Military One Source and DSTRESS, then smaller ones run by the corps under MCCS, and finally nonprofits like FOCUS. I'll explain all these crazy acronyms shortly.

I'll start the discussion off with one of the big, overarching programs. Military One Source. Military One Source, hence referred to as MONS to avoid confusion with MOS, should really say what it doesn't do rather than what it does. I'll try my best to break it down. MONS is for active and reserve military. MONS has informational coverage in these three big areas: family, personal, and financial. Its smaller function deals with deployment.

On the family side, they understand what it means to have a loved one in the service. They offer employment information and training for spouses, dealing with separation, locating child care, finding local schools, parenting advice, moving, commissary and exchanges, dealing with troubled teens, and communication advice. On the personal side, it gets even better.

MONS can advise you on coping with stress, marital communications, dealing with family separations, and problem solving. You might ask what type of counseling might be available for problem solving. Well, if your wife has ever asked you questions like, "Honey, how do I unlock the car?" or "What's the best way to stack my boxes of heels in the closet?" or even the most mundane like "How do I get the straw in our daughter's Capri Sun?" MONS can help. I'm sure you've been annoyed by types of questions like that. That's what MONS is for. Just refer your wife to them and request help with problem solving all on ole Uncle Sam's dime. Now for communicating between our aircraft when we need to go fly, that's another story. Our radios are constantly plagued with problems.

Back to the program. On the financial side they come with a mighty punch too. They can help you manage your budget, save for that car, and provide you with financial calculators for adding utility bills and the like, building an emergency fund, saving for retirement, and many, many more. For the deployment side of things, they advertise helping families reunite, deal with separation, combat stress, grief, and loss of not having that special Marine around. What I just gave you is just scratching the surface. Don't take my word for it. Go visit the website yourself: *www.MilitaryOneSource.com*. MONS is DoD funded so when you hear this talk on the news of people wanting to cut our budget in the DoD, just think long and hard about losing MONS.

You thought I was done, didn't you? I saved the best part of MONS for last. They have counselors on call 24/7. You can call them at 1-800-■■■■■■■. The number is so important that it is on every page of the six-part foldout brochure you can pick up your units. You can get six private counseling sessions and they can tailor the counseling to individuals, couples, families, and children. Every counselor is licensed and knowledgeable of military life. The website has numbers for Spanish speakers as well.

The brochure I just mentioned is very well laid out. In addition to summarizing everything I just spoke about, it has pictures of people just like you who have been helped or could be helped. The front cover has the token single mother with her daughter. The inside front fold has some good shots of what appears to be a counselor, mid-twenties hot blonde, helping a middle-aged woman. The bottom of the same fold has a couple sitting across from one another with satisfied smiles on their faces. Between them is a white man in a suit who, from the looks of it, has helped them with some of their issues.

The top of the page has a plump black woman just cheesin' for no real reason. The middle page has ghosted images of random people smiling. The last page of the inside has a few Latino service members. One is a female Marine wearing her camouflage uniform and another is a middle-aged male with a towel around his neck. Behind them are some shrubs or bushes of some kind. I thought it rather offensive to put the Latinos near some landscaping since most of their relatives work in that field. The back side of the brochure has similar pictures, with the most notable being a white guy one-percenter closing the deal with a handshake with a smiling couple.

A similar project is the Military and Family Life Counselors or MFLC. A DoD-funded program, their brochure is rather bland but it gets to the point. Starting with the premise that military families face unique challenges, they infer that deployments cause stress and the family can take a toll from their Marine or sailor being away. MFLC counselors can provide you with non-medical, cost-free counseling and psycho education to help military service members deal with deployments. They can even provide these services off military installations and administer them to individuals, groups, families, and couples. The counselors are at the minimum master's or doctorate level, licensed, and likely failed life coaches that stumbled into the explosion of programs in the recent years.

Per the MFLC brochure, on the military lifestyle side they deal in deployment stress, coping skills, homesickness, relocation adjustment, re-integration, separation, building resiliency, sadness, grief, and loss. On the life skills front, they serve counseling for anger management, communication, relationship issues, conflict resolution, parenting, and decision-making skills. MFLC was begun in 2004 by MHN Government Services Inc. as a pilot program then released fully in 2007 after winning a contract.

Next.

Navy and Marine Corps Marine Relief Society. Not much here. This one has actually existed much longer than any other program. They stay pretty low key and the only service they provide that I know of is an emergency loan for families that can be paid back without interest. Every year they have a loan drive and have a billboard with a bar graph near the base gates to show their progress.

The FOCUS project is based in Los Angeles at the UCLA Semel Institute. From their website: "The Jane and Terry Semel Institute for Neuroscience and Human Behavior is an interdisciplinary research and education institute devoted to the understanding of complex human behavior, including the genetic, biological, behavioral and sociocultural underpinnings of normal behavior, and the causes and consequences of neuropsychiatric disorders. In addition to conducting fundamental research, the institute faculty seeks to develop effective strategies for prevention and treatment of neurological, psychiatric and behavioral disorder, including improvement in access to mental health services and the shaping of national health policy."

The stress of the operational deployment tempo has resulted in the Bureau of Medicine and Surgery of the Department of the Navy to create a new initiative. The core mission of FOCUS is for Marine family resiliency. By utilizing group and individual family settings, participants are given the skills to cope with their emotions, solve problems, set goals, and communicate. Some of the buzzwords associated with FOCUS are assist, provide, help, and enhance. Parent, child, and family sessions are available. FOCUS has on office on Kaneohe for your convenience.

Marine Corps Bases Hawaii also has an Equal Employment Opportunity Program or EEOC. This program was planted by the Feds as an offshoot of the U.S. Equal Employment Opportunity Commission. Title VII of the Civil Rights Act of 1964 prohibits employment discrimination based on race, color, religion, sex, and national origin. With respect to age, a law was passed in 1967 to protect applicants over the age of 40 from discrimination. For the disabled the Rehabilitation Act of 1973, Americans with Disabilities Act of 1990, and Americans with Disabilities Amendment Act of 2008 protect individuals on the basis of mental of physical disability. Defined, disability discrimination is not making an honest attempt to accommodate the known physical or mental limitation of the requesting individual.

The Genetic Information Nondiscrimination Act of 2008 protects applicants and employees from discrimination based on genetic information. The Hawaii office can also look into sexual harassment, which is unwelcome sexual advances, requests for sexual favors, and other verbal or physical conduct of sexual nature. I think they may be a little off here. Physical crosses the line into sexual assault. The front of the pamphlet has a good mix of blacks, Asians, whites, male, and female.

Three counselors work on the base, all in different buildings so they can ostensibly spread their workload around. Now the insiders won't tell you this, but the real reason they are in different locations is in case of a massive terrorist attack. If one of them gets taken out, we'll still have two equal opportunity officers functioning. Could you imagine if we lost all three of them in an attack? The base commander would likely surrender.

They are all female as well. They will be totally neutral in all alleged cases of sexual harassment or assault. Did you know that each squadron and battalion also rates an Equal Opportunity (EO) rep? You heard it right. In addition to these paid counselors the Marine Corps has you covered with no-shit Marines acting as EO reps. One might ask why do we need EO reps when in order to call yourself a Marine your character has to be vetted by the hardest indoctrination course of any service, enlisted or officer?

The answer is that the Marine Corps takes its warfighting principles of 3 on 1 to the EO realm too. We only fight when we outnumber our enemies 3 to 1. And as noted above, we have three levels of coverage for the fight against discrimination in the workplace. That average Marine, then his unit's EO rep, and then the Equal Opportunity Program on base. Semper Fi!

The EO push isn't from the Marine Corps only. It's being initiated at the highest levels and with lethal effects. Jessica L. Wright, the acting undersecretary of defense for personnel and readiness, spoke at an event less than 30 days after the shutdown titled "Mission Critical: Transatlantic Security and Diversity."

She stated that the DoD must be committed to diversity and inclusion, which are integral to mission success. Specifically, "It is a security imperative for military leaders to proactively advance diversity and inclusion (D&I) best practices" because of the "rapid demographic change [and] advances in gender and LGBT equity and a new generation of veterans in NATO countries."[2]

Nothing like trickle-down D&I practices. Errhhh!

Now I'll move into the programs maintained by Marine Corps Community Services or MCCS. There are four categories: family readiness, family care, personal and professional development, and behavioral health. I'll start with behavioral health programs, the largest of which is the Family Advocacy Program or FAP. They decided, correctly in my opinion, to merge FAP with the Victim Advocate Program. So think of Military One Source like DoD wide, but FAP is just with the Marine Corps. An Air Force dependent can get MONS care but not MCCS. Trackin'?

Great care was taken to ensure there wasn't any duplication of effort, confusion, or wasted taxpayer money. The stated goal of FAP is to provide a variety of programs and services to military members and their families to "enhance life skills." The big three areas they hit are marriage disputes, argument resolution, and parenting. Since the family is the focus of this group, the victim advocacy part was attached as well. Whereas MONS had counselors on call any time of day, FAP is more classroom focused. The Cage the Rage class is put on every Tuesday. It helps its students manage stress and keep it at an acceptable level before it becomes anger. Each series is six parts. Make sure you make it to that first one so you can follow along in the class.

Building healthy relationships is an eight-parter that draws on all the wickets that build the foundation for healthy relationships: assertiveness, self-awareness, communication, and listening. The last class FAP dishes up is Marriage Skills Workshop. This one is only a one-day deal and held the third Wednesday of each month. It is for the recently married or planning to get married. Just the other day I saw a flyer for a related event, the Relationship Enhancement

Retreat for Couples. It was put on by MCCS as well, but was catered more for those not yet married.

Be careful about sending the married lance corporals here though. Just like when you run a casualty evacuation or CASEVAC, you have to triage and decide who has a reasonable certainty of making it and who isn't. Same thing goes for the lance corporals who fell in love too early. Use common sense. If your lance is 19, drives a 2014 Dodge Ram that he bought new on credit for $50,000, has two kids with two different women, and just fell in love and got married, that is equivalent to a routine casualty. He ain't gonna make it. Save the class for the sergeants who have demonstrated common sense but maybe are struggling with an entitled wife who hasn't left their couch in a few days and routinely raids the commissary for bean dip, caramel apples, and Starbucks while taking the kids to Gamestop.

Lastly the FAP has uniform victim advocates or UVAs. Now each squadron or battalion's Table of Organization or T/O is to have two Sexual Assault Prevention Response (SAPR) officers in their ranks. They attend a school to get trained and are responsible for reporting any accusations of sexual assault. But like my old XO Squib said, "You can never have too many SAPR officers." What he really meant to say was that you can never have too many UVAs. Our squadron had four. Two enlisted and two officers.

The UVA is one of those positions that functions as that good no-kidding middle man or woman between the victim and medical, legal, emotional, and support networks. Now there is only one Sexual Assault Prevention Coordinator or SARC. They serve as the overseer of the UVAs in the unit and report to the next highest commander in the chain of command. Now I can't confirm this, but I was told by a SARC that will remain anonymous that each SARC is given the personal cell phone of Senator Gillibrand. The senator likes to hear about the assaults before the commanding officers. That way she can destroy the careers and character of Marines before the justice system can discover the truth.

The ground side of things is a little different than the wing. From a friend of mine in 2nd Battalion, 3rd Marines, each *company* in the battalion is supposed to have a UVA. Sexual assault in an all-male, overtly heterosexual organization is low, on the order of only one in the past several years. That doesn't mean it can't happen, just that for some odd reason straight males tend to not sexually assault other males. Weird, right?

Keeping straight males together is an old and outdated way to run the military and by having a UVA per company, they are just getting ready for the hundreds of sexual assault cases that will occur once females are forcefully integrated into the infantry ranks.

This elaborate framework of coverage and responsibility might seem confusing, but they headed the problem off by publishing an SAPR newsletter that is published three times a year or tri-annually. I accidentally found the first shipment of the letters when I was frantically searching the squadron for some 20 millimeter chain gun rounds to shoot in my Cobra. After I found the newsletters instead of lethal ordnance, I hung them up all over the bulletin boards. As of the publishing of this corpus, the SAPR newsletter is published on a monthly basis. Semper!

The Community Counseling Program or CCP has licensed professionals to help families, couples, or individuals deal with emotional health, the stress of military life, and relationship problems. Note the subtle difference here. The FAP is aimed at helping married couples or those about to be married. The CCP focuses more on overall relationships.

Maybe your dog hates you for neglecting him, or your daughter calls every other man Dad except you because you are never around. CCP can help with that relationship trouble that is more general in nature. Be careful not to mention that you have problems with yourself though. Any hint of going internal or hinting of depression will initiate an immediate and forced referral to suicide counselors, which is a rather unpleasant experience. Believe me, I know.

Rounding out the behavioral programs of MCCS, we have New Parent Support Program (NPSP) and the Substance Abuse Counseling Center (SACC). These should go without explaining. I would like to note how considerate the Marine Corps is today. You have to pass a drug test to get in. In fact they breathalize you when you go to the Military Entrance Processing Station or MEPS to get your physical.

Apparently some guys signed on the dotted line drunk so they had to make sure you are of "sound mind and body" when you sign. However, if you slip and smoke a doob or rave a little too hard and eat some Ecstasy, they will help you with your abuse problems. On Hawaii all of these counselors and appointments can be made at Counseling, Advocacy, Awareness, Relationship, Enhancement or CAARE Center, Building 216. Look up the local CAARE equivalent on your base.

The family care division of MCCS is what it sounds like—all about the family. The first sub-unit of the family care division is the Child Youth and Teen Program or CYTP, which provides full- or part-time day care as well as education for children ranging from six weeks to 12 years. Next, there are several Child Development Centers throughout the Hawaii area that provide child care from ages 6 weeks to 5 years. Keep this one in mind if the spouse finds a job and then the kid needs day care. Speaking of getting that job, MCCS has the Family Member Employment Assistance Program or FMEAP. FMEAP is a referral service for the family member to get in touch with employers as well as an educational service to attain skills and write resumes. See your local Family Readiness Officer or Military Family Life Counselor for more information.

The Exceptional Family Member Program assists Marine families who have a member with special needs. Once the member is entered into DEERS, special consideration can be given for moving, relocating, and deploying. Most of the programs I'm listing are useful, but I personally think the exceptional family member program is too much, but that's just my opinion.

The last big item in family care is the School Liaison Program or SLP. This group helps families in the military compare which type of schooling is best for their kids. Should we put them in Hawaii local schools, on base schools, or maybe even home school them?

The second tier of the MCCS hierarchy is the Marine Corps Family Team Building or MCFTB. Their biggest program is LINKS, or Lifestyle Insights Networking Knowledge and Skills teams. These teams cater to helping the family understand what it means to now be part of the biggest, baddest, most expensive military in the world. LINKS caters to spouses, the individual Marine, and the Marine's children. Moving from the civilian world can be tricky. A lot of spouses and family members might not be used to free housing, healthcare, subsidized commissaries, schools two blocks away, or even air-conditioning for our Appalachian Marines.

LINKS will ease this transition and make them dependent and entitled faster than you can say Semper Fi. For the actual Marine, LINKS helps them allot their basic pay, setting up moves, and transitioning out of the military. LINKS children fills the parenting gap by helping them prepare for their parent's deployment.

LifeSkills is solidly in the realm of Marine spouses. As mentioned above, once they acclimate to living on base and having a house and garage on Uncle Sam, they will be itching to be productive members of society. LifeSkills provides Marine Corps spouses the opportunity to further their personal and professional growth.

They put on several workshops that focus on communication, goal setting, personal empowerment, and business management and leadership. The workshops focus on understanding your personality type and others, improving communications, dealing with difficult people, and improving your team-building skills.

Rounding out the MCFTB is the Family Readiness Program or FRP. They are the in-house production school for our FROs. Each battalion and squadron unit rates an FRO. I mentioned above what the FRO's job description entails.

The Marine Corps is a competitive organization. And like any competitive entity, wants to be first. It should come as no surprise that we have a few programs of our own. The first is DSTRESS. It was developed by the corps to "provide professional, anonymous counseling for Marines, attached sailors and families when it's needed most."

DSTRESS revolves around the hotline, and is exclusively for Marines and attached sailors. The topics are broad and include relationships, family, work, personal, and financial. The counselors are anonymous and DSTRESS is unique in that it has veteran Marines acting in the role of counselor.

Another more recent program is the Operational Stress Control and Readiness or OSCAR. The basics of this gem are summarized in a no-shit MARADMIN 597/11. The goal of OSCAR is to create teams of Marines, chaplains, and medical personnel within each unit to identify the signs and symptoms of combat stress as early as possible. All battalion level or equivalent commands had to have a team in place by 31 January 2012.

The team has to consist at a minimum of 5 percent of the unit's personnel or 20 personnel, whichever is greater. The basic certification training for the team is six hours while the advanced certification lasts four days! The team members all have their own billets within the team. The "Oscar mentors" are the trained unit Marine leaders; the "extenders" are the unit medical and religious ministry personnel; and "mental health professionals" is pretty much what it sounds like. Ideally the "Oscar mentors" should be men of sound character and leadership qualities who have prior combat experience. Check out the MARADMIN for more details; there are a lot.

Now I've made it sound like these programs exist off in cyberspace or in some obscure hole in a non- profit office in Washington. Nothing could be further from the truth. Pamphlets for almost all these programs can be found in every nook and cranny of every Marine base. First check out the boards outside the FRO's office if you are in a battalion or squadron. Next go to the local chapel or medical. They always have large stacks of the stuff. The squadron I was in did a good job of putting material above the urinals in every head and on the majority of corkboards. No matter which way I turned, there was a picture of our squadron's UVAs on the walls.

Even when I took a shit it was on the inside of the stall door, staring me in the face, subliminally warning me to be careful of how I used the weapon dangling between my legs.

During most safety stand-downs and pre-deployment briefs, they would have a base representative come by and give a talk about their respective program. If you look carefully, they hang the stuff as a poster or banner from fence parking lots. Lastly, for the junior guys, don't be afraid to go talk to Staff Sornt about it. I will caveat that with be careful about talking to Gunnery Sornt and God forbid you talk to First Sornt or Sornt Major. Just use common sense.

Sometimes we suffer wounds we never recover from and our FRO was no different. Less than a year later, on 24 September 2014 our commanding officer whose call sign is Utah sent a squadron email alerting us to her resignation. I personally think she suffered from a broken heart. She followed up shortly after with a farewell and an appropriate "Hooyah." Maybe for our corpsman, since Marines say "Oorah," I'm not sure. This wasn't the end of her influence though. Turns out our commanding officer and the FRO had a falling out that led to her resignation. The CO had the audacity to demand she function in a certain way in the squadron. He obviously didn't understand the power that she righteously held.

Before the door hit her in the ass, she was inadvertently included in the email chain for the letter of instruction for a party our squadron was having in October 2014 in El Centro, California, during a training evolution. These parties take the form of a mock Kangaroo court. Our community calls them Cobra courts or K Court for short. The commanding officer hears various charges brought forth to shame other pilots. Videos are played, beer and food are thrown, fights break out, people bleed, and insane amounts of alcohol are consumed.

It's the new guys battling to make fun of the senior guys and receive call signs. Our squadron had one in our house in Kaneohe, Hawaii, and I remember standing at attention in front of our commanding officer. He told me how awesome a K court we had and I proceeded to projectile vomit onto the floor. It was a hell of a good time and one of the last truly politically incorrect outlets for the officers. Dash and GYCO finished the party by throwing the leftover pizza into the running ceiling fans and slinging the stuff all over our house. I had to mop the tile floors three times to get the film off.

The letter of instruction the FRO was included in contained the rules of the court and some insensitive language and was found to belittle the younger pilots in the squadron as well as useless majors. Every court has a theme for costumes. For the court we had in Kaneohe the theme was '80s movies. The young guys were drifters from *Mad Max* and so had leather and chains. With this letter of instruction in her hand, she took it to the inspector general, a civilian lawyer who investigates wrongdoing in the military.

An investigation followed the FRO's complaint and on 1 December 2014, Brigadier General Rudder, the head of 1st Marine Aircraft Wing, relieved Utah, our commanding officer. Utah had served 19 years to country and corps. Turns out it was for hazing. Good thing they reinstated her when they did; if not we would have fun at work. All fun was promptly secured until further notice.

Why It Pays to Be a Cobra Pilot

Late October 2013

After my first year in the squadron, I took a look at my aviation logbook. It's a hard copy of your flight hours. The first entry is my first flight in the T-6B trainer during flight school. It contains what day you flew, what aircraft, what events you did, hours of visual or instrument flying, approaches, and crew. At the bottom of each page there is a spot for cumulative monthly hours, total hours, as well as hours for the year. One of the guiding documents we use in naval aviation is known as the OPNAV 3710.7U. It has general rules for all things concerning naval aviation. It covers flight-planning rules, air-traffic control procedures, safety, and even aeromedical issues.

Specifically it mandates that in order to attain an "acceptable *minimum* level of readiness and enhance aviation safety" (my italics) pilots must fly at least 100 hours per year.[1] And by year that implies fiscal year so October to October. If not, you have to obtain a waiver that basically explains why you didn't get 100 a year.

The reason I took a look at my logbook is because I had to fill this waiver out and wondered how it was that I wasn't getting 100 hours in a year. As I scanned the pages, it became clear. When you only fly three to four times a month, at 2 hours a flight, that comes out to about 8 hours a month or, multiplying by 12 months in a year, gives 96 hours. Now some months you might fly 20 hours, then the next only 4. But for some reason in my first year, I only got 94 total hours and hence had to do a waiver. I was upset but at the same time I was elated because while I was doing the easy mental math, I took it a step further and thought about my pay and how it relates to flying. After all, my job first and foremost is to fly my helicopter.

To keep things simple, just round my hours up to 100 for the year. Taking my pay as an O-3 after taxes, I was getting about $4,200 every two weeks. That comes to roughly $100,000 a year. Everyone wants to talk hourly wages these days so let's do that. Take $100,000 per year, then divide it by 100 hours per year. The units work out so you get my pay per hour. It's just a matter of cancelling zeros. My pay per hour for the time when I was actually on the clock for doing my stated military occupational specialty was $1,000 per hour. Winning. But it gets much better.

What if I dig deeper? On the average flight I manipulate the controls about half the time of a 2-hour flight. It is true that sometimes I would fly almost the entire time if sitting in the back and shooting rockets. More on that in a second. And sometimes I hardly touched the controls at all if sitting in the front and doing command and control or terrain flight. So on average the percentage of a 2-hour flight that I actually manipulate controls is 50 percent. Apply this to my yearly total and I'm "flying" 50 hours a year. This translates into $100,000 a year divided by 50 flying hours per year or $2,000 an hour. Nice. And yes, it gets even better.

The role of the Cobra helicopter is to employ ordnance. To shoot things. Guns, rockets, Hellfire, and the like. It is a pure-attack helicopter. Not many countries can afford a pure-attack helicopter. Instead they add some guns and rocket pods to transport helicopters and call it good. The Huey is a good example. Not so in 'Merica. We have a pure-bred attack helicopter in the AH-1W Cobra.

It doesn't carry troops, it doesn't deliver aid or rice or water or tarps or transport cargo. Its one job is to kill. And if you believe this reasoning, it should follow that the only proper training of Cobra pilots is to prepare them to employ this killing machine. When we aren't deployed and the enemy isn't before us, the only thing we can do is practice shooting. How many hours a year would you say the average Cobra pilot shoots? Well, in my first year I counted 7 events during which I had trigger time for a total of 14 hours. And as mentioned above, for rocket shoots the flying pilot is the shooter. We'll say I practiced shooting rockets and guns for 14 hours in my first year. The other 86 hours was either simulated ordnance, terrain flight, or the two heavyweight favorites of Hawaii, Tactical formation (TACFORM) and familiarization and instruments or FAM/INST.

TACFORM is just a silly circus dance of max performance bank turns and climbs with a partner aircraft. Think dancing with the stars but attack helicopters instead of celebrities. Sounds gay, right? Believe me, it is. Familiarization and instruments is doing standard procedures like a normal or steep approach, or a no-hover takeoff. Flight-school-type stuff. Instruments is what it is. You reference only your instruments as if in a cloud. We do so much of this stuff because higher allots us a certain number of hours to be flown per year. With only so many rockets to go round, you end up just flying around the island doing TACFORM or FAM/INST to burn the hours and make mission. And by mission I don't mean being good at shooting, I mean being good at logging as many hours as possible regardless of the mission.

Back to shooting. So if I trained to shoot for 14 hours in a year, that comes out to about $7,100 an hour. These fast-food protestors need to stop breeding like rabbits, get their shit together, and become Cobra pilots. They won't complain about their hourly wages here. No sir. And once again the story is sweeter still.

But what is the point of us shooting? Why do we practice the doctrine known as Close Air Support (CAS)? In the definition of CAS, there is a requirement that air missions are taking place in close proximity to friendly forces and the missions require detailed integration. If that doesn't exist, it's called Deep Air Support or DAS. Marine air prides itself on being masters of CAS. We admit the Air Force is better at DAS. They can just run in a few B-52s and destroy everything. But friendlies aren't close so no big deal. Not so in CAS. The reason we do CAS is for the guys on the ground, the maneuver element. We are but one piece in the puzzle. When Marines are closing on an objective they need cover until their weapon systems are in range. That range being the several hundred meters of an M16 rifle. We pound the enemy as they get closer.

So after soaking that in, how many hours would you say I employed live ordnance with actual Marines on the ground maneuvering toward an objective in my first year of the fleet? The answer is one flight or two hours. It happened at Integrated Training Exercise in Twentynine Palms, which is the most badass training range in the world. Nothing but miles of desert and tank hulks. I shot a Tube Launched Optically Tracked Wire Guided (TOW) missile while some Marines in Amphibious Assault Vehicles (AAV) rolled toward an objective. So if my job is to fly an attack helicopter, and an attack helicopter's job is to shoot stuff, and a *Marine* attack helicopters job is to shoot stuff while friendlies are close by and in need of support, I did my job for 2 hours in one year. You get the pattern and with that logic I'm making $50,000 an hour. Burger King flippers eat your hearts out.

I should mention that it costs over $1 million to train each naval aviator from check-in—think *Officer and a Gentlemen*—to getting their wings.

Drones anyone?

You could also go down the road of percentages. If I am at work 40 hours a week for an average 48 weeks out of the year, that is 1920 hours a year. If I fly 100 hours a year, I'm actually doing my "job" for 0.05 percent of the year. I'll leave the rest of the iterations to the reader if they so choose.

One may ask, "But what about the majority of your time? What do you spend the majority of your time doing?"

I pondered this question and attempted to write but became immediately suicidal and hence stopped. But if you've made it this far into the book, you already have an idea of what is a priority in the Marine Corps. Chapters 3 and 4 provide some insight.

A few weeks later I found myself standing duty as the squadron duty officer on a Saturday night. My post is just sitting at a desk waiting for phone calls. Despite the stipulation in "The Reawakening" that all duty standers carry weapons, I am still unarmed. That and I'm standing the duty in a business uniform known as service Charlies. The civilian equivalent would be dress slacks and a collared shirt. Definitely my first choice if I'm going to physically challenge an intruder to our base or squadron.

I was trying to pass the time by perusing motorcycles online, the mindless news, or some useless, resource wasting annual training. It was a Saturday and something was bound to happen. Something *had* to happen. I was having a good conversation with my duty driver, a young lance corporal, about Harley Davidsons, cougars, and the upcoming deployment.

As I drifted in and out of sleep in my chair, the phone rang about 0130. Here we go, I thought.

"HMLA-367 SDO Captain Groom speaking, how can I help you, sir or ma'am?"

"Good evening, sir, this is Sergeant Watson with PMO . . ."

PMO are base policemen. They are Marines too.

What could it be, I wondered. Someone probably got arrested for fighting or was drunk at the front gate.

"Sir, I am calling to report a suicide ideation. We are at Corporal Barnes' house here on base. We were told by his wife that he locked himself in their bathroom with a knife about half an hour ago and threatened to cut his wrists."

"Is he still in there?"

"No, sir. His wife said he took off about 30 minutes ago in his car."

"Okay, I'll be over there in 15 minutes and I'll try to get ahold of him."

I looked him up in the recall roster and attempted to give him a quick call. One ring then it shifted to voicemail. Well, that means at least he is still alive, I guessed. I sent him a quick text then took off to his residence.

His government home was slightly off the golf course in a quaint little neighborhood. I saw the PMO vehicle several hundred meters out and pulled up behind them. I met the PMO sergeant. It turned out Corporal Barnes was there too. He looked dejected and was standing off behind the PMO cruiser with another policeman.

The sergeant began to explain, "Sir, looks like he just went for a walk. His car has been here the whole time."

"Did he have a knife on him? Did he try to cut himself?"

"No, sir. His wife said he was threatening to cut his wrists, but what had happened was they had an argument about their kid so he was mad and locked himself in their bathroom."

"So the suicide ideation is not true then? His wife just made it up?"

"Yes sir, that looks to be the case at this point. We talked to him. He is upset, he isn't suicidal."

I got a chance to talk to Corporal Barnes. He looks malnourished and is very thin. His demeanor comes across as genuine and concerned. It is obvious at this point he had no intention to cut himself. He said his wife was threatening to leave him and go back to the States and take their son. They had a fight and he was upset so he locked himself in the bathroom and she called the cops to make some stuff up about him trying to kill himself.

PMO recommended that he stay in the barracks for the night to cool off. Seemed reasonable. I mean his wife just lied to the police about her husband trying to kill himself. He was obviously in the wrong and should be penalized. I escorted him along with PMO up a metal staircase to his residence so he can grab some things to stay the night in the barracks with all the other single Marines.

The house was a side-by-side duplex split down the center of the building with single-car garages below and the living quarters above. The night was clear and perfect. At the top of the stairs was a massive pile of old newspapers, probably two dozen, scattered and rotting. They were still in their bags. The storm door was missing its screen and didn't have a damper installed and so swung open 180 degrees as he entered. As we proceed in, I get a smell of body odor mixed with some type of mildew. His wife was sitting with their child on a futon that is in bed mode. Next to it is a loveseat sofa with multiple tears. A few toys were strewn about on the floor.

The place was fairly barren. No kitchen table, no crib, no TV, no shelves. The kitchen had dishes strewn about and I could see the room that Corporal Barnes entered. Clothes were strewn about all over almost like a tornado had recently passed. The wench was playing with the kid on the futon while texting on her oversized smartphone. Her ethnicity can be best described as an Asian mixture. She was mildly overweight, carrying most of the excess in her legs and lower stomach. She was wearing inappropriate yoga pants and a turquoise workout tank that exposed her heinous muffintop. She was lying on her back texting as the baby writhed around next to her wrapped in a ratty-ass horse blanket. Her hair was short and black and her demeanor was that nothing was amiss. She had a tattoo across her chest that was visible because of her shirt. It covered pretty much her entire upper chest above her breasts and was a circular mural type of some underwater scene. I thought I could make out a dolphin or two swishing about.

She didn't acknowledge me nor pay a lick of attention to her husband as he entered. I sort of hung out between her and him, occupying a neutral ground in the family room. Corporal Barnes left the door to his room open as he packed. He grabbed a sea bag, the classic cylindrical military green bag, and started stuffing random clothes in. I escorted him to the barracks. I asked him where he met his wife. Turned out it was in a bar. There weren't any vacant rooms so he had to shack up with another Marine we unfortunately had to roust from his sleep.

Since he couldn't fight the system, I decide to take out his frustration for him. As I drove back to the squadron around 0300, I threw my McDonald's dinner bag and drink out the window of my moving truck and onto the street. As the half-full drink, which was still teeming with ice, shattered over the pavement, I began laughing hysterically. Fuck 'em.

The next day I called him to see how things were, but didn't get a reply. Later that day, I saw his number calling on the duty cell phone and answered. It was his wife, wondering who was calling her husband, in a very accusing manner.

My last month before deployment was uneventful.

Dash and I decided to visit Maui over the Veteran's Day holiday in November. The trip started off poorly with little to see or do. I mean it was just another tropical island in the Pacific. However, Dash rallied and creeped on some L.A. chicks that were staying in the same hotel as us. We had a pool party and both slayed our respective chicks, never to talk to them again. In fact we left our hotel so quickly the next morning we ignored their calls that they needed to get back into the room to grab a sandal they forgot.

In mid-November 2013, I deployed to Okinawa, Japan, to join the 31st Marine Expeditionary Unit or 31st MEU. The 31st MEU is permanently based in Okinawa, Japan. A MEU is basically a combination of navy ships that can launch amphibious assault vehicles full of Marines as well as aircraft to take a beach by force. These boats are commonly called the Gator Navy. Remember that, Marines depend on the Gator Navy, not aircraft carriers. They include the LHA- and LHD-class assault ships, but not aircraft carriers. Besides jet pilots and their mechanics, no Marines are on aircraft carriers.

Our squadron, HMLA-367, sent Huey and Cobra pilots along with dozens of maintainers and support personnel. Upon arrival, we became part of an Osprey Squadron that is based in Okinawa. VMM-265. We were joined by CH-53 Super Stallion pilots and maintainers as well. VMM-265 then became VMM-265 Reinforced. The reinforced squadron then acted as the Aviation Combat Element or ACE in the 31st MEU.

Twice a year the 31st MEU does what is calls a "patrol." They basically load all the Marines and their gear as well as aviation and logistics elements onto several ships. The patrol does something different depending on the time of year and what exercises are being held. Power projection is the name of the game. There is a spring patrol and a fall patrol.

Diversity Training

"It is a security imperative for military leaders to proactively advance diversity and inclusion (D&I) best practices" because of the "rapid demographic change [and] advances in gender and LGBT equity and a new generation of veterans in NATO countries." The Defense Department not only talks "about diversity in terms of race and gender, and ethnicity, but it is much more than that in my mind." Diversity includes "your thought process, how you grew up, [and] what you can add to the greater good because of your background."[1]

- Jessica Wright, undersecretary of defense
for personnel and readiness, 2013

"One team, one fight!"
- Anonymous bigoted Marine officer (likely a white male)

Mid-February 2014. Marine Corps Air Station (MCAS), Futenma, Okinawa, Japan.

I was all settled into the bachelor officers' quarters (BOQ) on Futenma. We had been doing some flying with the reinforced squadron over the past couple months.

I rolled into the office early enough, about 0730. Bleeder, our detachment officer in charge, summoned me as I walked past his office.

"Hey, Bigsby!"

I spin and simultaneously sounded off, "Sir," and entered his office.

"I have a unique tasker for you. I got word from the public affairs officer that we need a driver, but not just a lance corporal. Apparently General Wissler is going to be taking a VIP around tomorrow. We don't know who. They are asking for a Marine captain. Most other guys are tied up, you're not on to fly. I want you to drive them."

At first I thought he was joking. He was known for being a prankster.

"Uh, yeah, um, where do they need to go? Should be pretty cool, I bet I'll get a coin. Generals always give coins."

He paused and frowned as if about to yell at me then quietly replied, "Apparently they are doing a press conference, then after that I'm not sure. Obviously just do what they say. Imagine, and believe me this is a hypothetical, he was in your aircraft. You just do whatever he says. I'm guessing they'll want to see a few bases. We don't have anything scheduled for flights yet like VIP Lift, erh, I mean battlefield circulation flights, but don't be surprised if they wanna see the Osprey."

"Roger that, sir. What time and where do I need to show up?"

"I'll forward you what you need, and don't fuck this up. I might let you sign for an aircraft and fly around the pattern for a few hours during daylight with no ordnance if you do a good job. Sexual assault training, weather, maintenance, and ground training permitting, of course."

I could hardly contain my excitement. Me. A Marine captain. Aviator. Flying an attack helicopter with a peer captain, all alone and unafraid *in the pattern* of Marine Corps Air Station Futenma. Bleeder is essentially offering to throw me the keys to the family car. He was like a proud papa and I didn't want to let him down. Just the thought of it stoked the joy of a kid inside me. I tried to hide it and respond quickly, "I'll do a good job, sir."

I turned and practically floated to my office. I was on cloud nine. I was the first one in at this hour and snagged the first computer near the door. As the trons moved to log me in, I paused and stared over at our three printers that were currently down. We had no ink for one, and the other two were given to us broken. All our printing had to be sent to the ready room with its huge scanner printer.

I signed into the computer and I opened Outlook, our email system. A few Marines that worked in the shop came in, shot me a cursory greeting, then lethargically took their seats at the small central table in the room. They then initiated their daily ritual that lasts all day, playing on their smartphones.

I hadn't checked my email since the week before because we were planning the previous week at Camp Hansen, which is north of Futenma. A few minutes ticked by as the inbox loaded and filled in quite a few emails. I started at the top and began scanning. The emails were sorted by date, with the most recent being at the top. I zeroed in on a few emails as they catch my attention.

From: "Navy"
Sent: Friday, February 14, 2014 1:29 PM
To: 31st MEU All Hands
Subject: National African American History Month Fact of the Day

In 1954, the U.S. Supreme Court handed down its ruling in the landmark case of Brown v. Board of Education of Topeka, Kansas. The unanimous decision overturned the 1896 Plessy v. Ferguson decision, which allowed for "separate but equal" public facilities. Declaring that "separate educational facilities are inherently unequal," the decision helped break state-sponsored segregation and provided an intricate piece to the civil rights movement.

Reference:
http://www.history.com/topics/brown-v-board-of-education-of-topeka

Well, I'll be damned, I didn't know that. I clicked the link and read up on it. Pretty crazy it took that long. I scrolled to the next email.

From: "Navy"
Sent: Thursday, February 13, 2014 9:59 AM
To: 31st MEU All Hands
Subject: African American/Black History Month

The Department of Defense has designated the month of Feb each year as African American/Black History Month. The theme for this year's African American/Black History Month is as follows: "Civil Rights in America"

This year, America will celebrate the 50th anniversary of the Civil Rights Act, one of the greatest legislative accomplishments of the twentieth century.

Take a minute to look at the attached Presidential Proclamation. For more information go to the DEOMI website at the link listed below:

http://www.deomi.org/SpecialObservance/MonthlyFactsoftheDay.cfm

R/S
NAVY SEL; E.O. Representative
Command Element
31st MEU

Another good email, I think. If we aren't constantly reminded of this stuff, we'll forget.

From: "Navy"
Sent: Thursday, February 13, 2014 12:04 PM
To: 31st MEU All Hands
Subject: National African American History Month Fact of the Day

Mississippi was chosen as the site of the Freedom Summer project due to its historically low levels of African-American voter registration. In 1962, less than 7 percent of the state's eligible Black voters were registered to vote.

Reference:
http://www.history.com/topics/freedom-summer

R/S
NAVY SEL; E.O. Representative
Command Element
31st MEU

Hell yeah, I thought, fight that disenfranchisement. Seven percent. America should be ashamed. We are such a racist, imperialist, bigoted country sometimes.

From: Capt X
Sent: Tuesday, February 11, 2014 8:06 AM
To: VMM 265 ALLHANDS
Subject: African American History Month

Ladies and Gentlemen,

Good Morning! The DOD has designated the month of Feb as African American/Black History Month.

This year's theme is as follows: "At the Crossroads of Freedom and Equality: The Emancipation Proclamation and the March on Washington." This year's theme commemorates two events that changed the course of the nation-the 1863 Emancipation Proclamation and the 1963 March on Washington.

The first celebration of Black History Week occurred on February 12, 1926. The Library of Congress, National Archives and Records Administration, National Endowment for the Humanities, National Gallery of Art, National Park Service, Smithsonian Institution and United States Holocaust Memorial Museum join in paying tribute to the generations of African Americans who struggled with adversity to achieve full citizenship in American society.

Please take a moment to review the attached websites.
http://www.biography.com/people/groups/black-history
http://www.history.com/topics/black-history-month

V/r
VMM-265 FlightLine OIC
Equal Opportunity Representative

Mass. It's a war-fighting principle of the offense. To win an assault you have to mass your forces at a particular point on the enemy. Same way for equal opportunity and Black History Month. To keep it in people's minds, you have to mass the emails. I expect a few more, but they switch it up a bit.

From: "EO Rep"
Sent: Tuesday, February 11, 2014 9:05 AM
To: 1MAW All Users
Subject: 2014 III MEF Military Women's Leadership Symposium
Importance: High

Ladies and Gentlemen,

The attachment with details is for the 2014 III MEF Women's leadership Symposium that III MEF host every year. There will be two dates it will be held: 21 April 2014 at the PALMS and 2 May 2014 Surfside.

Please pass on to any senior females (0-3 for officers and E-6 or above for enlisted) who you feel would be able to contribute in a positive fashion. Thank you very much for your time.

If there are any senior females 0-3 through 0-6 who would be interested please let me know so I can pass the name onto MGySgt X.

NOTE: Men are more than welcome to attend this training. (You would not be the first)

MSgt X
1st Marine Aircraft Wing,
Equal Opportunity Advisor

I open the attachment.

III MEF, Okinawa Japan

2014 MILITARY WOMEN'S LEADERSHIP SYMPOSIUM

Overview

- Situation
- Mission
- Execution
- Administration and Logistics
- Command and Signal

Situation

Maintaining combat readiness is largely dependent upon the ability to mentor and provide preventive education to military personnel. The absence of mentorship that specifically targets issues unique to the female gender have been identified as one of the factors that prohibits combat readiness among our service members.

Mission

- Provide guidance/mentorship targeted to issues that are negatively affect female service members.

- Instill education/measures that will allow female service members to empower themselves and make wise life choices.

- Increase unit cohesiveness/maximize positive command climate.

Execution – 2 May

Agenda

☐ 0730-0740	Welcome	MGySgt X
☐ 0740-0745	Invocation	Chaplain
☐ 0745-0800	Opening Remarks	TBD
☐ 0805-0830	Guest Speaker	TBD
☐ 0830-1130	Workshops	All
☐ 1130-1300	LUNCH	All
☐ 1300-1500	Workshops	All
☐ 1500-1555	Leadership Panel Discussion	TBD
☐ 1600-1620	Closing Remarks	BGeneral Y
☐ 1620-1630	Benediction	Chaplain

Execution – 21 April

Agenda

☐ 0700-0710	Welcome	MGySgt X
☐ 0710-0715	Invocation	Chaplain
☐ 0715-0730	Opening Remarks	TBD
☐ 0730-0800	Guest Speaker	TBD
☐ 0800-1130	Workshops	All
☐ 1130-1300	LUNCH	All
☐ 1300-1500	Workshops	All
☐ 1500-1600	Leadership Panel Discussion	TBD
☐ 1600-1620	Closing Remarks	LtGen X
☐ 1620-1630	Benediction	Chaplain

Administration and Logistics

Workshops

- **The Person Within**
  - Self-Respect/Self Esteem
  - Goal Setting/Remaining Focused
  - Sexual Harassment/Assault
  - Coping w/isolation

- **Let's get to Work**
  - Proper Civilian Attire
  - Uniform Regulations
  - Appropriate behavior –vs– Expected treatment

- **Finding the Balance**
  - Relationships
  - Starting a Family
  - Family Care
  - Career Choices

Administration and Logistics

Collaborators

- Marine Corps Community Services
- Equal Opportunity Advisors
- Family Readiness Officers
- Family Advocacy Program
- Chaplains
- Career Planners

Administration and Logistics

Marketing

- ☐ Combat Camera
- ☐ FROs
- ☐ Posters
- ☐ OkiMar
- ☐ OkiNews
- ☐ Social Media, E-Mail

What a great way to get the girls together! Serving in a mostly-male organization snuffs out feminism. They need this. They need to have workshops about starting families and the like. Good for them! I unconsciously shifted a little in my seat; I was so excited for these girls. One of the Marines heard me stir a bit in my chair, glanced up, then immediately returned to his smartphone.

The next several emails appeared to be a chain so the original was lower and the responses were on top of the e-mail. I scrolled down to what looked like the original email. It seemed to be a brief with another general for some Professional Military Education (PME). Looked like they got the word out to all the people of the 1st Marine Aircraft Wing (MAW). The MEF is Marine Expeditionary Force, basically all the Marine assets in the Pacific fall under Third MEF. General Wissler is the commanding general of Third MEF.

From: MSgt X
Sent: Wednesday, February 5, 2014 01:23 PM
To: 1MAW All Users
Subject: PME with LtGen Wissler INFO

ALCON,

All minority officers and women officers have a PME with LtGen Wissler on 4 March. See below email chain for coordinating instructions.

Time: 0930 - 1030 (Field Grade)
1045 - 1145 (Company Grade)
Location: Butler Officers Club (Main Ball Room)

Task:
1. All sections provide list of personnel meeting the requirement; highlight those unable to attend with justification and submit to the S-3. (Suspense: 1200, 28 Feb)

2. S-3:
- Compile master roster from all sections/shops
- Responsible for all CG officers with justification

3. S-4
   - Arrange for transportation to and from the Butler Officers Club

Please let me know if you have any questions,

Respectfully,
Master Sergeant X
1st Marine Aircraft Wing, Equal Opportunity Advisor

The good news just keeps coming. I read on.

From: LtCol X
Sent: Thursday, February 6, 2014 6:41 AM
To: MSgt X
Cc: Recipients
Subject: Re: PME with LtGen Wissler INFO

MSgt,

Is this for every unit in the MEF or just those on Okinawa? I don't think we'll have a means to fly all our minority and female officers down from Iwakuni unless some aircraft are going to be fragged for that purpose.

Thanks,
LtCol X

Fucking bigot, I think. He's probably a white guy. He just won't let the minorities have a little piece of the pie. Thank God DoD is pushing this stuff. No one else would if they didn't.

From: MSgt X
Sent: Friday, February 7, 2014 10:28 AM
To: 1MAW All Users
Subject: RE: PME with LtGen Wissler INFO (Iwakuni and Hawaii WING Units)

Ladies and Gentlemen,

Female and Minority officers from Hawaii and Iwakuni do not have to make the trip for General Wissler's PME. His intentions are to travel to those spots for the same brief. I spoke with the general's SSEC and at this time there is not scheduled time for this, I am sure it will be sent out as soon as a date and time is determined.

Master Sergeant X
1st Marine Aircraft Wing, Equal Opportunity Advisor

I've got some flight hours and gas to spare. I'd gladly give them up so the general can put on this PME all over Asia. Next email.

From: MSgt X
Sent: Monday, February 10, 2014 01:23 PM
To: 1MAW All Users
Subject: PME with LtGen Wissler INFO

Ladies and Gentlemen,

I have fielded numerous calls on the below e-mail and the purpose of it. I understand the concerns that have been brought to my attention and have got clarification from III MEF on what the exact purpose of the PME is about. The following is why the PME is only requesting minority officers and women.

A few months back the Marine Corps was tasked with diversity training. While in that training it was noted Marine Corps Wide that the Marine Corps has been less successful with retention of minority officers as well as female officers. It also was found that less minority officers and female officers were reporting sexual assaults, therefore giving General Officers a tasker from HQMC to work on the issue at hand. If there are any other questions that may arise please free to contact me again.

Master Sergeant X
1st Marine Aircraft Wing, Equal Opportunity Advisor

I was not surprised. An organization ruled this long by white men is bound to push back. Just like the South did. Good on DoD, I think, to have some "preparatory fires" in the form of the Black History Month emails and the women's symposium. Change didn't come willingly to the South and it ain't gonna come easy to the corps either. Luckily we are under civilian control.

Not really sure about the "less reporting sexual assaults" part. I mean are Senator Gillibrand and her aides really getting into the weeds that much with sexual assault reporting? I wonder if they were analyzing who reports the sexual assault based on race or sex as a percentage of total reporting and then comparing that to the percentage of females or minorities in each service or branch? And if those two numbers aren't close, do they see a problem?

I did a quick lookup of the facts for sexual assault in the military. I found the Department of Defense Annual Report on Sexual Assault in the Military. It's a doozy of a document and 2012 had two volumes, the second of which is 795 slides of tediously made Excel graphs and pie charts. They covered just about everything with respect to sexual assault.

Turns out in 2012 there were approximately 12,000 *reported* cases of unwanted sexual contact of females, which can include rape. This translates into about 6 percent of the 200,000 active-duty female force. However, the total number of assaults was around 26,000, meaning 14,000 *men* were *victims* too. But since our government smartly counts percentages and not people, those 14,000 men only comprise 1.2 percent of the military's 1.2 million men.[2] Six percent is greater than 1.2 percent. So I'm not really sure where this "less minority and female officers were reporting sexual assaults" came from. I guess in sheer numbers, yes, females did report fewer sexual assaults, but as a percentage they reported more and that is what grabs headlines.

The premise has to be that they don't believe the data and the "true" number of assaults, or alleged assaults, is much higher. I dug into the civilian statistics and discovered that a comparable age group of 18- to 34-year-old females in the civilian world reported a sexual assault rate of 0.4 percent for 2012. If that percentage held true in the military, there would be less than 1,000 women reporting assault.[3] The same study found the male on male assaults weren't due to gays but rather "prison-style rape." There is no evidence to back this claim up, but it makes sense to me. The military is very similar to prison, lots of living in closed spaces with other men. A pecking order develops outside the idea of rank and you gotta take a bitch or be a bitch. The natural progression is rape. I also stumbled upon a stat that says in 2012, of those 26,000 reported cases, only 0.9 percent, or 238, were convicted. All but 2 percent of assailants were men.[4]

As I was pondering these issues, one of the other captains in the squadron walked in to ask for some more printer paper. An Osprey pilot, he is Chinese, originally from Hong Kong, and he looks every bit of it. His call sign is Ngrsh and for those that can't figure it out, it's making fun of Asian accents. Imagine a very heavy-accented Asian trying to "speak the English." Most likely you'll hear something like "speeka da ngrsh." Based on what I've just been mortified reading, I decided to ask him if he is attending the training.

"Hey, Ngrsh, have you been tracking this female and minority PME? I take it you are going?"

Ngrsh has a unique mannerism. When he gets worked up about something, he does a half shrug and moves both arms up while pinching his thumbs to his fingers. My question pushed him into this mode and he started ranting,

"I canna fookin berieve dis, dis is fookin bullshi. How dey gonna force peepole to go to a confence based on only race and da genda? It's a fookin bullshi. It's illeregal, dey can't hold a confence for a certain kinna peepole. It's again everyting we stan fo. Whatta if we hadda confence for all da white guy? Woulda dat be okay, fook no! Whatta da heil happin to dis idearah that we taykuh the basic recruit or candideyt for offica and we giva dem da title Maween? We donna care wherea you came from, what you religion, or wace, we justa breaka you down and giva you title maween. We donna need diversity in da corps, we needa unity."

I responded before he got too carried away.

"Yeah, but with an organization run by white guys so long, don't you think we need to sort of forcefully change the hierarchy to allow for more minorities and women to climb the ranks? It's obvious to me that the Marine Corps has a glass ceiling for minorities and women. You saw the email, minorities and women don't stay in as long as white guys. Shouldn't we address that injustice?"

He had been watching me the whole time holding his outrage pose and nodded slowly to show he is taking it all in. Before he can reply, I sprung some facts that I'd been researching. I just wanted to show how far we have to go before we have equality in the military.

"And since we are on the topic of injustice, how about this. Females comprise about 15 percent of our total military but presently they have only accounted for 2.5 percent of the fatalities in Iraq. And in Afghanistan as of May 2012 they only comprised only 1.5 percent of casualties.[5] So you can see from these statistics, we have some work to do in order to put them on equal footing. To be frank they just need to get killed more often. That's why I'm all for them being placed into combat arms. We should relax standards to make it happen."

He stopped nodding and pondered what I have just laid at his feet. He decided to avoid the topic.

"What's unrust is dey fact dat dey axe peepole to a confence because a dey only a certain race or genda. That's diskimination, prain and simpull. I dona give a shi about race or backgroun. Ifa yu da best main you getta da job. Peepole needa to stop been so poriticarry correct. Looka at my call sign. It Ngrsh, I dunno care, I think it funny."

"So is the XO making you go or not?"

"No, no fookin way, I gotta too much ta do here. I canna be takin a day off to go and hang outta wit a buncha femayo and shi. What are dey gonna do? Axe peepole why dey get out and conwince dem to stey?"

I didn't want to get him more fired up even though I disagreed with him so I just went along, "Yeah, I see what you're saying. It would probably be very boring anyway."

He nodded, grabbed his printer paper, and hurried out.

I glanced down at my screen and deleted all the emails. A few seconds later Bleeder's email arrived with the details for driving the general and his VIP. I dug into it and prepared myself for the next day's journey. The Marines at the desks were playing Angry Birds.

A two-star general was on deck for a few minutes in the hallway and I overheard him talking to a few of the MV-22 Osprey pilots about how Bell and Boeing are trying to sell their aircraft to anyone that will buy, even Egypt. He said he had an airshow to attend in Singapore on the fifteenth and sixteenth and hopefully someone buys it so we can bring costs down because right now they stand at $72,000,000 apiece.

Ambassador Caroline Kennedy Visits the MCAS Futenma Barracks

21 February 2014

U.S. ambassador to Japan Caroline Kennedy, following her appointment by President Obama in July of 2013, made her first stop to the island of Okinawa to "gain perspective of the bigger picture of Japan, and Okinawa is very important for accomplishing that."[1]

She was received at the Camp Foster Community Center. She was escorted by the Third Marine Expeditionary Force Commander, Lieutenant General Wissler. After reading Bleeder's coordinating emails, I was ready to serve. I checked out a special up-armored Cadillac SUV—I'll call it an Urban Assault Vehicle or UAV—from the motor pool and met them at the Community Center. I got a firsthand glimpse of what was going on when they were introduced. They first met backstage prior to press exposure. After quickly introducing myself, I sheepishly held a corner of the room and observed.

"General Wissler, so nice to meet you, I've heard so much about your work out here."

The ambassador offered her gnarled hand to the towering general. The general is a wise-looking man, hardened by years of having to prove himself and hold himself to a high moral standard.

"Yes, ma'am, I've only recently taken command, but we are instituting some good changes here. Before we continue, I think you have something on your nose. It's like a brown smudge or food or something. There is something brown on your nose."

She stopped immediately and reached into her Burberry Small Salisbury Tote, a modest $1,000 purse, and grabbed a makeup mirror. Sure enough, right on the tip of her nose there was a brown splotch of some kind.

"Oh, that's just leftover from when I supported the President at his 2008 convention speech." She took a Kleenex and using her mirror, wiped it off.

"Very well," the general says in a neutral, matter-of-fact way. "Let's go meet the press."

At this point I moved out into the seating area and awaited the remarks. There were mainly politician types in the crowd as well as a healthy dose of reporters.

The graying general made his way to the stage first.

"Ladies and gentlemen, I would like to introduce to you an amazing American. Caroline Kennedy stands before us today. She sacrificed greatly over her life in service to her country, and to numerous Americans both at home and abroad and continues to serve all of those who serve Japan. She's applied her education as a passionate advocate and a leader for education, the arts, civil liberties, and democracy. Looking at the past of Ambassador Kennedy, there is no doubt that we are in the presence of a great leader and certainly a true inspiration. We are honored that she can be here with us today.[2] She has written many books promoting liberty and rule of law including *In Our Defense: The Bill of Rights in Action* as well as *The Right to Privacy*."

The general had a habit of incessantly massaging his hip with his right hand.

"Her political pedigree is impressive, stretching back many decades in the American northeast. She is new to this part of the world, so let's give her a warm welcome. Ladies and gentlemen, Ambassador Caroline Kennedy."

A small rolling applause lightened everyone up and she confidently moved to the center of the stage and took the microphone. She reached down to talk, but was a little awkward and her beak nose poked the microphone and static shrill sound scintillated the audience and few jumped slightly in their seats. She backed away and adjusted her head to speak at 45-degree angles to avoid hitting the microphone.

"Thank you, General Wissler, for that introduction. My reputation certainly precedes me. To be honest, I am humbled to be holding this position, given my limited political experience. Initially I was interested in Hillary Clinton's Senate seat in 2008, but in an interview I volunteered for on television I said 'you know' 168 times in a 30-minute window.[3]

"After that I figured I should defer to nepotism to advance. I was good friends with the President so when I heard about this job, I jumped on it. I have to admit I was a little upset when the revelations of the traitorous Edward Snowden concerning the illegal and unconstitutional constant surveillance of Americans by the NSA were uncovered earlier this year. As the general mentioned, I've published books about privacy and our Fourth Amendment, but ultimately I trust the government and I trust the president. Our military members out there will no doubt empathize with my conundrum. Follow your moral compass or follow orders? The World War II generation will be familiar with the phrase, 'Loose lips sink ships' or for the Twitter crowd out there, 'Loose tweets sink fleets.'"

The crowd had a good laugh amidst flashes of smartphones and recording devices. The general had a one-thousand-yard stare as he sat motionless behind her.

"One of the first things I did in Okinawa was tweet my mortification with Japanese dolphin drive hunting and how inhuman it is to drive together a bunch of mammals and keep penned up before killing or transporting them. How you can keep such tender creatures in cages or pen them up like that is the utter cruelty. My father said that while serving on his PT boat, they would come up to the boat and do tricks and sing to his crew. They are just like us!"

On the "us" she struck the podium fairly forcefully and caught herself getting angry, recomposed, then changed subjects.

She started again, narrowly missing the microphone with her hooked nose.

"For all of us Americans here in Japan, we are all ambassadors, so it is great to be in your presence. I look forward to meeting all of you individually. You have all done such a magnificent job. You are on the front lines of the twenty-first century. It may not be easy, but it is incredibly important in spreading peace and prosperity. Whether it is through environmental cleanups, reading to children, your capacity and service is truly an inspiration.'I know that's why you all joined the world's most pre-eminent warfighting organization. To clean, read, and inspire. You have adapted so well to the needs of the corps in Japan. Hooyah!"

There were only a few Marines in the audience including myself. I'm not sure how they were selected to be present. The reporters in the crowd were feverishly writing things down. After a few seconds' pause she opened the floor for questions. A young woman from MSNBC raised her hand and was called upon.

"Ambassador Kennedy, what is the U.S. policy with respect to the Senkaku Islands and China's recent establishment of an Air Defense Identification Zone encompassing the East China Sea?"

A fair and pointed question, I think.

"I'm not really ready to weigh in on the U.S. policy toward China's territorial claims. What is an Air Defense Identification Zone, by the way? Those pale in comparison to the problem of the ancient Japanese practice of dolphin drive hunting. You can follow me on

#AmbassadorKennedy to see the latest updates in our drive to stop this barbaric practice of penning up mammals like dolphins and treating them like caged wild animals."

Before the reporter could reply, General Wissler interrupted.

"Okay, ladies and gentlemen, thank you for your time. The ambassador has several more stops to make today so we must be going."

A few more flashes of the cameras and the two were off the stage. I rushed through the side door and beat them back to the original area I saw them meet. I escorted them outside to the UAV and politely opened the door for the ambassador.

As I opened the door for the general, he shot me a smirk that said, "Can you believe I put up with this shit?" I smiled back and closed the door, hopping in the driver's seat and taking off. I could see their interaction using the rearview mirror and my peripherals.

"Okay, General, now I'd like to see some of the Marine bases and maybe get a feel for how they live from day to day. Which base would you like to see? I personally would like to see the air station on Futenma."

The general had trouble hiding his aversion to the idea. As she was speaking, he nodded slowly while pursing his lips and rearing his head back slightly.

"Ma'am, that sounds like a great idea, but our schedule has us going to a lunch reception at Naha City Hall for you to make another speech. I recommend we stick to the plan."

"Nonsense! I insist. What better way to show the Marines we care about their welfare than a surprise visit to Futenma. Besides, in a few years that facility will be taken back over by the Okinawans."

Maintaining his bearing, the general shifted from the benign warnings of breaking schedules to inciting fear for personal safety.

"Ma'am, if we visit unannounced, there is no telling that your safety could be adequately prepared for. When ambassadors visit, we give the bases at least a month's notice so they can have quiet hours, establish roadblocks, have a few safety briefs, knock out some delinquent ground training and the like. To just show up I cannot condone."

"General, surely if the Marine Corps is in a high state of readiness, me showing up unannounced will not be cause for concern. Is it not true that we should inspect what we expect? Isn't that what the Marines say? And as a matter of fact, I already planned this out."

"I beg your pardon, ma'am?"

The general was beginning to fume inside. I could see him grind his teeth. He better be careful, she could get him fired.

"That's right, General, one of the old family friends from the New England area works in the Department of Commerce, specifically the U.S. Census Bureau. Her father knew Uncle Teddy so that's how I know her. Once she heard I got the job out here, she requested I help her with one of her projects."

The ambassador paused for a moment to gauge the general's reaction. The general had to compose his response. Definitely didn't foresee this at all.

"Uh, well, okay, what kind of project are we talking about here?" The general's body was beginning to tense slightly and he shifted a little on his side of the opposite facing benches in the UAV. He soothed the tension by leaning over his shoulder and directing me, "Captain, change of plans, we are going to Futenma. You know where that is, right?"

"Yes, sir, that's home for now, in the old bachelor officers' quarters."

"Good, man," he said genuinely and turned his attention back to the ambassador.

The ambassador smelled the lack of confidence and relished every second of it. She then proceeded with confidence.

"It's called the American Community Survey or ACS. I have a pamphlet with me. Here."

She reached across the open space between them and handed him the pamphlet along with several papers. All held together with a paper clip. As she moved toward him, I can't help but think she resembled some twisted-ass ostrich-type creature. After coming to grips with being told what to do, the general composed himself and forcefully dropped his cold eyes down toward the pile of papers she just handed him. He sifted through them for a minute or two then handed them up to me.

Sure enough, the pamphlet seemed legit. A large American flag with one of those impressive weeping willow-type fireworks going off in the middle on the front page. The title of the pamphlet is "Frequently Asked Questions for Facility Administrators: American Community Survey Group Quarters." On the lower half in yellow is "Your Community's Key to the Future." The bottom left sealed the authenticity with the U.S. Department of Commerce Economics and Statistics Administration. I was praying for something of apocryphal origins, but this was not. I turned the page and began reading slowly under my breath during the long stops at red lights and traffic.

The pamphlet is organized utilizing the question-and-answer format. The first question is, What is the American Community Survey? "Conducted in every county . . . provides current demographic, social, economic, and housing characteristics . . . does not count population . . . reflects what the population looks like and how it lives . . . vital for states and local communities in determining how to plan for schools, roads, senior citizen centers."

What kind of arcane shit is this, I wondered. What are they gonna do with this information? I still read on.

How long has it been conducted? "Began in 1996 . . . began sampling group quarters in 2006."

How does this group quarters and its residents benefit by answering the American Community Survey? "Provides up-to-date information for your community . . . communities need data about the well-being of children, families, and the elderly to provide services to them . . . used to decide where to locate new highways, schools, libraries, hospitals, and community centers, and to determine the goods and services its residents' need."

What type of group quarter facilities are included in the ACS? "College dorms, residential treatment centers, nursing facilities, group homes for adults, military quarters, correctional facilities."

How many times during the year will the Census Bureau sample my facility? "Depends on the size . . . large facilities may be sampled multiple times throughout the year."

The first thought across my mind is this might be a good thing. Let's talk to the Marines in the barracks and see what they think. But I immediately had second thoughts. They all fucking hate Okinawa, and good God! If they see the living conditions, the general might be fucked. I know that was his reason to keep her out of there in the first place, to avoid having her interacting with the Marines. And now she is toting some bureaucrat who will finger-fuck our entire system of incarceration. I stumbled back into reality and hear the general.

"Okay, this seems reasonable. Where are we picking this representative up?"

"He is meeting us at the CoCo's Curry house. He just ate lunch. We'll swing up north, grab him, and head back down to Futenma. Shouldn't take but five minutes out of the way."

"Good to go. Let's show him the base and get these surveys knocked out. Son, did you hear that, we gotta hit CoCo's first."

"Roger that, sir," I said.

We spotted him from a few hundred meters out. A rotund Asian man but not Asian Asian; he's American Asian. He stood erectly at the edge of the street, looking off to the northwest probably at the big Ferris wheel at the heart of American Village a few kilometers away. He stared blankly at the murdered-out UAV as if it was just another vehicle passing by and he was people watching.

Looking into his eyes, I felt like I was connecting with the mind of a dog. There wasn't much intelligence behind them. Just the involuntary brain functions were churning up there. I pulled over and stopped for him to get in and also seized the moment to grab a drink from a vending machine that was in an alley for all practical purposes.

The ambassador narrowed her eyes in confusion and said, "General, where is he going?"

"Looks like he is just snagging a drink. You are actually allowed in Okinawa to pull off to the side of the road in traffic, stop, go grab a drink from a vending machine, then continue."

"Oh, they sure do love vending machines."

I hop back in with a 24-ounce can of blue-and-white Aquarius water.

"That's good stuff, right, Captain?" The general was trying to be normal.

"Oh, yes, sir, it's like grapefruit-flavored Crystal Light. Coke actually bottles this stuff, so why they haven't launched it back in the States I'll never know. I drink at least three a day when it gets really hot like today. God, where are my manners? Ma'am, did you want anything? They have all kinds of stuff. Iced small coffee? Or your guest?"

"I have my Evian here. I'm fine, but thank you." The ambassador tapped her large Evian bottle.

"I'll take one of those small iced coffees, man."

The census rep eked out his request as he folded over his own gut getting in the vehicle. He sat in the third set of seating in the vehicle in the back.

The general responded while still staring at the mass of flesh that just rolled itself into his UAV.

"I'm good, Captain."

"Coming right up, sir."

I sprung out as a small gang of scooter riders buzz by. I was back in two minutes, raging with excitement over what I saw coming. I bought a small rainbow-colored can of coffee that said "Boss" and had a man with a mustache on it.

"Sir, your coffee."

"Arigato," he said as he took it.

The representative greeted the ambassador with a short "Konnichwa, Ambassador. Atsui deska?"

Ambassador Kennedy immediately cocked her head to one side, wearing an inquisitive expression.

"I said good afternoon, and isn't it hot here?"

The representative lowered his head slightly as he clarified so his one chin becomes two.

"Oh, of course, yes, it's just stifling. Much more humid than Nantucket. I'm just feeling dreadful. I'm still picking up my conversational Japanese."

"Mr. Chang, this is General Wissler."

The ACS rep slowly moved an open-faced palm with outstretched fingers toward the general.

"Pleased to meet you, sir. I'm Ryan Chang." He struggled to reach over the chasm between the two men but offered his business card in his left hand and his right was open for shaking.

"Nice to meet you too, Mr. Chang. What level spice did you get at CoCo's?"

The general took a few seconds to scan the business card he now possessed. He handed it to me after he was done. At the top: U.S. Department of Commerce U.S. Census Bureau ▮▮▮▮▮▮▮ Way, Suite ▮▮ Van Nuys, CA 91406. Ryan Chang, Field Representative, Los Angeles Regional Office. A cell and office phone were listed as well.

"Oh, I got the 4 to play it safe, and even that was too much."

"I've worked my way up to a 6, but it took awhile and countless hours of training on the toilet seat. So I understand you will be administering this survey for the ACS program?"

"Thanks, yes, sir, actually I have a few more documents you can scan as we drive to Futenma."

As he finished his sentence we were rolling again and did a quick U-turn to head back south. The general was passed three pages of official-looking papers. He then began reading the first page. It was addressed to the facility manager. After the meeting, I snagged the papers and read them.

"Your facility has been randomly selected . . . participating in this survey is important and also *required* by law (Title 13, United States Code, Sections 141, 193, 221, and 223) . . . a field representative will contact you to discuss the survey . . . answers are confidential by law . . . if you want to learn more visit Census Bureau website at census.gov/acs."

The second page was thicker than the first and very official looking. It contained the laws mentioned on the first page.

"Title 13 and Title 18 United States Federal Code June 2010 . . . U.S. Code is a way to organize by topic the laws Congress passes . . . U.S. Code is divided into 50 titles . . . Title 13 and 18 relate to laws specific to the U.S. Census Bureau . . . Title 13 contains authorizations to conduct Census Bureau data collection programs."

Lots of superfluous legal jargon filled the rest of the page so the general flipped it over.

Section 223. Section 3571 Title 18 Amendment.

"Whoever, being the owner, proprietor, manager, superintendent, or agent of any hotel, apartment house, boarding or lodging house, tenement, *or other building*, refuses or willfully neglects, when requested by the secretary or by any other officer or employee of the Department of Commerce or bureau agency thereof, acting under the instructions of the secretary, to furnish the names of the occupants of such premises, or to give free ingress thereto and egress therefrom to any duly accredited representative of such Department or Bureau or agency thereof, so as to permit the collection of statistics with respect to any census provided for in subchapters I or II of Chapter 5 of this Title, or any survey authorized by subchapter IV or V of such chapter insofar as such survey relates to any of the subjects for which census are provided by such subchapters I and II, including, when relevant to the census or survey being taken or made, the proper and correct enumeration of all persons having their usual place of abode in such premises, shall be fined not more than $5,000. (3571 (a)(7))."

The last page was basically a piecemeal summary of the former two pages, but it was addressed to the property manager. "Bureau of Census conducts surveys each month involving thousands of households and businesses throughout the country . . . used to continuously monitor and assess social and economic trends . . . information from the surveys supply in-depth and current information on characteristics of the American people such as labor force participation, income, crime victimization, incarceration rates, and measures of health."

I couldn't help but think of how valuable surveying enlisted Marines will be. Labor force participation? They are all employed. Income? Look at their ranks. On to the next paragraph. It's just a bolded excerpt from the legal page, "You risk a fine up to $5,000."

"I trust you will extend our field representative the time needed to conduct the survey. If you have any further questions, please do not hesitate to call the Program Supervisor at (800) ▆▆▆▆. Sincerely, James T. ▆▆▆▆, Regional Director."

The general paused for a moment as if still reading, just to breathe a little and maybe think of a way to avoid what he saw coming. No solution was materializing in his mind, just not enough time to mock up something normal in the barracks. He closed his eyes, brought his head back to level, and opened them.

Both the ambassador and Mr. Chang were happily looking out the heavily tinted windows at the run-down streets of Okinawa. The expression and countenance of Mr. Chang reminded him of that little creature thing that always accompanied the mad scientist in South Park. Both of them just blink, stare, blink, stare, exist, nothing more.

"Mr. Chang, I believe we can get you a list of the Marines living in the barracks and from that you can pull your sample. Just curious, why do we provide a roster of Marines in the barracks and then you pull a sample. Why don't we just give you a random sampling?"

"Sounds good, sir, it should only take 15 minutes or so. We do that so we avoid picking too many white guys. Turns out they have less crime victimization and incarceration rates and they are a larger portion of the military. Plus if the survey showed no one was in need for schools, libraries, and the like, I'd be out of a job. No one really says it, but our real goal is to create the perception of need, whether that is based on reality or not."

"That's cool. We can talk about it some other time but we are in the works for starting a female and minority officer symposium here to figure out why more of them get out early and don't stay in for 20. The project looks promising."

I felt an urge to chime in at this point and related my recent battle with "Ngrsh" the day before about diversity and the like. I decided to stay silent.

Now I never spoke to the general, but I assumed he figured to attempt a Hail Mary for avoiding the coming train wreck. Let's get them an Osprey ride first; they'll bite off on that while we work the barracks situation. He got out his Blackberry and texted who I only imagine can be the Futenma Commanding Officer to ask whether the barracks was still in "Condition 1," as they call it. The hope of salvation had injected him with a shot of energy and he began furiously pecking on the Blackberry.

"Something wrong, General?" the ambassador quipped.

The ambassador was sitting cross-legged in the back of the SUV with an undeniable coquettish smile, sipping her Evian bottled water.

"No, ma'am, just trying to keep us on timeline with this detour."

"General, did you know Demi Moore washes her hair with this stuff? I'm good friends with her. She visits my estate in Nantucket often. We eat soft shells and sip Kendall Jackson Merlot."

"No, ma'am, I hadn't heard that," he replied.

He didn't even look up from his Blackberry. The UAV made a left turn off the 58 abeam the old but proud-looking sign of MCAS Futenma. There was a Yamaha scooter shop on the left corner. The hill to climb up to the base was fairly steep and had several winding turns. As soon as we made the left turn, they spot about a half-dozen protestors on the sidewalks.

The local police were out to ensure the civility of the demonstration and avoid direct confrontation. A few of the protestors had signs. A few were just there to hoot and holler at the passersby. Their big gripe was with the Osprey. They didn't like the new aircraft one bit. Several had pictures of the aircraft on their signs. Another sign said "No US troops on Okinawa." One man had what looks like a Star Wars Jedi-type sword and as each vehicle with U.S. military personnel passed by, he made a slashing gesture. He had hatred in his eyes. The ambassador glanced up at the commotion.

"I had heard about these protests. It was in during my turnover for the ambassador position. What is their problem with the Osprey, it has had a safe record during its time here?"

"Well, ma'am, the Osprey is a new technology, the first of its kind. It can fly like an airplane but land like a helicopter. It was first conceived after the hostage crisis in Iran to have a long-range raid capability. Its first flight was in the early '80s, but after cost overruns and some problems selling it to the Marine Corps, we got it done. The fact that Dick Cheney tried to cancel it shows how troubled a program it had become. As a matter of fact, he tried four times in four years to end the program.[5] The Marine Corps just couldn't end its love affair though."

"What do you mean by that, General?"

The interest shown by the ambassador was one of envy rather than moral indignation.

"Well, ma'am, the Marine Corps can't seem to get away from Bell Textron products no matter how shitty they are or how much Bell Helicopter fucks us. Our UH-1Y Hueys you are about to see can't even fly in the rain because their tail rotors have a composite that expands when it gets wet. Bell sold us an all-weather helicopter that can't fly in the rain. Having said that, the Osprey has had a perfect safety record here in Okinawa. I think the protests are about ignorance rather than knowledge."

After this short conversation, the UAV had made its way to the top of the hill and to the entrance to the base. The Marine working the gate was young, maybe only 19 years old. He snapped to attention and saluted when he saw the ID of a general. Since he couldn't get eyes on to see a return salute or acknowledgement that he could cut his salute, he just held it. As the SUV drove straight through the four-way intersection just after the gate and past the Subway and Anthony's Pizza Shop, the Marine was still holding the salute and other guards have had to step up and forcefully move his arm down from the salute position.

The general was beginning to visibly perspire at this point. Something was wrong. He had ceased and desisted from pecking away on his Blackberry and he was consciously observing the ambassador. Unbeknownst to the ambassador, the general was praying she didn't decide to check out one of the enlisted barracks. *Just get her to the officer barracks. Anything, anything, God, but the enlisted barracks*, I think. He decided to try reverse psychology on her. Just something to buy him some time.

"Well, here we are, ma'am. May I suggest we conduct the survey at barracks 431? It has all the enlisted Marines up through the rank of sergeant who work on the flightline. It would give you a good idea of their living situation. Or we could get you up in an Osprey? I made a few requests on our way and they are all ready for you to go up. We can do the survey after. Mr. Chang, you can go as well."

For a moment he looked relieved, proud, and satisfied. Surely this will get them away from those Goddamn barracks. I prayed for his sake that it worked. As he snapped back to reality, his face showed his worry. It seemed to say, *Did I just zone out in front of her?*

"That's so very nice of you, General, to arrange for a flight for me on such short notice. However, I am very scared of planes. Ever since my brother crashed a perfectly good airplane into the ocean and killed himself and two other gold diggers, I haven't set foot in anything other than a commercial airliner that is commanded by true professionals. Hey, General, wanna hear a JFK Jr. joke?"

"Uh, are you serious, ma'am?"

The general could hardly believe what he had just heard.

Is this really happening, I think?

"Oh, yes, that was many years ago and the pain has passed. Ready? Why did JFK Jr. not take a shower before his last flight?"

"I don't know, ma'am." His face was hardened and bore the countenance of an ill person.

"Because he figured he'd wash up ashore. Get it?"

The general paused for a few seconds to gauge if she was fooling him. She had a smirk on her face showing him it's not a ruse. I was glued looking at the two in the rearview mirror and was about to burst. Mr. Chang was still doing his best South Park–creature pose and was oblivious.

"Bahahhahahahah."

Wissler folded over and started slapping his knee repeatedly. I took the cue that it's okay to laugh and almost lost control of the car. I was convulsing with laughter so hard.

After the general regained composure, he confessed, "Jesus, that's hateful as hell. I'm beginning to like your style, Ambassador. Got any more?"

"You bet. Why did the search and rescue team know JFK Jr. had dandruff?"

"God, I can't wait. Why?"

His face was transformed from a brutal killer to a kid in a candy shop.

"They found his head and shoulders in the wreckage."

"Whoooaaaaaaaaaabahahhahahahaha. Stop, stop, holy shit."

This time the general's head reared back as he belted out strings of joy. I had to pull over this time and recompose myself.

The general had been so occupied with the jokes that he lapsed on his previous fear.

"So enough with the jokes, like I said, I would like to check out the barracks, please."

The general was simply reserved to his fate. There was nothing more he can do. I pulled into the small lot in front of Barracks 431. As they entered the building, a smell of barn animal pervaded the small entranceway. The duty was asleep, slumped over the latest copy of *The Marine Corps Times* with a picture of Mad Dog Mattis on the cover and some story about crazy re-enlistment bonuses and a new CrossFit workout. A thirty-two-ounce Gatorade bottle was half filled with dip spit. Several grainy pieces of tobacco clung to the inside of the bottle. As we moved close, I caught the sharp smell of Grizzly wintergreen chewing tobacco. The general moved right by without saying a thing. He grabbed the duty binder and thumbed through it to grab a roster then went up to the second floor. There was a long hallway. No one was out or about. It was very quiet. The hallway tiles were very worn down and had dozens of stain marks.

"Well, ma'am, as you can see, it is pretty quiet right now. Most Marines are at work. The only ones that are here should be night crew. You see, maintenance is continuous so they need Marines to work on aircraft from sunup to sundown. After the flights for the day are over, the night crew comes in to work on any broken aircraft or do maintenance to get the birds ready for the next day."

She mulled this information over for a bit, but still seems perplexed. The general noticed so continued.

"Night crew Marines rack up with other night crew Marines. This allows them to all sleep during the day before they go into work."

"What time is the night crew shift?" she inquired.

"I'd have to double-check that, but I think it starts around 1600. They have a changeover with the day crew to pass any pertinent information from the day."

The clock on the wall said 1530. Steps could be heard on the stairs below. The squishing sound followed by creaking alerted the general to be none other than the sound of Corfams. Someone on duty was approaching. It was fairly dark in the hallway, but as the Marine passed into light, there was a glimmer and a daggone shimmer—it was an officer. A captain of Marines!

He was wearing his duty belt with a Beretta M9 automatic machine pistol with a 45-round clip. One in the weapon, the other in a holster ready to go. Also on his duty belt was a Taser, pepper spray, bear mace, handcuffs, and a retractable baton. His service Charlies were looking sharp, his chest adorned with the national defense and "global war on terrorism" ribbons. Above them were some shiny naval aviator wings. He noticed the two figures in the hallway and approached them. As soon as he could see the stars of the general, he snapped to attention and rendered an appropriate greeting.

"Good afternoon, General."

"Good afternoon. Are you the officer of the day, son?" The general was feeling relaxed now. He was a man who has accepted his fate.

"Yes, sir, this is only the second week of us working the officer of the day and the staff duty officer concept. It's part of the Reinvigoration."

"You mean the Reawakening?"

He blushed Marine Corps red for a second then corrected himself.

"Oh, yes, sir, the Reawakening."

"What is that?" asked the ambassador.

She had gone internal for a few minutes. The sight of the living conditions had shaken her. The last time she saw things this dirty was when their last maid was deported and they went without for two days.

"Ma'am, due to some behavioral problems in our corps, we have had to come out with a few new policies to correct the deficiencies."

"Oh, really, I love policy. Tell me more. The great thing about policy is that no matter what aspect of day-to-day operations, we have to have a policy. So what's the policy?" Her voice cracked high on the last sentence for some reason.

The ambassador could hardly contain her excitement.

"Well, let me tell you what the Reawakening isn't about. It's not about creating anything new. No new orders, training, buzzwords, or sayings. We have a small but not insignificant number of Marines who aren't upholding our standards. We have defeated our enemies on the battlefields and have exceled there, but at home in garrison we have begun to slip. We are committed to using the non-commissioned officer core of our organization to reenergize us. We want to make it clear that the identity of the Marine Corps is one of sacrifice. We fight for our country and each other. We are trusted by the nation to uphold the ideals of liberty and freedom."

She looked intrigued so he continued. I shot a quick glance at the duty officer and he just rolled his eyes.

"Marines are America's force-in-readiness focusing on fighting conflicts with aggressive and expeditionary forces, ready to go when our nation calls. We are ready to go to war, fight, and win in order to provide options to our leaders. We are trained and confident across our mission essential tasks and we will have units ready to fight and win in any clime and place. We use maneuver warfare, which allows us to function effectively in an uncertain, chaotic, and fluid environment. We are an island-based force that can conduct amphibious breaching operations, the last of which occurred in 1950. An iterative, diverse, purposeful, and challenging training program guides our development, sustains our readiness, and prepares our leaders at every level to make decisions under the pressures of combat. In addition to our training regimen, our standard operating procedures capture best practices, enable us to execute complex actions with increasing speed and tempo, and support effective tactical decision making.

"We have an innate bias for action and are offensively oriented. Our preference is to fight at night, negating the darkness with the green light of our night vision devices. The key to our combined arms warfighting abilities lies with putting our enemies on what we call the horns of a dilemma. From here the situation becomes untenable for the enemy and . . ."

"General!"

The ambassador cut him off abruptly and in a tone that didn't hide her dissatisfaction: "Why are you insulting my intelligence? I know the ethos of the corps. You think I haven't heard that boring-ass monologue you just recited before? I have to deal with generals all the time. I've seen the lava monster commercial, for Christ's sake. Oh, and that one with the 'Which way would you run?' with all the guys sprinting across open terrain in full combat gear to deliver USAID boxes full of water and rice. I've seen it all. Now please stop patronizing me and tell me *what . . . the . . . fuck* the Reawakening is about!"

Her head bobbed up and down on each word of the "what the fuck."

The captain duty officer was just frozen with fear. Or maybe it was fascination. It was hard to tell. I for one was just snapping my head back and forth between the exchanges.

"Okay, ma'am. I'll get down into the nitty-gritty of what exactly our course of action is. We are mandating that all single corporals and sergeants return to the barracks. They can no longer live out in town. Company-grade officers and senior staff non-commissioned officers will be armed at all times while on duty and will make their presence known at the barracks, especially between the hours of

2000 to 0400. We will have two non-commissioned officers on duty and a fire watch on every deck. An interior guard is to be established and will be trained up by the SNCO of the unit. All duty standers, officer and enlisted, will be in either service Bravos or Charlies.

"The overall goal here is to fight and win in the barracks, ma'am. Every morning at 0730 instead of reveille we will play 'Back on My Regimen' by Stic.man of Dead Prez feat. Divine on the barracks emergency broadcast system to get the Marines in the mood to work out. Following this the duty SNCO or officer will lead the men in physical training. We will install security cameras in every barracks. Every officer or SNCO that has Marines in his or her charge will download the app, 'What's My Marine Doing?' from the Google Play Store.

"This app was developed by Marine Corps Cyber Command in conjunction with GoPro specifically to meet the intent of our security camera policy. When you open the app, you sign in with your military .mil email address and it knows which barracks your Marines live in. Each respective unit has a security camera manager. It's an inspectable program. The manager ensures each .mil is synced to the correct security camera where their Marines live. To allay any privacy concerns, cyber command developed annual training. All users today are annual security camera manager training complete, I might add. If they aren't, they can't sign into the app. Anyways, kind of like it sounds you can view each Marines barracks hallways, rooms, bathrooms . . . everything. Want to see it in action?"

"Uh, yes, I guess."

Ambassador Kennedy was a little confused with all the buzzwords but seemed to get the gist of it. Mr. Chang held his position a few feet behind her and seemed to just turn his head ninety degrees to the left, right, and up every twenty seconds and surveyed the situation.

"Actually, better yet, Captain, let me see your phone's app, I take it you have it operational? The Blackberry I use can't run apps. We keep the contract with them though because a retired one-star got on their board of directors."

"Yes, sir." The captain pulled out his iPhone and turned on the app. It fired up right away and as it is warming up, a little caption popped up saying, "Watching those who can't watch themselves."

The initial screen is two drop-down boxes in addition to a spot for an email address. The first is the base, he scrolled to MCAS Futenma. Next is the building, 431. Lastly at the bottom, there is a button that goes from gray to green once both are entered and meet the criteria of being in range and having the correct credentials. The button says, Supervise.

"Captain, select floor two."

"Yes, sir."

The duty officer moved to the upper third of his screen and there are a few tabs. One is labeled floors. One is labeled rooms. He selected the floor tab and selected 2 then hits the Supervise button.

Lo and behold an image appeared, albeit a slightly grainy one, of the hallway they are standing in.

The ambassador was delighted and clapped her hands together a few times while jumping up and down a bit as she said, "Oh, how clever."

"Ma'am, as you can see, this just jumps up to the third floor. And this tab labeled rooms."

He trailed off and shot the general a hard stare. The look on his face conveyed that he is seeking approval. He wasn't sure if he should show her this.

"Go ahead, son." The general had suddenly become confident.

The captain pressed the room button and another image appeared of inside a room on the second deck. The sight of the room was hard to discern only because it was so implausible and audacious. There were three large cages, about the size you would keep a large dog, equally spaced about the room. There appeared to be desks and cabinets. In all the cages you could make out the profile view of a person in the fetal position. There appeared to be some bedding in the cages as well.

"General, what is inside those cages?"

"Those are the Marines, ma'am. Looks like they are still sleeping. Night crew most definitely. Actually," he glanced at his watch for a moment, "It's getting close to 1600, they should be rousting here shortly. Mr. Chang, here is the roster. You can take your sample from this. Just make sure they are on night crew. There is a column on the left side of the roster that says if they are day or night crew." The general had to physically walk over to hand him the roster because he was out of it.

"General, why do you keep them in cages like that? I assume they stay in there for their own personal safety? Surely this base is secure. I mean I was kinda scared when that protester took a fake swipe at me with his samurai sword, but we have gate guards, we have cameras, and we have this duty officer here."

"Well, ma'am, after a navy sailor raped an Okinawan woman a few years ago, things have never really been the same. And recently a Marine got drunk and broke into an Okinawan's home to just pass out. The real story behind that one is the Japanese woman was cheating on her husband and didn't expect him to come home. When her husband found the cheater, she claimed he broke in.

"They tend to ignore the fact that if it wasn't for the U.S. presence here, Japan and Okinawa would be a Chinese territory. Tokyo would be like Nanking was in 1937, a place of genocide. And if that scenario didn't pan out, Japan would definitely have to make tanks instead of Toyotas and ships instead of Sonys without us here to defend them. World War II has shown us that it's better to have the Japanese focus on capitalism rather than militarism. They are good at whatever they focus on. So in order to appease the Japanese government, we had to institute some protective measures to shield the local population from our savage Marines.

"As of today we do not allow drinking off base unless it is with a meal, so no bars. That's only for officers. For enlisted below the rank of sergeant, in most cases, they have to be back on base by 2200. They are not allowed to stay overnight in hotels or friend's houses. We use a card system. Red cards are for what I just described and gold cards are for the former description. Every night at 2200 we hold accountability for the red cards at the barracks. Just recently we instated a policy to have Marines sign in and out of logbooks when they go to places as simple as the gym or the post office. Just our way to keep tabs in case someone goes missing or whatever."

The ambassador immediately countered, "But didn't they earn the title Marine? Aren't they given the benefit of the doubt to act in a way that is honorable? Shouldn't we assume that they will act in the right way until they prove us wrong? If we treat them like this, what was the point of boot camp? Isn't there a vetting process?"

The general kept his bearing but my jaw dropped at the precision and accuracy of her question. The ambassador had just taken a massive diarrhea squirt shit on his OODA loop.

"Ma'am, I'll try to answer those individually if I can. Yes, they have earned the title of Marine and we take that seriously. We don't let anyone become Marines. You have to prove it and earn it. We don't want to punish the group for the actions of a few bad individuals. However, Okinawa is a different situation, an incident in town here goes high order very quickly. Someone getting into a fight near Camp Pendleton with a Mexican isn't newsworthy. A Marine fighting an Okinawan is. It quickly becomes an international incident.

"And international means you have to be involved. Imagine how much paperwork and drama you would have to deal with if we just let Marines raid the local bars and establishments every weekend. If they beat the shit out of each other because of their pent-up rage with being locked in cages, it's transparent to you. We deal with it at the unit level and it never spills out into the international arena."

"Yes, I see, General, thanks for not giving me grief. Between learning about Japan, dolphin hunting barbarism, and managing my estates, I have a lot on my plate. So why cages though?"

"We learned from flash reports after on-base incidents that most fights between Marines happened in the room and within plus or minus one hour of lights, otherwise known as bedtime. It turns out when Marines get tired, their depression with Okinawa deepens and they start fighting each other. The cages are a way for us to de-conflict the fights. I will say we have actually slackened off a bit on our initial policy. The cages are known as Condition 1. When we first started it, was more punitive for everyone so the Marines had to sleep naked to harden them. That was Condition 0. Now that incidents have decreased, we have allowed clothes. What we see here is Condition 1. Oh look, they are beginning to stir, right on time, it's 1545."

On the captain's iPhone you could see the shapes slowly writhing out from under their covers. The lights automatically came on. The three Marines slowly made their way out of their cages and began dressing. They each took turns grabbing a Red Bull and a can of Grizzly out of their mini-fridge. Within five minutes, they were dressed and on the go.

"Captain, escort Mr. Chang here and assist him in any way that he needs. He'll be conducting a survey on several Marines. I suggest waiting at the bottom of the stairs and calling out names, take them into the lounge to fill out their questionnaire. Drop my name if they are late for the maintenance turnover meeting. Trackin'?"

"Yes, sir, it will be done." The captain clicked his heels, saluted smartly, and escorted Mr. Chang down the stairs.

After the survey the group decided to exit the back gate in order to see the entire flight line. The road took the rough shape of a U with the runway in the middle. As we wrapped around the bottom part of the U, several small schoolchildren can be seen glued to the outer section of fence. They gazed mesmerizingly onto the air station.

"General, why do those children do that?" the ambassador asked. Mr. Chang was sleeping peacefully using his chin as a pillow.

"There was a time, ma'am, when Marines knew the Okinawans in a neighborly sort of way. Back in the '60s and '70s, I think, I was here, but it seems like a dream you struggle to remember. Some guys back then would go out and visit the battle sites without tour guides. We would bring beer to them and they would sit down with us and tell us about the battle. There weren't feelings of resentment or blame or anger or hate. Imagine the atmosphere of cookouts back in the States. We learned something about each other's humanity and how the Okinawans hated the Japanese occupying them but almost equally hated their island being destroyed by the U.S. Most estimates put Okinawan civilian deaths at over 100,000. It is hard to quantify the loss of life, welfare, and innocence that took place here. The Okinawans aren't anti-U.S. military; rather they are anti-military in general. They would hate the Chinese just as much as they hate the Marines.

"But with time comes a fading of memory. Slowly but surely the diplomats and ambassadors assigned here were more interested in present-day political correctness and fleeting politics than starting with a baseline of common humanity. Cultures clash but humanity always remains. They were afraid to tell the Okinawans who we are and in turn ask them to tell us about who they are. It's like two neighbors that live in black boxes right next to each other and one has no idea who the other one is or what he does. So to answer your question, the kids look at us now not as humans but as some type of caged animal. Sort of like a zoo. They come to observe the Marine animals that live on Futenma."

"Interesting take, General. Can we stop for some more Evian, it's hot here."

"Captain, next vending machine stop for drinks."

"Aye, aye, sir. Sir, these machines don't carry Evian, only Dasani."

"I guess it'll do, Captain." The ambassador rolled her eyes.

Boarding the Boat and the Tactical Recovery of Aircraft and Personnel

Late February 2014

We had been conducting workups the past several weeks. As usual it is a crawl, walk, run approach. First the missions launched from the island of Okinawa. Then we briefed as if we are on the ship. And then finally we actually embarked onto the ship and run the missions. The enemy is always a communist-backed insurgency on the northern end of the island. We practiced most of the missions of the MEU. Mech Raid, which is using amphibious assault vehicles to assault an objective. Helo Raid, inserting a large number of troops by helicopters. Even a little Non-Combatant Evacuation Operations or NEO are conducted. Think what *didn't* happen at Benghazi.

We slowly but surely loaded our gear onto the ship, driving it from MCAS Futenma up to White Beach about an hour north. After the logistics Marines do the loading of the heavy stuff, we ourselves made the trek with our personal gear. As we were walking down the long pier toward the ships, I noticed how massive the mighty USS *Bonhomme Richard* was. She towered over the USS *Denver* opposite her. And in the shallower waters were small Japanese patrol-type boats. Definitely large ships, the size of pleasure yachts, but fishing boats in comparison to the American ships behind her. I smiled inwardly and recited the words of Rudyard Kipling:

Send forth the best ye breed,

Go bind your sons to exile to serve your captives need.[1]

Worker bees of all types were busy loading gear and supplies onto the ships. Food, tools, weapons, and personnel baggage were waiting their turn to be craned onto the ship. Further back in the line of things to be lifted were a few curiously large wooden crates. There were two distinct types of crates. The larger ones were about 8 feet long by 5 feet high and 3 feet wide. The smaller ones were about 3 feet long by 2 feet high by 1 foot wide. I quietly broke away from the main pack of my group and investigated the crates. As I drew closer, the smell of barn animal was present.

I got close to one of the larger crates and I could hear what almost appeared to be labored breathing of some large mammal. I gave one of the smaller crates a gentle kick and immediately I could hear rustling inside. What the fuck were in these crates, I think? If I had to guess, it was some kind of live animal. Before I could dig deeper, one of the guys in our group called me back and we boarded the ship to unload our belongings. A few days later we flew our helicopters to the ship and we commenced the Okinawa 500, as it is called. Just laps around the island of Okinawa.

Within a few weeks we conducted the MEU Exercise III. Same missions except as noted above we were now on the ships. Once those were complete, the next hurdle was Certification Exercise or CERTEX. Kind of like it sounds, CERTEX is an evaluation exercise. Marines from another higher unit of III Marine Expeditionary Force board the ship and observe our planning and execution.

There was considerable pressure to perform in order to certify the MEU as full mission capable. Our squadron CO had warned us earlier that if we drop every last mission for CERTEX, we still passed. We were not to take any unnecessary risk. Keeping this in mind, I was tasked with taking part in one of the less well-known MEU missions: Tactical Recovery of Aircraft and Personnel or TRAP. This was a training code I needed in order to progress as an attack pilot.

Pre-mission planning went about as expected. I got with the Osprey pilots who would be flying the recovery force a few days prior to hash out our plans. The Skids would be launching a Cobra and Huey. The Osprey guys were as usual on the ball. They told me we would just "flex" and do a strip-type brief because to be true mission capable, we would be on strip alert for TRAP.

Knowing this, I went to my Assault Support Tactical Standard Operating Procedure manual and got a digital version of the TRAP template. The TRAP template allows you to overlay an objective area that is centered on the survivor, complete with battle positions and holding areas for rotary wing aircraft and fixed wing initial points.

As I was coming up with my brief, I realized I had some "resource shortfalls." For the non-aviation readers out there, a "resource shortfall" is some type of asset you need for the mission but don't currently have. For instance, if the enemy situation includes MI-24 HIND attack helicopters, you need to deal with those. The best way is with some friendly fixed wing with air-to-air missiles like an AV-8B Harrier or F/A-18 Hornet. Or if you need persistent Intelligence Surveillance and Reconnaissance or ISR, you can request an RQ-7 or Global Hawk or a similar drone that can loiter for hours.

Since we don't actually have those assets, we just fairy dust or make believe those assets are there. You just go to your instructor and ask for the asset and they say "Approved." You then put that asset in a PowerPoint slide with *whatever* weapons you want and an on-station time that facilitates your mission. Another important point to remember about today's military is our love of PowerPoint slides. We love to give briefs and have meetings along with pretty charts and quantitative analysis. As long as you include what your plan is on that PowerPoint slide, regardless of how infeasible it is, the slide is all that counts. We rightly assume that when a war happens, we can just pass those slides along and then those assets will appear since it is the real thing. Gone are the days of learning by doing, as long as the slide looks good, the system will reward you even if reality won't.

One of the most memorable PowerPoint moments occurred before we began our float on the ship. I was standing Operations Duty

Officer. The ODO gives aircraft assignments, weather, and other pertinent information to fly. Some of the Osprey pilots were in the room practicing their brief to become Night Systems Instructors or NSIs. They had an NSI with them to coach them on their brief, which was one big PowerPoint presentation. As they slowly clicked through the slides, their fellow NSI stopped them at their slide showing the overview of the island of Okinawa. In order to represent the cultural areas, which would be bright at nighttime, they used a type of freeform shape that looked like a mini explosion with a red outline and yellow fill.

These shapes were strewn all about the island and placed in the appropriate areas. The NSI reviewing their slides said when it came time for their check ride, or the final flight in the NSI syllabus when they would be evaluated, the instructors wanted to see more cultural lighting. The NSI said on his check ride they hit him on his brief on that particular slide because he didn't have enough little yellow explosions to signify well-lit areas. The students took down some good notes to add more of the shape to the slide. That's the detail that PowerPoint allows you; it's a great tool.

And the great thing about make-believe assets is you will never get turned down. And their beauty is in the fact that they do whatever you need to perfectly, zero friction. They show up on time, with the ordnance you requested, and for the time you wanted. And they never miss. For example, I want the Harriers to use AIM-9 Sidewinder missiles to attrite the MI-24 HIND threat. As soon as we start flying, the instructor lets me know the Harriers have engaged and destroyed the HINDS. A make-believe asset destroys another make-believe asset. It's that simple.

As I was in the wardroom writing my brief, it occurred to me how fake our training was and I became sad. After eating four cookies, two brownies, and a sundae from the wardroom, I still didn't feel better. Just bloated.

Then the usual evening announcement came on. This civilian on the ship was tasked with giving us motivating pep talks every night, it seems. She has a large, ugly, dumb head and runs her mouth a lot.

For the song of the night they began playing "You Got It" by Roy Orbison.

"One look . . . from you . . . I drift . . . away . . . I pray [*pop pop*] . . . that you [*pop pop*] . . . are here . . .to stay. Anything you want, you got it, anything you need, you got it. Anything at all, you got it, baaaaabbby."

I realized this song fits perfectly with my training shortfalls. Anything I want or need I got it, no questions asked. I was overcome with grief and in an attempt to end it all, I ran up to the ice cream machine and invert my head, mouth open. I pulled the handle full down to open the spigot of chocolate malt. However, after about 15 seconds, the brain freeze was too much and I passed out.

When I came to, I was sprawled out in a puddle of brown, sticky goo on the floor. I slowly rolled over and sat up. A fat captain by the name of Fitzgerald didn't even notice me as he was eating two plates of food for midnight rations. I gathered my sad self together and headed back to my stateroom.

At next morning's breakfast, I noticed the ship's little bi-weekly newsletter. In it is the commodore of the Amphibious Ready Group cutting some cake with a bunch of female navy personnel . . . hmm. Turns out March is Women's History Month, no wonder I've been hearing a daily inspiring story about females in the military. Fifteen minutes before my brief, they tell another story.

"Today's female history highlight goes out to Jessica Lynch. Jessica was from West Virginia and wasn't sure what to do with her life. All the men went to work in the coal mines or joined the military. She decided to join the National Guard while studying for her degree in organizational leadership. She didn't plan on a war happening and in 2003 she found herself in Iraq, part of the push to Baghdad. While in a convoy to support logistics her unit was ambushed. Quickly taking action she grabbed her well rusted M16. As the men around her engaged the enemy and chaos ensued, she assumed command of her fear and calmly curled up into a ball in the back of a Humvee. When she came to she was in possession by the enemy. The Rangers ended up rescuing her and after a million dollar book deal she is a motivational speaker for how to overcome adversity. The men who fought and died were lost in the back pages of the newspaper."

Finally the brief was allowed to commence. Overall it was uneventful, typical stuff of the Osprey guys mixing their section brief with the flight brief. The big unknown was the survivor information and location. We were not sure how or when we would receive this information. Usually you would get an ISOPREP from the S-2, which gives you specific information on how to authenticate a survivor. After about an hour of waiting around and hearing a few more PA announcements for Women's History Month, we got the call to stand 15-minute TRAP alert. That means we have 15 minutes from the time we receive the order to launch the TRAP until takeoff. We assembled our suits and gear and headed to the flight deck of the mighty USS *BHR*.

We spun up and were awaiting a launch order, but still no ISOPREP. Finally one of the Osprey pilots, call sign Beeboop, appeared on the flight deck looking commanding as usual with a short, unsure composure and voice tone similar to a mouse. He was approved to move underneath our rotor arc to give us our ISOPREPs. As this was occurring, my instructor was busy talking to Tower Flower to make sure we were on the same sheet of music for the execution checklist. Tower Flower has no procedural control. He is just a fellow aviator that can help you out with aircraft status or mission questions. Turns out they have one checklist per the MEU exercise and we have another. ISOPREPS have specific questions only the person who filled it out would know. Then when we authenticate them, we can be sure we have the right guy. The one that sticks out to me is "My Marine recruiter was busted for child porn."

I immediately began laughing but the instructor shut me up and called for a takeoff checklist front seat. I rolled through it.

I instinctively took a last sip of water, set the comm, nav, squawk, and gave the signal for chains. After we were unchained, I slid my hands right under my ass. We were off and 10 minutes later we were feet dry over Okinawa looking for the survivor. I tried to make a few good points, but the instructor as usual just ignored me and went internal. Eventually we spotted the survivor, running down a hardball road being chased by dogs. We tipped in and at this point I "simulate" mowing them down with 20mm. However, my hands were so numb at this point I couldn't even use them. I tried shaking them out, biting them, and wringing them quickly to get the blood back. It was not working.

The instructor was trying to attack some vehicles near the pickup landing zone while the Ospreys were slowing approaching at 100 feet and 5 knots. I told him they were not in the scenario and not fair game. He just repeated the question as if I wasn't even in the cockpit. After the survivor was extracted, we began searching for other targets. We saw some guys lounging around near a road intersection. The instructor asked me to take controls so he can write an attack brief down. Being the sandbag that I was, I didn't want to upset him, so I take them.

I figured out I can just set the torque on the collective with my wrist then use both wrists on the cyclic to control. In keeping with the tradition of not interjecting during flights, I just kept my mouth shut even though I think I should say something. Luckily the instructor didn't notice the shitty control movements and somehow the feeling started easing back into my hands. I flew us back after the pick and as we approached the boat I thought I might actually get to land. Right before we broke across the bow of the ship, the instructor said, "Tell ya what, this might get kinda complex with the Ospreys, my controls."

After passing controls I passed out from boredom and the next thing I remember is sitting in the ready room for a debrief. The Osprey guys had already broken beer out and were slapping each other's backs talking about how they flexed. The section lead gleefully proclaimed, "We didn't brief to it, we didn't plan, but we flexed . . . good job, guys."

I learned a lesson that day: Even when things don't get briefed, you still need to play out all possible scenarios. I would have never guessed my hands would cease to work like they did. On subsequent flights, I learned to switch which hand was under my ass to make sure one was always awake. I also brought a camp pillow to take naps for those long lulls holding in battle positions and holding areas.

Afterward we still have 20 minutes before lunch was over, so we rolled down to the wardroom. They were having chicken parmesan and spaghetti. I joined Dash and My Friend who were sitting with some unfamiliar Marine officers. Not even a minute after sitting down, my My Friend was preaching another round of our recruiting pitch for three-percenters. The officers My Friend was speaking with seemed to be ground officers.

One was a captain, another a female first lieutenant. The female had a habit of wearing a ridiculous amount of makeup with lots of red in the cheeks. So much that I actually bestowed on her a call sign of JD or Joker's Daughter . This was among friends and not to her face. I simply listened to My Friend indoctrinate.

He was good at it.

My Friend started.

"Do you know what percentage of the American population took up arms against the British in the Revolutionary War?"

The captain shrugged and replied, "I dunno, like 20 percent."

Joker's Daughter fancied that answer and added a little.

"Thirty percent."

My Friend just stared at them for about two seconds and said, "Three percent."

"Really? Damn I woulda never guessed."

The captain was genuinely impressed.

My Friend glanced around the room at bit for theatric effect then continued, "Did you or did you not take an oath to defend and protect the *Constitution* of the United States against all enemies, foreign *and domestic*?"

They both answered in unison, "I did."

One more second of pause. My Friend dug deeper, "Do you think our government is currently representative of the people of the United States?"

The captain immediately jumped on board. "Fuck no, our government is corrupt as shit. Special interest has taken over. Look at this exercise, for God's sake."

Joker's Daughter was looking at a makeup mirror so My Friend ignored her and focused on the one with potential. He nodded in agreement with the captain and dropped the last line with force.

"Will you stand with me, when the time comes?"

Again the captain jumped at the chance.

"Hell yeah, give me liberty or give me death! Where do I sign up?"

"Welcome, 3 percenter."

My Friend looked at me and I was proud.

We continued our meal.

Brigadier General Mullen and Lieutenant Colonel Roesti Address the Ready Room

2000L 27 March 2014

The ships comprising the 31st MEU are known as the Amphibious Ready Group or ARG. They had made their way to the waters of the Korean peninsula and were on station for the exercise.

We'd flown a few TACFORM missions on our way up to the peninsula. Other than that, it had been the same regimen of eat, workout, study, sleep.

A few hours after reading the email from our Executive Officer concerning the political nature of this exercise, we assembled in the ready room, awaiting our VIPs. I would suggest re-reading the email in the first chapter if necessary.

Our squadron commanding officer delivered a quick prep talk to all the officers assembled in the ready room. Keep up the good work, this, that, and the other. He couldn't say why the long string of VIPs were speaking tonight, but was told it was very important. The word "critical" was dropped several times. The first speaker was Brigadier General William Mullen, director of the Capabilities Development Directorate.

His journey has been long and he just landed aboard the USS *Bonhomme Richard* a few hours before. Earlier that day, we were told he took a tour of the island of Okinawa aboard an MV-22 Osprey from the squadron. On our flight schedules, this is known as a VIP Lift, but this quickly became distasteful. Lifting a VIP on an aircraft that has little to no visibility for passengers and costs $32,000 dollars an hour to operate might raise a few red flags. So they simply changed what we call it on the schedule. It is now Battlefield Circulation. Same mission, different name.

As we all stand to the position of attention, I noticed he is accompanied by the executive officer of the MEU, Lieutenant Colonel Roesti. The general put everyone at ease and we took our seats. I arrived early and occupied a seat in the second row.

The general began. "Gentlemen, we are on the brink of some changes in our corps. I'm sure many of you have questions regarding the current exercise we are preparing for: Ssang Young 2014. The shift to the Pacific has been good and bad for us gents. Good in that we have so much awesome history whipping the Japs back in the day and even back to the days of ole Smedley Butler and the Boxer Rebellion in China. We were truly at the top of our game during the Korean conflict. Minimal time to deploy, an overwhelming horde of Commie bastards rolling south, and freezing cold. We still won. So naturally our pedigree gives us a leg up on pushing out the competition like the army.

"I was recently answering questions at the Center for Strategic and International Studies in Washington last July. I explained there what I'll try to explain here is that with the budget the way it is, and with the nature of future conflicts the way they are, we have had to put priorities in places we maybe didn't want to. We're in a state of flux right now, as you can probably imagine. Our commandant's priorities right now are crisis response, at the expense of major combat operations. With regards to a true amphibious assault, if we absolutely had to do it, we certainly would, but it'd be a stretch.[1]

"Our well-known Amphibious Assault Vehicles (AAV) are aging rapidly. We had the Expeditionary Fighting Vehicle (EFV) coming down the line, but it was canceled due to other reasons which following speakers will discuss. As hard as an amphibious assault would be, we absolutely have to keep that capability in our pocket. If you don't have a credible ability to do that, that gives people who don't like you very much room to maneuver. We have to have the ability to do something, either V-22s or a combination of V-22s and connectors.[2]

"We are fighting some internal battles right now over the Amphibious Combat Vehicle (ACV) 1.1. I'm sure many of you read the article published in the *Marine Corps Times* by Colonel Magee concerning the ACV's shortcomings. I would recommend taking a look. I happen to agree with Colonel Magee's big points. We have to prove that it swims. We don't know that for sure, engineering specifications appear to say that it does, but we can't say that for sure.[3]

"I brought Lieutenant Colonel Roesti along to give you a little more relevant picture of the challenges we face in the twenty-first century. Being the XO of the MEU, he has a better firsthand account of what goes on out here. I'm just back in Quantico and Washington most days making coffee for fucking major generals. Liutenant Colonel Roesti, the floor is yours."

Lieutenant Colonel Roesti traded places with the general and confidently assumed the central position of the ready room. He was a large but not tall man and had a high and tight haircut, which instantly made me want to not trust him, but his countenance made me think he is a great American.

"Thank you, sir. Gentlemen, I'd like to expand upon what the general said and talk a little more tactically since that's the level you all find yourselves in. I'm currently writing a short piece about the Anti-Access Area Denial or A2/AD defense posture our potential adversaries are taking these days. Borrowing briefly from Colonel Magee and Major Duvall's recent work, assume we are 100 NM from the enemy shore. Anti-ship missiles in the Exocet class could reach the fleet in 5 to 6 minutes. Missiles like the supersonic Soviet Sunburn will reach us in 3 minutes, and the newest iterations of

Carrier Killer missiles the Chinese have travel hypersonic and would reach us in less than a minute.[4]

"Enemy threat missiles have come a long way. No longer do our objectives allow us to loiter within visual range of the enemy. If some of you history buffs will recall from the study of World War I, the general thinking prior to the war was you could use gusto and courage, what the French called *elan*, to overrun your enemies. The last major war in Europe before World War I was the 1870 Franco-Prussian war. The Prussians simply outmaneuvered the French despite inferior weapons. The notion of defense was thought to be irrelevant. History shows that the defense is indeed strong. We have to allow for proper standoff if we don't want our fleet to come to rest in Davy Jones' locker.

"The latest Expeditionary Force (EF) 21 vision released by the corps has moved our offshore distance to 65 nautical miles from the previous 12 nautical miles.[5] EF 21 is guiding document for the future operations of the Marine Corps and was released less than a month ago on 4 March 2014. Colonel Magee and Major Duvall seem to think the 100-mile distance isn't farfetched given the proliferation of anti-ship missiles.[6] We'll go with the 65 nautical miles that EF 21 espouses. That is over a dozen times the distance our current amphibious assault vehicles are designed to swim.[7] It used to be 12 miles and . . ."

He was cut off by the phone ringing at the briefing desk. Rookie mistake on our part, I thought to myself. We should have put an underling at the desk to answer the phone when it rang. Lieutenant Colonel Roesti isn't the type of officer who is above anything menial, so he answered the phone.

"Lieutenant Colonel Roesti speaking, how can I . . . no, this isn't the number for Force Protection, this is the ready room. What? Okay, calm down, what is your name? All right, LS2 Simmons, so you think you may have been sexually assaulted?"

There was a perceptible stir in the room.

The lieutenant colonel grabbed a piece of paper to take some notes and simultaneously asked the crowd, "Do we have any Uniform Victim Advocates (UVA) in here?"

I instinctively glanced behind me and about fifteen guys and three females stand up. Let me remind you, there were about 70 people in the room. That's the usual ratio. The lieutenant colonel summoned the closest UVA in the front row, a female captain from the CH-53 community. Without passing the phone, he began to take the 5 *W*s of who, what, when, where, why.

"Okay, so you were sort of seeing this guy before the ship was underway and you continued to hang out on the ship."

He jotted a few notes then listened, interjecting every few seconds with an *mmhmm*.

"Let me read it back so I see if I get it right. You both ate chow together and you invited him back to your room, you were sober, and you asked him to lay in your bed. You took off your panties and sat on his face. That's correct? Okay. Next question, did he ask you to? He didn't. Okay. So you just climbed up on him?"

His expression turned from semi to super serious.

"All right, what happened then? Oh, okay, he licked you on your huha. That's definitely sexual assault, cut and dry. Where are you now? Still in your room, all right, stay put. Don't take a shower."

He turned to the UVA,

"You hear all that?"

"Yes, sir."

The female captain was red with anger and disgust for this vile sailor that would do such a deed.

He moved back to the phone.

"Where is the perpetrator now, LS2? He went back to his rack? Okay, we need his name and rate."

He finished writing on the pad then told the LS2 that the authorities will be with her soon to help her and hung up. He quickly dialed Force Protection, the cops of the ship, and summoned them to the ready room. Meanwhile he gave the waiting UVA a quick brief.

"All right, Captain, should go without saying this will be an unrestricted report. Here are the 5 Ws. Get to her room quickly and comfort her. Tell her that she is the victim of sexual assault. Can't stress that enough. Instill that victim mentality in her. Take her to the ship's doc to get checked out then report back to me in my stateroom and I'll push this up to the ship's XO. From there he'll let the Amphibious Ready Group Commander know and likely after that have a conference video with the chief of naval operations, the secretary of defense, and Senator Gillibrand."

The captain took the pad and swiftly left. A minute later Force Protection arrived.

"Gentlemen, here is the name of your suspect. Expect him to be trying to wash off evidence. He will stick out like a sore thumb with all that box juice on his face, nose, and possibly neck. Make sure to swab it to get a match. I want swabs of his mouth, nose, and eyes. Apprehend him and take him to the brig. No food and water for 24 hours. We will interrogate him soon. Make haste!"

They took the paper, turned, and left, making a change jingling sound as their instruments of force swayed to and fro on their hip belts.

"All right, where was I, oh yes, the range of anti-ship ballistic missiles. So Coastal Defense Cruise Missiles or CDCMs have proliferated greatly. No longer is it just NATO countries; Iran and North Korea have them and places like Yemen and Egypt ain't far behind. The carrier battle group stays around 400 miles away to honor the CDCM threat. As Colonel Magee and Major Duvall stated in their piece, if the goal of the amphibious task force is to protect the carrier, where will that leave us, the Marines, hanging out at 100 miles off the coast? Launching the AAV from 65 miles as stated in EF 21 is ludicrous even in calm seas.

"The Amphibious Combat Vehicle 1.1, our interim solution, as General Mullen stated, isn't amphibious, has wheels, and is damn heavy. It would rely on some type of navy connector like a Landing Craft Air Cushion (LCAC) to get ashore. The navy isn't interested in procuring the LCAC fleet. Even with LCACs we are looking at around three hours from ship to shore.[8] If we can't get the world's finest fighting man ashore, how can we justify our existence? Until Congress says part of our job description isn't the seizure of advanced naval bases, what are we gonna do?"

He paused and panned about the room, taking in everyone's reaction. I personally was struck by how honest and shocking this all was.

"My goal is to not scare any of you into thinking we will become irrelevant. We have some friends in high places, uhruh. Like any business that sees its market shrink, we just have to change our business model. We are a bureaucracy, and like any good bureaucracy, we'll search out other things to be responsible for. Believe me, there is plenty of business out there, we just have to adapt to get it and where necessary create our own business in the model of the self-licking ice cream cone. Here to help explain how this transition will happen, we have two very special guests, the secretary of defense and the secretary of state."

Secretary of Defense Chucky Hagel Speaks

A perceptible shuffling in chairs could be sensed all around me. Really? The secretary of state and the secretary of defense, here, on the 31st MEU? Something really important must be happening for them to show up. The general moved and took one of the reserved seats in the front row while the lieutenant colonel shifted to the door to keep watch for the next VIPs.

Naturally during this pause, we started to chat softly with our neighbors about the odd situation we found ourselves in. The MEU XO compensated for the last mistake and posted one of the young lieutenants on the phone. I think he was a DASCateer, a Direct Air Support Center guy, who would be responsible for setting up the aviation element's communications if we went ashore for a battle. Since we aren't doing this he spent all day either eating, working out, annoying the pilots with stupid questions, or sleeping.

About a minute went by and the lieutenant colonel glanced outside, back in, and said, "Standby . . ."—we all scooted to the edge of our seats—"attention on deck!"

Chucky and Kerry strode confidently into the room. Chucky had the command presence of a military man. Kerry had his usual long, gaunt, and tired face paired with sunken eyes. They were both wearing slacks and polos with undoubtedly freshly issued USS *BHR* ball caps. Kerry had an aviator jacket on. Maybe to make us feel more at ease with him, I don't know.

Chucky put us at ease and we took our seats. He gazed at the crowd for a few seconds then began.

"Gentlemen, I'm sure you are all wondering why myself and the secretary of state are on your ship right now. I promise there is a good reason. First, I want to say thank you for what you do and your service. I know you all probably have some questions about this exercise as it approaches. I would be upset if you didn't, to be honest. We operate on the enemy, not on ourselves, and this exercise is putting that to the test. Putting myself in your shoes, I bet more than a few have some heartache with the Marine Corps putting on a brigade-level exercise off the coast of an allied, wealthy foreign country.

"Interventionism has its bonuses. A recent poll by the *Wall Street Journal* and NBC news found 47 percent of Americans want us to be less involved in global conflicts. The American people are tired of war and understandably so. They have seen their taxes increase tremendously to fund our foreign wars and foreign aid. They want us to just mind our own business. However, turning inward, history teaches us, does not insulate us from the world's troubles. It only forces us to be more engaged later—at a higher cost in blood and treasure, and often on the terms of others.[1]

"Although Americans today are increasingly skeptical of foreign engagement and global responsibilities, it is a mistake to view those responsibilities as a burden or as charity. Let us remember that the biggest beneficiaries of American leadership and engagement in the world are the American people.[2] In the period of 2000 to 2012, shipments of real defense goods rose 41 percent compared to a 4 percent increase in total manufacturing shipments.[3] That was good for the American economy and Americans making those weapons. Yes, it's true, we have lost a huge amount of our manufacturing base. From December 2000 to December 2010, we lost 5.5 million manufacturing jobs. It's okay, Uncle Sam picked up a lot of the slack.

"In 2011 there are around 22.5 million people working for the government and around 11.5 million in manufacturing. Contrast that from 1960 when 15 million were in manufacturing and 8.7 million worked for the government.[4] Times change. It's okay. The secretary of state will expand upon that shortly. The point is, we can't shy away from the world in a military way. Walking away from the world, and our relationships, is not an option for the United States.[5] Even after the drawdowns in Iraq and Afghanistan, we have 400,000 troops in over 100 bases around the world.[6] What would happen to Europe if we took out our 68,000 troops? Russia is practically knocking on Europe's door. Forgot for a moment that the GDP of the EU is ten times that of Russia and that if Europe had to truly to defend itself, they could.[7] Think more of consumerism. The Germans would have to go back to making Tiger tanks instead of BMWs. I personally love my M3."

He paused when he saw a few faces begin to frown. I personally just unconsciously did a puppy head roll to reveal my confusion.

"Sorry, I got off on a tangent there. Secretary Kerry will flesh that concept out here shortly. I'm here to give you a hint of what the future holds. I want to talk about our presence in the Pacific. I recently sat down with Chris Uhlmann of the Australian Broadcasting Corporation. He logically questioned how we could pay attention in the Pacific while we have raging problems in the Middle East. We have over 360,000 military personnel in the Asia Pacific region and over 200 naval ships.[8] There is a good damn reason we have your capabilities out here. Marine blood has been spilled by the buckets in the fight to defeat the Japanese in World War II.

"As mentioned by the general and Liuetenant Colonel Roesti, the amphibious assault was the culmination of Marine daring and ingenuity and helped to win the war. We have retained that ability to do an amphibious assault despite the increase in the enemies' defensive technologies like anti-ship missiles just mentioned. Even in World War II without anti-ship missiles, amphibious assaults were dangerous operations and they remain the hardest of all military operations. At Tarawa our Higgins boats didn't have enough draft of water and got hung up on coral hundreds of yards away from the beach and had to wade under intense enemy fire to the beach. Only the risky commitment of the reserves the next day allowed the Marines to overwhelm the Japanese. Marines, you are a service who is known for being blunt and up front, so I'm going to lay some cold truth on you. The fact is . . ."

The phone rang again and Chucky just stopped cold and turned. The average man can only assume it has to do with the sexual assault that just happened. The hapless first lieutenant at the desk picked up the phone and answered with his name and rank followed by the cursory, "How can I help you, sir/ma'am?" We all just watched him gaze off into space as he absorbed the noise on the other end of the phone.

"Okay, sir," he said as he cupped the mouthpiece and shouted, "Attention, gentlemen, I've got the ship's XO on the phone and he needs Sexual Assault Prevention Response training rosters from each Marine unit."

The rosters showed that everyone in the unit has been given the required training. It's just bookkeeping really, but God help the commander whose Marines aren't trained. Dash was our unit's ground training officer and learned from experience that it isn't good ground training until you have a roster. As soon as your name is on the roster, it really doesn't matter what happens because higher can produce that roster for his higher to "prove" all his Marines are trained.

Remember, in today's military, being good on paper is being good enough. As long as you can provide paper copy documentation and the boxes are checked, that suffices for readiness.

The squadron CO, without being asked, stood up. This doesn't mean much because he's about 4'10", and directed, "Okay, I need all H-1 and CH-53 detachments officers in charge to get me those rosters in five minutes, I've got our roster on me, I had a feeling this might happen."

He reached into his lower flight suit pocket and produced a folded, laminated roster.

The various Sexual Assault Prevention and Response representatives within the detachments scrambled out the door to head back to their workstations to retrieve their rosters. While we are waiting in an awkward silence, the first lieutenant has hung up and the XO came onto the PA system.

"Good evening, BHR, this is the XO. Higher is asking for our SAPR training rosters, with the exception of the Marine Aviation Combat Element who is in a meeting right now. All divisions of the ship need to get me their rosters in person or via email no later than 1900. The captain is requiring 100 percent accountability. We've had, and I've counted, four SAPR training sessions in the past three months so there is no excuse. If you don't have 100 percent accountability, I need to see you in person no later than 1915. The captain would like to say something."

A slight garble can be heard as they changed positions, then the captain spoke in an unmistakably Southern accent. This captain being a navy captain, so the Marine equivalent is a colonel.

"Hey BHR, just wanna say we are BHR, thanks for all the hard work. This is just a hiccup we'll get through. We are BHR Cap'n out."

Chucky looked up toward the intercom to await another possible message, gave the phone another cursory glance, then resumed, looking annoyed.

"All right, I was on subject of the amphibious assault. The bottom line is that it's a relic. It's a thing of the past. The last actual no-shit assault against an enemy actively holding a beach was in September 1950 during the Korean War. 64 years ago. Sixty . . . four . . . years ago."

The creaking of the old flight chairs in the room can be heard as Marines turned their emotional disturbance into a physical one. He paused for dramatic effect, scanned the back of the room then back to front, and continued.

"Now some of you astute history buffs may say, 'Secretary Hagel, we conducted a successful amphibious invasion of Grenada in 1983.'

"You would be right, but that landing was essentially unopposed and on an island nation being defended by pussies. Per the Joint Pub JP-3.02, there are five kinds of amphibious operations. Amphibious raids, demonstrations, assault, withdrawal, and support for crisis response.[9] The Grenada operation would be something between a raid and a demonstration. Let's just say it was a landing even though there is no such technical term. Ssang Young is a demonstration. I'm talking about big war here. Amphibious assault.

"Instead of just hearing it from my mouth or thinking I'm just dropping this in your laps all of the sudden, consider the actions of the man who previously held my position, Robert Gates."

The secretary took a folded paper Kerry handed him from his aviator jacket and reached for his spectacles in his right Docker pocket and began paraphrasing. He maintained a good cadence of reading, pausing, and making eye contact with his audience.

"Secretary Gates ordered a review of the future of the Marines in August of 2010 to be conducted by Commandant Amos and the Secretary of the Navy Ray Mabus to determine what role your force will play in future wars. The conflicts in Iraq and Afghanistan have removed you from your amphibious roots and relegated you to a second land army. As Gates said and I'll reiterate now, ya'll don't want to be, nor does America need, a second land army.

"The review's intent was for what an expeditionary force in readiness would look like. He did mention that the review should not lose sight of the Marines' greatest strengths of being able to move ashore under uncertain conditions and protect and sustain themselves quickly. Gates asked whether large-scale amphibious landings like Inchon are even feasible.[10] Let's be honest, we can't pull off an amphibious assault of China if we went to war.

"The review was completed in 2011 but didn't do much to quell bickering in the beltway about how the corps is going to change and adapt. All it really recommended was cutting the size of the force, which you all know about. We were up to around 202,000 Marines and are falling back to the 180,000 man range. In this age of fiscal austerity and budget deficits, the cutters always look for low-hanging fruit. It doesn't help that you are a subset of the navy and hence get unfairly subjected to budget battles with the bigger services. But with a small budget and a small force, it's hard to have much fiscal inertia. So with that short background, you can see why the future of your core trump card doesn't look so promising.

"In a piece written in the *Fiscal Times* in May 2013 titled 'Why Afghanistan Might Be the Marines' Last Fight,' the point was made that all future threat assessments don't include amphibious assaults. They include counterterrorism and cybersecurity, neither of which Marines have skill sets for.[11] The replacement for our current AAVs, which entered service in 1972, was the Expeditionary Fighting Vehicle or EFV. It was designed to have three times the speed and twice the armor of the current AAV. The EFV was easy picking for the Pentagon planners, who don't see an amphibious assault any time soon as well as tax watchdog groups.[12]

"The U.S. Public Interest Group and the National Taxpayer Union published a report in November 2010 that called the program wasteful and recommended it be cut.[13] I would say it was slightly wasteful, had a high failure rate in testing and hence needed a fresh infusion of millions, but that's defense spending for you. Who is complaining about the Joint Strike Fighter? No one right? That's because Lockheed has 1,300 suppliers spread out in 45 states creating 133,000 jobs to make the thing.[14] A windshield here, a landing strut there, an avionics computer here. They gutted the will to cut the monster by using pork-like intimidation. That same report that called for axing the EFV also called for axing the JSF.

"But the EFV got the ax anyway. Gates cancelled it in January of 2011 while it was scheduled to be operational in 2015 after having been delayed for introduction since 1993.[15] Besides the cost issue, think about the tactics. If we have to stay 65 miles away from a beach like EF 21 says and it can travel at 28 miles per hour, you are still looking at a 2-hour boat ride to assault a beach. Then what happens to our support elements? Are we just gonna speed ashore a few dozen rifle squads in EFVs, hope they secure the beach, then behind them send in defenseless Navy Landing Craft Air Cushions carrying tanks, heavy weapons, and Humvees to an unsecured beach? Jumping back into the JP 3.02 on amphibious operations, the key for an assault is the 'swift introduction of sufficient combat power ashore.'[16]

"A ride of over 2 hours to drop a couple hundred Marines on a hostile beach doesn't sound swift nor sufficient. And that 65 nautical miles is still well beyond the EFV's designed assault distance of 25 nautical miles.[17] That alone is enough to can the project. As the general mentioned, we are exploring the ACV, but it's a long ways from getting in the game and for God's sake we don't even know if it floats.

"Let's say the problem with the EFV was budget and costs even though I just showed it is tactics and relevance. The official story in the corps is it was too expensive. So follow the logic here. A vehicle that has been developed since the mid-1980s and was scheduled to be operational in 2015 is canceled due to cost overruns. They had two decades to research, test, and validate the EFV and keep cost under control.

"By the time it got the cut 3 billion had been poured into it. And it couldn't be done. So the solution is back to the drawing board after 20 years and 3 billion? That is laughable. If the vehicle is fast, it has to be light and hence lack heavy armor protection. Unacceptable. If the vehicle is heavily armored, it will be super slow. Also unacceptable. No balance between the two was found in over 20 years of research and development. Barring some super material that is light and protects or a propulsion system that has incredible speeds for a heavy vehicle, the technology isn't there.

"The ACV 1.1 by its design is supposed to rely on connectors like an LCAC or a CH-53. They have already given up on trying to get it through the water on its own power to the beach. ACV 1.2 is supposed to be able to self-deploy and swim like an AAV while still keeping the protection of troops needed in the ACV 1.2. What this resembles is an act of desperation. They are trying to bring capability in 'incrementally' because they know it can't be done in one vehicle. Even if you get the ACV, the plan is to keep 392 AAVs until 2035.[18] Your 40-year-old AAV is here to stay for quite a few years to come."

One of the guys in our squadron who lives and breathes Marine Corps threw up behind me. I didn't like him anyway. Had a high and tight haircut. I guess the truth was sickening. Chucky just kept going.

"Let's dig into Expeditionary Force 21 for a few minutes. The 65-nautical-mile standoff previously mentioned has to be honored. Next EF 21 says if we can 'reduce' the Coastal Defense Cruise Missile threat, we can move to around 30 to 50 nautical miles.[19] They don't define reduce. They don't give a percentage or threat degradation quantification. Can we accept a few CDCMs? How about one? To reduce the threat, we are talking shaping fires here. Bombers, Tomahawk cruise missiles, or a Standoff Land Attack Missile from an F/A-18 or the like. They have to take out the CDCM threat or 'reduce' it so the ships can move closer. Who is observing these fires from 65 nautical miles away? Who is providing the Battle Damage Assessment? Who is saying 'Yep, that Tomahawk just took out a CDCM site go ahead and move closer to launch the AAVs?' Thirty to 50 nautical miles is still too far for launching AAVs. Remember the old number was 12 nautical miles.

"And here is the worst part. Say we do 'reduce' the threat. EF 21 says there needs to be a 'careful calculation of risk by the involved commanders.'[20] In today's military, where the zero-defect mentality has infected us, do you really think a navy skipper would move his ship into the threat ring of an anti-ship missile? The man who commanded the Revolutionary War Bonhomme Richard, John Paul Jones, would likely try it. But he would never make it in today's military. Too abrasive.

"It only takes one missile to take out this ship or completely disable it. The navy has defensive systems, but I doubt they rely on those when facing the possibility of several CDCMs flying their way. Losing a few Marines to take a machine gun nest, as heartless as it sounds, is acceptable as long as we win the battle. Losing an entire amphibious assault ship, her Marines, sailors, and equipment is unacceptable regardless of the end state. The ships alone are on the order of 3 to 4 billion dollars apiece.

"The next step in EF 21 is when the CDCM sites are 'neutralized.' Again no quantitative numbers are given. The problem with these terms, reduce and neutralize, is they sound great on paper. They are on some fancy-looking PowerPoint slide. They allow us to continue with our problem framing but they are showstoppers when you apply even a conservative dose of reality.

"On a PowerPoint slide is where they should remain. The only time we can use those terms is if we are dealing with some manmade Chinese island that has been so extensively bombed and destroyed by shaping fires the only thing left to seize is some charred land and Chink corpses.

"And last but not least, the ACV is a Marine Corps—only program. No one else wants or desires it. The Marines are in charge of its development, procurement, and testing. It's hard to keep an irrelevant project alive if the Marines, the smallest and most underfunded service, are the only ones demanding it.

"Your service was allocated about 34 billion at its height in 2010 and this includes overseas combat operations costs. About 60 percent of the budget that isn't combat operations is devoured by personnel costs for pay, retirement, and benefits. If you think that isn't much, consider that in 2000 you were getting 12.5 billion a year and based on the current downward trend in 2015, that will be around 25 billion a year. Both in 2000 and 2015, the overseas combat operations chunk of the budget will be gone.[21] The wars are over for the Marine Corps, but your budget is double. Why does anyone think we won't be cut further? Needless to say, you don't have the fiscal weight to get your way with acquisitions."

"It always amuses me when I hear your generals, Toolan is one that comes to mind, talk about how our allies in the Pacific want to create an 'amphibious capability.' That is nothing more than propaganda to attempt garnering a larger piece of a shrinking financial pie that was just mentioned in your budgets. It is saying, 'Hey, Congress, look, we have lots of customers in the Pacific that want to learn our trade we deserve more money.'

"The Marines are the pioneers and flame holders of amphibious assault and we are putting on a dog-and-pony show. You don't practice the real thing. So what makes you think the Malaysians, Filipinos, and Indonesians can do amphibious assault? They are poor as shit and their militaries as a whole are essentially dog-and-pony shows. Malaysia doesn't even own an AAV equivalent.

"Are we going to sell them 40-year-old AAVs that chug along at 7 knots in the water? It's like trying to sell VHS tapes 10 years after the introduction of DVDs. It will be hard to move units and if there is truly a market for AAVs, the United States Marine Corps wouldn't be the only ones trying to develop them. Plenty of countries make planes, tanks, and ships. There is competition to create a machine for a real need in the marketplace. No such competition exists for AAVs. Only the USA makes AAVs. Why is that? And God help us if the Malaysians or Filipinos try to launch dozens of AAVs from some magical amphibious assault ships they don't have. That will quickly degenerate into a humanitarian and disaster relief mission, which we are becoming masters of."

The SAPR representatives noisily returned with their rosters, handed them to the squadron CO, and he departed.

"So let's review. You don't have the correct vehicle to get you ashore outside the range of anti-ship missiles, there are no viable vehicles being developed, and the replacement was cancelled. This exercise does nothing to honor the threat and is nothing more than a water version of a military parade. There are no tactical considerations. The secretary of defense cancelled the EFV because no future threat assessments say amphibious assault is a mission essential task. Now, as compelling as those arguments are, one might say it's just rhetoric and politics. If money didn't matter, we would have our EFV. Where is the physical proof?

"Well, we do indeed have physical proof. The ship we stand on right now is a LHD ship. LHD-6 to be exact. Known as the Wasp class, they are an improvement over the Tarawa class, which we are now retiring in stages. She has a well deck and holds dozens of vehicles, including your precious AAVs. We flood it to a certain degree, float the toys, and they go chugging out into the water and presumably to the beach. What does the future hold? Well, the future is now.

"The newest amphibious ship in the fleet is the LHA-6, the *America*. She will be acquired by the navy shortly in early April. Just a few weeks from now. Guess what she doesn't have? A well deck. And why do you think that is? Why would the navy build a 3.4-billion-dollar ship that doesn't even have a well deck and hence no AAVs? The navy saw the writing was on the wall just like Gates did. Their vision of future conflicts was one where coastal waters close to an enemy beach would be mined or protected by the reach of anti-ship missiles.[22]

"The logic was the future conflicts from the sea would rely solely on air assault. Despite the Marine Corps complaining that they needed a well deck, the navy went forward with it.[23] The fight didn't end there. Secretary Kerry will explain. Enter the MV-22 Osprey. It was a troubled aircraft for a troubled service. The corps needed to stay relevant so they found an aircraft that has two times the speed and four times the combat radius of the CH-46 Phrogs they were replacing. Now they could still fulfill the role of 'taking the beach.' But the story isn't so cut and dry as it sounds.

"In building the *America* as an aviation-centric ship, the space where the well deck used to be was used to enlarge hangar spaces as well as add more storage for fuel, parts, and even ordnance.[24] Several articles concerning the *America* have mentioned the 'significant' size difference between the MV-22 and the CH-46 that necessitated the enlargement of maintenance facilities.[25] The only problem with that statement is it is untrue.

"Yes, when unfolded and ready to fly, the Osprey is much larger than the CH-46. However, have you seen how nicely the Osprey folds and can be stored on this ship? The wings pivot ninety degrees and all the blades fold along the length the aircraft. Quantifying the numbers, directly from the NATOPS manuals for both aircraft, will make it clear. The MV-22 is 18.5 feet wide, 63 feet long, and 18 feet tall when folded up.[26] The CH-46 when folded is 15 feet wide, 46 feet long, and 17 feet tall.[27] The only large difference is length, which doesn't matter when you line aircraft up side by side on the starboard side of the ship. They don't go past the foul line and hence don't interrupt flight operations when stored.

"Additionally, if the Osprey is so 'significantly' larger than the CH-46 and if the *America* was designed to accommodate this, then why does the *America* carry 12 MV-22s and the ships she replaces, your BHR LHD class, carry 12 CH-46 Phrogs? The only advantage the *America* has is that she can carry 9 F-35B versus 6 with the LHD class.[28] But both can take 4 CH-53Es, so draw there. Even if she could carry more, you can only launch so many aircraft at a time with spotting six aircraft in the launch positions on the deck. And finally the Osprey carries the same amount of troops as the CH-46. 24 combat loaded Marines.

"And I saved the best for last. The Osprey's blessing is its curse. Because it can fly so fast, cruising at 240 knots, traditional rotary wing escorts like the Cobra and Huey, which fly half the speed, cannot escort the assault waves and protect the package from a ground threat. It wasn't a problem for the slower CH-46 and CH-53. But now that we have to launch assaults from so far away, we have no hope of escorting them other than jets like the AV-8B and F-35B.

"Here is another problem. So the logic is we have to stay far away from a potential enemy coast because of mines and anti-ship missiles. It should follow easily that if an enemy can afford to mine his waters and purchase and operate anti-ship missiles, he should also be in the market for some pretty serious integrated air defense systems. Like the kind that will destroy the incoming waves of MV-22s."

I thought to myself that they will not have to work hard to shoot them down. The Osprey guys had trouble landing at the right grid, let alone worrying about surface-to-air missiles taking them out of the sky. And that landing was after they had waved off two to three times.

I began to hear soft sobbing coming from directly behind me. I could tell it was one of our Osprey pilots coming to grips with his fate. I wanted to turn around and tell him to shut the fuck up, but I was afraid of being yelled at so I stayed locked forward.

Chucky was on a roll and kept flowing.

"But hypothetically, let's say we use a combination of jets and tomahawk missiles to take out the most dangerous air defense systems, never mind the man portable surface to air threat which is ubiquitous these days. So we launch a few waves of MV-22s escorted by more jets and they get to their zones. We get about a company of Marines on the deck in hostile territory. Then what?

"The ships are still too far away to get any heavy equipment ashore like tanks or artillery or any type of fire support. The anti-ship missiles and mines have kept them at bay to the tune of 65 nautical miles. We have to take the beach before we can send defenseless landing craft with the heavy equipment. So we have a company of Marines fighting their way to some objective with no fire support other than 60mm mortars. No artillery support, no close air support from aviation, and no direct fire heavy weapons like .50 caliber machine guns or Mk-19 grenade launchers. Sounds like a suicide mission, right? As soon as they land, the enemy will be all over them. Okay, I'm sick of talking about amphibious ships.

"I'm sure this talk of being irrelevant scares you, but I promise the Marines are here to stay. In *The Fiscal Times* article, Gordon Adams at American University mentions that he thinks the Marines will survive because we can't let go of anything.[29] Plenty of phony patriots who have never served a day in their lives will come to the rescue of the service if it ever came to being disbanded. There is a plenty of other stuff we can have the Marine Corps focus on.

"Before I turn it over to the secretary of state, I'll briefly mention one of those and that is climate change. Rising global temperatures, increasing sea levels, and intensifying weather events will challenge global stability and could lead to food and water shortages, pandemic disease, and disputes over refugees and resources.[30] I'll be speaking at the Conference of the Defense Ministers of America this coming fall and will give you a sneak peek of my talking points."

A few more creaking chairs could be heard.

"The Pentagon will soon be releasing their '2014 Climate Change Adaptation Road Map,' which highlights how global warming will bring new demands on the military. Your bases that are all near the coasts will be more likely to flood and hence need upgrades; more frequent natural disasters will require more humanitarian assistance; and our equipment will need to operate in harsher and more severe weather conditions are the main wickets of the road map.[31]

"This road map shows how we are identifying—with tangible and specific metrics"—as he said metrics, he held up both hands with each hand's thumbs and index fingers parallel to one another about two inches apart and alternating rotated both hands; good visual communication if you ask me—"and, using the best available science, the effects of climate change on the department's missions and responsibilities. Drawing on these assessments, we will integrate climate change considerations into our planning, operations, and training.[32] Think of the disaster relief you just completed in the Philippines due to a typhoon. We must be clear-eyed about the security threats presented by climate change, and we must be proactive in addressing them.[33] The dangers of global warming will keep you guys employed for many years to come, I promise. Okay, that's just a sneak peek. As always, thank you for your service. I am so proud of all you. I'll turn it over to Secretary Kerry from here."

Secretary of State Kerry Speaks

Chucky silently moved to the spot Kerry vacated and Kerry traded him places and began immediately.

"I just want to begin by asking a question. How many of you guys actually practiced shooting with troops maneuvering? I mean like no-shit close air support practice? It's different if you do it in a jam or in combat, but I'm talking practice."

All the hands of the Cobra and Huey guys went up logically while none of the other guys do.

"Okay, now you—" he pointed at me—"how many *times* have you done it?"

I froze up, wondering why he singled me out, and immediately thought I've done something wrong. I scanned my memory in a split second and I think I eked out an "uh" to buy myself some time. The horror confronted me that the number he is inquiring about is one. I had to tell the truth.

"One time, sir, a TOW shot at Integrated Training Exercise in Twentynine Palms, California."

"Thanks for being honest. I think you, gentlemen, can see my point. Integration sounds great on paper, but it's just prohibitive most times. It's hard to get everyone on the same sheet of music. And that's with a simulated enemy, good food, rest, plenty of time to plan, and only self-induced friction. Imagine what a thinking, maneuvering, vicious enemy would do that is playing defense with little planning time on our part? Defense is always stronger, right?

"Anyways, that's just an aside. I'm really here to talk about why we are doing this exercise. If you didn't already figure it out, there is no enemy situation. To simulate a true enemy would place you all in too much danger. Real enemy means real tactics and that means integration, which is inherently dangerous. And as the young captain just illuminated, ya'll hardly practice it anyway. Deconfliction is the opposite of integration. Deconfliction is the name of the game here. I read the email your XO sent out a few hours ago. I totally approve and couldn't do it better myself. This is a political exercise, not a tactical one. I'm sure that unsettles some of you. Let me try to use some personal historical experiences to clarify what is going on here.

"For Christmas my family used to bake hams at my house when I was young. My mother used two pans and cut the ham in half first before baking. I never understood why she did that. We had plenty of pans large enough to fit the entire ham. One Christmas I asked her why and she replied that her mother always did that and since she learned to cook from her mom, she did it too. When Grandma came over for the day, I asked her and you know what her answer was? 'I never had a pan big enough to fit the whole ham.'

"We need to analyze why we do business the way we do with a special consideration of the initial conditions. We are holding onto this idea of amphibious assault like the initial conditions still exist. We are still using two pans when we have no logical reason to. I don't need to rehash on what the previous speakers said. To attempt an actual assault against an enemy in this day and age is foolish at best and downright suicidal at worst. The anti-ship missiles are to the machine gun bunkers as the amphibious assault and its ships are to the men waiting for the order to go over the top and assault. The analogy is pretty close.

"Now, outside of amphibious assault, I understand your method of fighting, combined arms, is unparalleled in the world. No other service or military puts the emphasis on integration of weapon systems with maneuver into an orchestra of death like you guys do. That is still relevant and even though it should be enough to justify your existence, it's not enough to the bean counters in Washington.

"We have 718,000 civilian employees working for the DoD, over three times the size of your Marine Corps.[1] They would still cut you first. Think of it like gangrene, you cut the extremities away first. You guys are out here, out in the field, out in harsh places while your overlords in Washington like me get cush six-figure salaries and live an easy life. But you are extremities; they are the core. They live in D.C.— you don't. They can protest when benefits are cut; you just follow orders. Fucked up, but that's how it will be. We need more justification for the Marine Corps to exist than combined arms warfare.

"To revert shortly to the points made by Secretary Hagel and expand upon them. The LHA-6 *America* as well as the next ship LHA-7 *Tripoli* do not have well decks. The tactical situation dictated the switch from well decks to aviation-centric ships and even they are checkmated by the inability to support an over-the-horizon air assault. You would think the next ships following these two would not have well decks either. The fact that they were built, to the tune of billions of dollars, shows there was some serious thought put into the feasibility of amphibious assault and they said no, thank you.

"However, in February of 2012 a memorandum of agreement was signed between Commandant Amos and the Chief of Naval Operations Admiral Greenert that restored the well deck to the LHA-8 and subsequent ships.[2] I can only imagine what that conversation sounded like. Here is my best guess."

He proceeded to impersonate the Commandant and the CNO having a back-and-forth conversation.

"Commandant: 'Admiral Greenert, listen, our number one weapon systems acquisition priority is the amphibious combat vehicle. If you keep building ships without well decks, where will be put them?'

"CNO: 'Commandant Amos, we built ships without well decks because the future of power projection from the sea is air assault. We will bypass enemy defenses and honor anti-ship missiles. That's why you have the MV-22 now. I hate to break the news to you, but Marines storming enemy-held beaches is history. Even in World War II by the time Okinawa was fought, the Japanese learned to retreat into the island's center.'

"Commandant: 'Okay, I see your point, but is it not true you need the Marine Corps to build these ships? Without Marines, the Gator Navy has no reason to exist. Whether we take the beach with planes or AAVs, you still need us.'

"CNO: 'That's true. Our job is to give you a ride to the fight. These ships do that, just by air now instead of AAV. So what is your point?'

"Commandant: 'The number one thing that keeps the Marine Corps alive is fueling the perception we can conduct amphibious assaults. Between you and me, I got it, it is irrelevant. But I'm talking about the survival of the organization I lead. If we don't have a place to put our ACV, they won't be developed or even introduced at all. If we lose the ability to move ashore from the sea, we are not much different than the army. The MV-22 option is a dead end too, but at least on paper it can be done. But if that is all we have, we will quickly drift into irrelevance. Look at South Korea. Why aren't Marines stationed in South Korea? Because if we were, we are no different than the army and hence couldn't be justified. It should be painfully obvious that the logical way to defend South Korea is to be *in* South Korea. Not launching a suicidal amphibious regimental assault into a defense that has been continuously prepped since 1953. If we aren't different, we can't exist in fiscally constrained times. We have to hang on to this notion that we will come storming off of navy ships and take the beaches if the North attacks. And so that brings me to my point. If you don't build ships with well decks, we won't get our ACV. When we are shelved as a military organization, the Gator Navy goes with it. The navy will lose huge. Money, assets, personnel, weapon systems, you name it. The fucking Air Force will complete their takeover of DoD. Our relationship is symbiotic. And to end my argument, I'll just say like with everything, it's all about the money.'

"CNO: 'You got yourself a goddamn deal, Jim. We'll put well decks on LHA-8 and the next ships. You better fucking get that ACV though.'

"Commandant: 'We will, now that we have a place to put it. Thanks, I knew you would understand.'

"Now that is my best guess, but you see the logic here."

"Don't fear though, we have a place for you after all. Just your presence here is enough to keep capitalism alive. That's right, I'll say it again, the U.S. military presence in the Pacific is totally economic. You are the mercenaries, the military strongmen, of international stock capital. When someone says our nation's interest, what they really mean is corporate interest.

"You really think someone could threaten the physical security of a nation that is separated by its potential enemies by two vast oceans? Not a chance. We need to talk about the difference between an attack and physical invasion. It's almost impossible to stop an attack on this country. Even with the NSA in place, we got the Boston Marathon bombing. Compare that to an invasion by a state-sponsored military of, say, Los Angeles. See the difference? The Soviet Union was the only industrial enemy we could have faced, but we won the Cold War not because of outright war, but because of the impossibility of Soviet socialism. They fell and we still stood.

"Today some people talk about China's rise and we have to stop China. No doubt they are modernizing. We spend 600 billion a year on defense; they spend 112 billion. But they are playing defense, believe me. They have 4 boomers, 5 nuclear attack subs, and 50 older diesel attack models, which are easily detected. We have 14 boomers and 55 nuclear attack subs, which honed their skills during the scary Soviet years and are undoubtedly the best in the world. They have one Russian refurbished aircraft carrier. We have 11 carriers.

"Terrain matters for the ground game, but it also matters for subs. To lash out from their home sub bases and break out into the open Indian or Pacific oceans, the Chinese have to make it past what is termed the first and second island chains. The first chain begins at the southern tip of mainland Japan, skirts the eastern edge of Taiwan, then hugs the western coasts of the Philippines and Malaysia. The second island chain begins around mid-mainland Japan and weaves to the southeast then southwest, terminating on the Indonesian side of the Papua New Guinea island. There are only a few straits they can use to break out, such as the Sunda, Lombok, or Luzon. These can all be monitored by our forces.[3] The only chance they have is to curtail the majority of our economy, which is consumerism. Do an enemy most likely course of action or EMLCOA on China. Would you really bite the hand of consumers that are feeding you? The Chinese own over a trillion dollars in U.S. Treasury bonds. You think they will get their money back if they start a war? Nope.

"The rise of China is directly a result of our country. We sent them lots of manufacturing jobs and our consumers send them billions of dollars every year. If Americans had a genuine 'Buy American' streak, they would take down China fairly quickly. The iPads and sneakers would start piling up at the factories and the Chinese would have massive riots and insurrection as their workers went unpaid or were laid off. No investment and no American consumerism means no economy for China.

"Capitalism is always racing to the bottom to find the best product for the best price. Think about what you are defending here. Imagine if Korea didn't have us here putting on fake exercises to scare the North? They would have to spend more on their defense budget and that means more taxes. More taxes means less money for business to invest in innovation, expansion, and jobs. I'm sure many of you enjoy your Samsung phones and televisions as well as Kia and Hyundai automobiles, many of which are now assembled in the USA. Sure, you might say the Koreans risk losing their freedom if they don't focus on their martial skills rather than business skills. It's up to them ultimately to be free or become enslaved. But the implications are deeper. Your actions here keep not only Korea churning but China and Japan as well. Japan isn't allowed to have an offensive military. Hasn't had one since the end of World War II. We take care of defense while they build stuff. Same goes for Europe and Germany. Japan doesn't import people either and they currently have the largest and fastest-growing percentage of citizens sixty-five and older of any developed nation. In addition, 42 percent of their marriages were categorized as 'sexless,' or no sex for a month or more.[4]

"As George Orwell stated in *1984*, it's all about who controls the working masses of the world. China's export miracle has been fueled by cheap labor and an artificially low peg of the yuan against the dollar, which didn't move an inch from 1994 to 2004. Investment is 50 percent of China's GDP while consumption is 70 percent of the U.S. economy.[5] Forget for a minute we have a third of Americans in debt collection and average retirement savings is 3,000 dollars.[6] If we don't keep the electronics and consumer goods cheap, we might have another recession if consumer spending falls and Southeast Asia might erupt in warfare.

"You make sure all the Asian countries play nice and don't have to worry about the next invasion or hardly their military for that matter. Shit, the Koreans, between me and you are just a bunch of minions, robots, waiting for their American puppeteers to control them if a war broke out. If Ssang Young 2014 didn't have its title already, it really should be 'Be afraid of us and keep making cell phones and tablets or else.'

"I want everyone in this room to think long and hard about the last few points I just made. You are the guardians of globalization. You are the security apparatus for this great race to the bottom. Without you it couldn't be done. You should be very proud. Don't think for a second that our 600 billion a year in 'defense'"—he made the quotation mark with his fingers and so I annotate it here as such—"spending isn't tied to our GDP. GDP is comprised of investment, government spending, consumption, and net exports. If our 'defense' spending here in Asia were to drop off significantly, you better believe our consumption would go down as less of the Asian economies went into factories and investment and more went to defense. Consumption goes down, so does GDP. American-made iPads would cost 3,000 dollars instead of 300 dollars.

"What would the pretentious hipsters in San Francisco do? Or for those of you with kids, where would they get their smartphones, toys, and video games? So if any of you get upset or complain that we have you participating in a dog-and-pony show, just know it's for one, the survival of your own organization. If we didn't put them on amphibious assault would quickly be relegated to the history books as the reality of the anti-ship missile technology says it should.

"And two, but more importantly, you are making electronics and consumer goods cheap for American companies and our citizens. Thank God 46,000,000 Americans have been on food stamps for over 37 months and can spend their disposable income on consumer goods to keep the wheels greased and the money flowing.[7] So when you guys leave this room, and I've talked to the Skipper about it personally and he will allow ample time, I want you to call back home. Call home, get ahold of your wife, kids. For the single guys, call your folks, significant others, siblings, friends, whoever. We've cleared the lines and made sure communications are working. I'm not telling you what the subject matter should be, but I'm insinuating that you should talk to your families to get an appreciation for how much these cheap electronics, cars, and clothes have changed our lives. Have them tour the house and look at your four or five televisions, I'm sure all households have at least two to three computers. Have them go sit in the garage in their Nissans or Kias and admire what you are a part of. I know your cell phones don't get reception, but fire them up anyway and play some Angry Birds or whatever your favorite game is. Okay, I'm rambling, but make that happen, okay?

"Finally I wanted to hit on fiscal policy. President Obama appointed Paul Volcker to lead the Economic Recovery Advisory Board in 2009. Mr. Volcker has been around finance a long time beginning his service at the Fed as a staff economist in 1952. He is most notable for taming inflation following the Carter years by raising interest rates to 19 percent in 1981. When asked about the U.S. current fiscal malaise, he counters that we can continue on our present course as long as we still have confidence in the system. If people are confident in the dollar as the reserve currency of the world, despite that it's been a fiat currency since 1971 when Nixon closed the gold window, then the dollar can sustain any period of uncertainty or crisis. If that confidence fails, then God help us.

"Despite our record deficit of 17 trillion and Federal Reserve bond holdings of 4 trillion, we have had under 2 percent inflation since 2008. Why is that? Because we in essence offshore our inflation by flooding other countries with our dollars in trade deficits, treasury bonds, and consumerism. Our money and debt doesn't stay local, it ends up over there. The countries with a pegged currency to the dollar have two options. They either print more of their own money to adjust for the influx of U.S. dollars in order to keep their currency weak relative to the dollar. This helps their export competitiveness, which is their model for prosperity.

"However, nothing happens in isolation and printing the home countries' currency leads to local inflation. Or option two, they don't print money and their currency gains value relative to the dollar, hurting their exports.[8] Your presence, and our military in general, is one of the number one reasons confidence in the dollar will continue. The Fed's Keynesian economic model is being propped up by you guys. Nothing says 'Deal with an influx of U.S. dollars and local inflation' like a floating armada of ships, subs, aircraft, and Marines right off your coast, right?

"This won't go on forever, of course. Eventually, and I can't say when, our debt will become so onerous it will become unattractive as an investment in the international marketplace. Interest rates on bonds will *have* to rise in order to attract the same amount of capital. The point will come when our trading partners can no longer balance dealing with local inflation in their countries with damaging their export competitiveness. Incredible sums of U.S. dollars in foreign countries will pour back into the U.S. These dollars will snatch up real estate, factories, and other tangibles in an effort to hold a physical asset instead of worthless fiat currency. Then we will see the inflation we have offshored with the blessing of the Federal Reserve.[9] But we can delay that day for many years by using the intimidation factor of the military. I dare the world to refuse the dollar as standard transaction currency of all international business. It might be dangerous for their national health."

I heard these words, but they barely registered in my head. I was still stuck back on the discussion of being used as an economic tool to control the working masses of the world. I was torn between the love of all my cheap electronics, clothes, video games, Ironman watches, and textiles and the love of country.

It's one of those moments when you are so focused on a faraway place or thought that the time seems to pass without you knowing it. Your mind leaves the body for an unspecified time then when it returns, you marvel at how the mind and body can be separate. My body that is left behind hears some strange things that I can only recall the concepts but not actual words.

Vice President Biden apparently came in and started talking about how he was honored to be speaking to the Thirtieth Annual Rothschild's Conference on a remote location on the Pacific Ocean. He mentioned something about how the International Monetary Fund's goals of forming a new world order are being aided by the continuous state of warfare the neoconservatives have been able to maintain and the media luckily hasn't questioned. For the meeting today, we would be discussing Protocol 8 from *Protocols of the Learned Elders of Zion* and specifically how to entrust responsible posts in the government.

He took a tangent about how when war becomes continuous, it ceases to be dangerous before none other than Paul Wolfowitz dashed into the room. Breathless and alarmed, with a copy of *The Protocols* in his hand, he whispered something into Biden's ear. Biden then straightened up and said something to the effect of he didn't know he was on the wrong ship and how could he have known with all the different ships floating around and swiftly departed.

After him a representative from Bell Helicopter showed up and basically sobbed to everyone about how it's not fair that the AH-64E Apache is leaps and bounds better than the AH-1Z Zulu and his feelings were really hurt that Korea chose the AH-64E over the AH-1Z.[10] He had to be led away, barely able to hold himself up.

Finally a guy wearing light brown khakis similar to Jack Hanna strolled in and gave us a brief about how to deal with any of the dogs and ponies if we happen to encounter them loose on the ship. The guys running the AAVs will be getting a more detailed brief.

When my mind returned to my body, Dash is staring at me from a few feet away. Everyone else had already left the ready room. A few minutes must have passed.

I broke the silence. "Dash, you wanna go call our families?"

He shook his head and said, "Nah."

And then we went to eat.

The good ole days. My time in Pensacola in training command were my best years in the military. On a ski trip with my best friends in Montana. From left to right: GYCO, the Creeper, and me. The Creeper was kicked out of flight school after he flew his T-34B trainer under the Pensacola bridge with the canopy open and sporting a 1920s Armani pilot scarf.

Our flight schedule the day of the government shutdown on 1 October 2013. The flight events with lines through them were cancelled. Higher headquarters was spring loaded to shut everything down in order to prove a point to the taxpayer that we keep our priorities straight and cut the fat first. The fat in this case being operational flying for an aviation Squadron. Our Family Readiness Officer was quickly, and in my opinion, wisely, reinstated by order of Chucky Hagel.

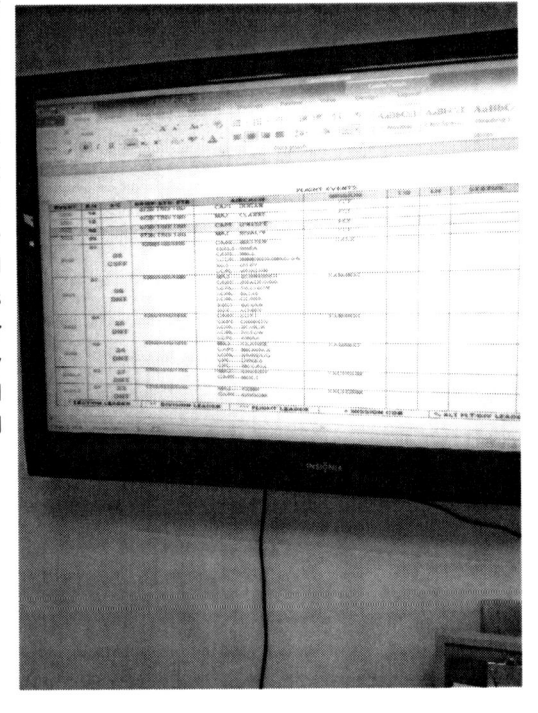

Here is an aerial shot of Ka'ula island, also known as K rock. Besides the Big Island it was the only land mass we could shoot at. However we needed three legs, one to get there, one to fly the mission, and another to fly home. The training was very permissive with a single final attack heading of 270 degrees, one target spot on the lower crest of the island, and a stay above altitude of 1,000 feet. At $7,000 dollars an hour to operate the Cobra and flying for 5 total hours you are looking at $35,000 dollars. Most times you take 14 rockets so each rocket shot is $2,500 bucks. One time I went there to shoot a Hellfire and boats were near the island for fishing so we had to abort the mission. Bye bye 35k.

While we were cresting the end of the runway while I was driving General Wissler and Ambassador Kennedy we saw local Okinawan school children peering through the fence at the Marine "creatures" that live and work on MCAS Futenma. The look on their faces was one of wonder.

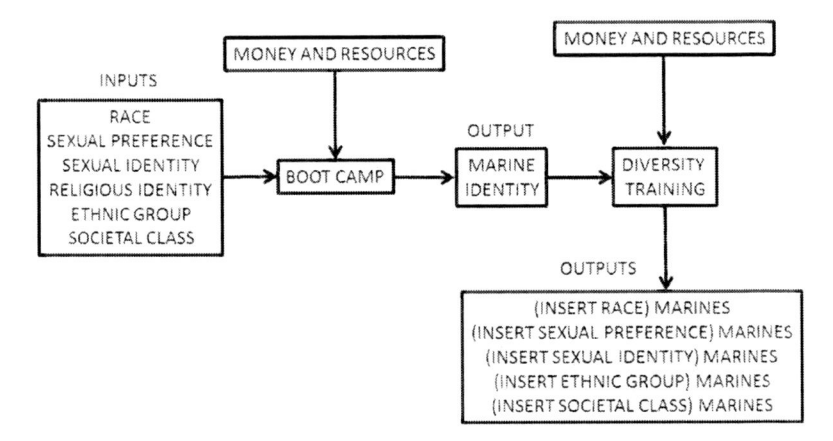

```
                    MONEY AND RESOURCES        MONEY AND RESOURCES
                            │                          │
      INPUTS                │                          │
      ┌──────────────────┐  ▼         OUTPUT           ▼
      │ RACE             │         ┌──────────┐   ┌──────────┐
      │ SEXUAL PREFERENCE│         │          │   │          │
      │ SEXUAL IDENTITY  │────▶│BOOT CAMP│──▶│  MARINE  │──▶│DIVERSITY │
      │ RELIGIOUS IDENTITY│        │ IDENTITY │   │ TRAINING │
      │ ETHNIC GROUP     │         └──────────┘   └──────────┘
      │ SOCIETAL CLASS   │                              │
      └──────────────────┘                    OUTPUTS   ▼
                                    ┌────────────────────────────────┐
                                    │ (INSERT RACE) MARINES          │
                                    │ (INSERT SEXUAL PREFERENCE) MARINES │
                                    │ (INSERT SEXUAL IDENTITY) MARINES│
                                    │ (INSERT ETHNIC GROUP) MARINES  │
                                    │ (INSERT SOCIETAL CLASS) MARINES│
                                    └────────────────────────────────┘
```

The logic of diversity training. The inputs to the Marine Corps are a diverse cross section of society. Boot camp destroys these divisions and replaces them with the identity of Marine. Applying diversity training simply reverses the process but puts the title Marine at the end of each division. The astute observer will note that boot camp and diversity training along with their associated costs could simply be removed and the result would be very similar if not the same.

Here I am with my best buddies from the deployment. We are at the Chiang Kai-Shek memorial in Taipei, Taiwan. Pictured from left to right: My Friend, me, Dash, and GYCO.

Me, GYCO, and My Friend went to Ie Shima one weekend. It is a small island off the northwest coast of Okinawa that has a Marine detachment to man an airfield where we practiced boat landings. GYCO knew the Officer in Charge. Here me and GYCO show our love for our fellow Osprey pilots with a sign captured from protestors.

Dinner the night before the show. Surf and turf, veggies, and baked potato. After being told we were fighting for American consumerism our morale was low so the ship decided to cheer us up with some good chow. Note the leftover lunch taco in the upper right corner.

"The appearance of U.S. Department of Defense (DoD) visual information does not imply or constitute DoD endorsement."

Amphibious assault vehicles treading ashore. Honoring the threat of anti-ship missiles, the ship that launched these AAVs is holding at Expeditionary Force 21's recommended range of 65 nautical miles off shore, and hence can't be seen.
http://www.3rdmeb.marines.mil/Photos.aspx?igphoto=2000803350
Cpl Lauren Whitney

We chose an excellent site for our dog and pony show. Note the flat terrain on the coastline, the water was deep and free of coral, and favorable seas for a launch. Pay particular attention to the equal spacing between the three tracks on the left and the three on the right. Also note how they are all online. In a real war with anti-ship missiles the AAVs would have just finished a 9 hour, 65 nautical mile swim at 7 miles per hour after having somehow refueled 3 times along the way and would be attacking a completely surprised enemy. One of our Cobras is flying perpendicular and is carrying simulated ordnance.
http://www.3rdmeb.marines.mil/Photos.aspx?igphoto=2000803344
Photo by Master Sgt Michael Schellenbach

So I guess there was an enemy situation. Here we have some South Koreans acting in the role of opposition forces or OPFOR. This would be the standard, logical defensive positon if an armada of ships and Marines were off your coast. Dig a shallow, unimproved, unconcealed hole 50 meters from the water and wait for the tracks to hit the beach. Then, if your unsheltered position survived the initial bombardment, employ your pea shooter assault rifle against armored vehicles as they hit the shore. The hole would conveniently double as a grave. These guys are lucky we fed the dogs and ponies prior to the assault, they would have been overrun and eaten. That is if they stayed in their hole to fight, I've heard humans have a natural aversion to horses.
https://www.dvidshub.net/image/1209502/rok-us-marines-intergraded-amphibious-assault-during-ssang-yong-14#.VU0xGpP-WDk
Cpl Sara Medina

Another good shot of the landing. The white smoke screens being emitted from the AAVs are well behind the vehicles and provide no real concealment as can be seen. They do however serve as a good aiming reference for the enemy for many miles out. The black smoke grenades exploding in a circular fashion are a theatrical effect that is synchronized at a certain time to add to the shock and awe effect of the show.
http://www.3rdmeb.marines.mil/Photos.aspx?igphoto=2000803344
Photo by Master Sgt Michael Schellenbach

If I could only put one picture in this epic novel it would be this one. This picture illustrates the political, not tactical nature of Ssang Young 2014. If I was flying and could talk to the South Koreans in those stands I would say, "God bless you for making all my electronics for cheap, the Samsung Galaxy S5 better live up to the hype God damnit." They got real low and looked cool and were de-conflicted from other aircraft. Note the AIM-9M Sidewinder air to air missile on the outboard station for engaging a possible air to air threat.
Lance Cpl. Katelyn Hunter

Here is Dash posing with the Cobra that has his name stenciled on it. Note how the part of the aircraft he has his left hand on is partially disassembled. The ordnance Marines were working hard to get this Cobra's laser designator working properly. Only one Cobra of our four could designate for a Hellfire shot. And only one of our four Cobras could shoot a Hellfire. So between the two aircraft we could find a way to shoot some Hellfire with one Cobra designating and the other shooting the missile. Despite these serious tactical and operational shortcomings I would like to add that all of our Sexual Assault Prevention and Response training was done on time and all rosters were submitted properly.

After our Squadron's marvelous performance for the dog and pony show one of our senior pilots, SWUD, decided to get some commemorative patches made. Our call sign for our time on the boat was Trogdor, a fictional dragon whose symbol is in the center of the patch. The color choices are important. Since the Blue Angels are the ultimate demonstration team we decided to follow suit and hence called ourselves the "Blue Trogdors". The helicopters we fly are all H-1 model, whether it be an AH-1 or UH-1. The SY is Ssang Young. I have amassed several patches over the years but this one is near and dear to my heart.

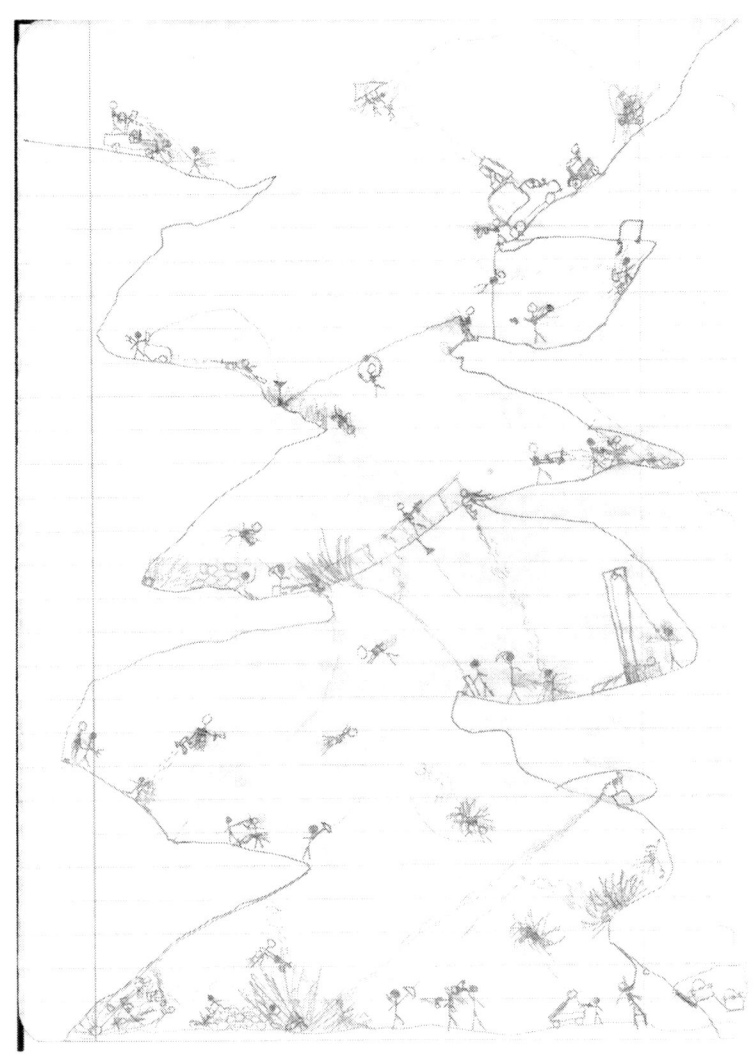

My grade school battle drawings. In this battle we have several notable items. Tactical vehicles, jet packs, and motorcycles. They also utilize zip lines to make their way down. The bridges were built by the natives. The treasure in the bottom right is their goal. Things to note in this battle are the Avenger missile system on the top right engaging the native in his glider, the jet pack assault in the lower half that is stalled by well placed fire arrows, and the native guillotine mid right in the drawing. The invaders almost made it to the treasure but the last guy steps on a booby trap and is decapitated. A ferocious defense by the natives has resulted in another win for their tribe.

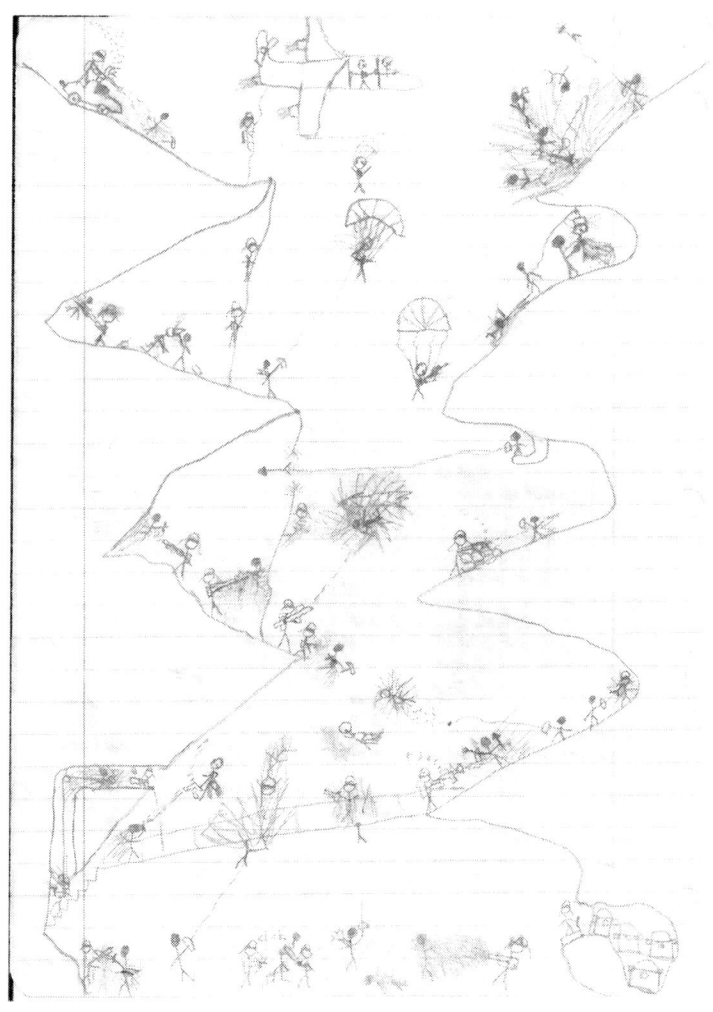

This is the battle that turned the tide. Here we see an airdrop, jet packs, heavier weapons to include HK Infantry Automatic Rifles or IARs (in the previous battle most men were only armed with sub machine guns like MP5s or UMPs), Stinger air to air missiles, and a man portable flame thrower. They were able to mass their fires and personnel at the correct time and overwhelm the natives in the lower half of the canyon and secure the treasure. If the natives can't use their bows they have to rely on close in weapons like the axe and sword, no match for automatic weapons. Some key features of this battle are the prepatory fires off the transport with a well placed AGM-114M Hellfire shot into a large group of natives, a Stinger missile shot on a glider, and the natives successfully blowing a section of the bridge rigged with black powder.

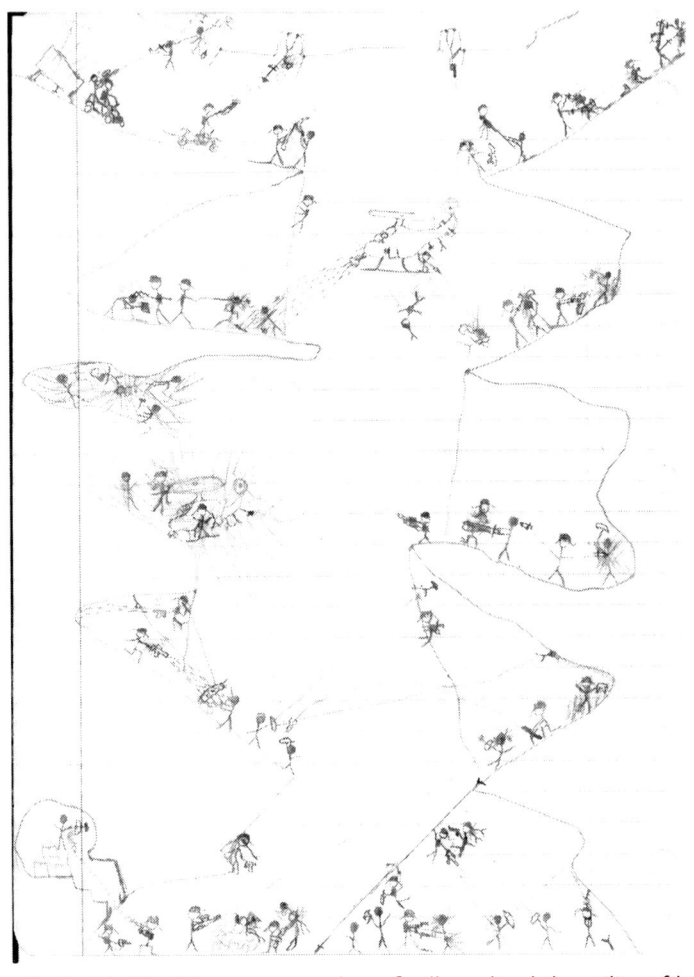

This was the last battle. The aggressors have finally realized the utility of helicopter gunships uruhh. They also aren't afraid to drop their weapons and reach for the blade and go hand to hand for God and country. I count six hand to hand kills. They also air drop a quadcon with vehicles. The natives are fighting with all they got but are no match. Things to note in this battle are many. The MI-24 Hind gunship middle picture chain gunning some guys, the MI-24 crashing after receiving numerous arrow strikes, the guy mid picture on the right side shooting across the canyon with his M-79 grenade launcher, the ledge below him a motivator is shooting the 60 mm mortar from the handheld and getting some, and across the ledge from the mortarman a native crossbow with multiple arrows. And last but not least the guy shooting the native leader guarding the treasure is using a rail gun, look at that corkscrew smoke trail! After this battle the natives were subjugated, given Christianity by force, then cordoned onto a reservation and given Casinos and whiskey to pacify them.

After admitting I was sexually aroused by a Hellfire explosion and recognizing the response as extreme risk for violence in the Violence Prevention Program Awareness Module I confessed to my chaplain. In order to rehabilitate me they sent me to the HA/DR course in Coronado. I am proud to say I am a cured man. Nothing gets me more excited than using loaned money from China to feed other countries while 46 million Americans are on food stamps.

Soon after we returned from the deployment Dash decided to take advantage of what we fought for out in the Pacific. Here he is in our family room with some of his most prized possessions. On his lap are two laptops, the one furthest to the right is an HP laptop and the other is a MAC book. In his left hand he has an Ipad and the other tablet to the left is a Samsung model. He is making a call on his Samsung Galaxy smartphone. The call is to order another HP computer. He hated the Apple computer because it was hard to use but his other HP laptop was over a year old so he decided to get a new one. God Bless those working masses!

The Hammer Speech

After the speeches, I was pretty shaken up. Honestly it's more confusion than emotional trauma. Why would we use the military to just put on dog and pony circus shows? Why don't we just change our tactics? I decided to pull aside one of our senior Cobra pilots who I have a lot of respect for.

V-Neck. As an aviator, officer, and student of history, I take his words seriously. He has a way of conceptualizing what's going on and thinks critically about everything. Plus he has been around. Iraq as a pilot, Afghanistan as a forward air controller, and several MEU pumps. As Dash and I were leaving to go eat, I saw V-Neck going the opposite way. I told Dash I would catch up with him in a second and headed after V-Neck.

"V-Neck, what's the deal? What was that all about? If our tactics are irrelevant, why don't the higher-ups see this and adapt. Either say to hell with amphibious assaults all together or develop new technology that gives us a reason to exist. The fact that we are still going through with this exercise makes no sense to me."

He stared at me very matter-of-factly and waited for another guy to pass by us and confidently began,

"You gotta understand, it's a hammer."

I should have let him continue, but I had to interject.

"What do you mean, a hammer? What is a hammer? The Marine Corps?"

"Listen, what we are dealing with is a massive machine, the military industrial complex. It is a beast and it needs fed. The things it produces like attack helicopters, missiles, bullets, ships, AAVs—they serve no other purpose than to hit a nail. When those weapon systems end up in our hands, that is the hammer."

"Okay, I follow that, but where are you going with this. If the industrial complex makes hammers, then they just need to make us a different tool for a different job."

He shook his head mildly while rolling his eyes to express that I'm naïve.

"Like I said, their only job is to hit nails, right? They only make hammers, that's it. The nails in our scenario is this notion of amphibious assault. Their hammer is us, the Marine Corps. They help us hang onto this irrelevant tactic. It's a symbiotic relationship. Our organization survives and in return they make money by providing us with our equipment. This happens all over the military, but this example is particular to the Marine Corps.

"At one point they made a genuine product for a genuine threat. That threat is no longer there. What good are AAVs other than amphibious assault? And would we still rate our AAVs if the Marine Corps and country came to grips with how irrelevant it is? Of course not. We have to keep on message that amphibious assault is plausible or else we will slowly die as an organization. Or start picking up gay missions like Humanitarian Assistance and Disaster Relief.

"You heard them in there, we don't need two land armies. Do AAVs make food cheaper? Life expectancy longer? They just keep this economic engine of cheap labor protected. The market for the hammer is nails and nails only. A hammer cannot be used for anything else. The hammer has no other purpose than to hit a nail, and since we are running out of nails, the power of the industrial complex makes it owns nails. The colloquial term of what we are dealing with here is a self-licking ice cream cone. The producer and the consumer are one entity. We tell the Koreans they need to do amphibious assault. And when they ask how they can learn it, we say we can show them. The military industrial complex's influence, in the form of lobbyists, politicians, war profiteers, and mainly the well-meaning but patronizing American public keep it fed.

"Our military, after being severed from the American public, is now nothing more than a tool of the national security state. James Madison himself said it. He was afraid of standing armies because they give our executive branch a hammer. Citizen armies are good, and professional armies are even better. But professional armies are good only as long as the leadership of the country has loyalty to the state or people of the country. Think like Germany or Japan in World War II. Obviously we didn't like them and their regimes were brutal, but objectively speaking, their leaders were undoubtedly ardent nationalists."

He paused as another Marine filed past us.

"Our leaders are instruments of corporate power and special interest. Far worse than Hitler or Hirohito from a governing perspective. Private interest is good for our citizens, not our government. Fascist and autocratic states can work as long as the leaders have the nation's interests at heart and hold themselves accountable because no one else will. But our fascist state is responsible to private interest. Either you need a citizen army like we had in World War II that is financially and morally connected to the people, or you have a professional army with selfless leaders and a populace that willing supports the state like Germany in World War II.

"Today America has the worst of both of those. We have a professional army that isn't connected to the people it represents and is commanded by a state that is run by special interests. The state doesn't need to raise taxes or ration gas or food or cut benefits to wage war. They don't even need to draft a single fat fuck. You know why? Because the second the state asks for sacrifice from the American people in the form of taxes, discomfort, or offering their sons and daughters, we would have riots like Vietnam and this machine would grind to a halt. The state is plenty happy to have continuous warfare. This beast thanklessly churns through the young and the idealistic as long as their bottom line looks good. Nixon won in 1968 by promising to end the draft. But did the war in Vietnam end? Nope. He was just getting the American public off his back. Same thing applies today. The industrial complex and the national security state have an interest, say a 600-billion-a-year defense budget interest, in keeping the cash flowing."

I knew I would open a can of worms.

"If it—and by it I mean the industrial complex and its beneficiaries—can't find a nail to hit it will *invent* them. We are dealing with a bona fide self-licking ice cream cone here. If it doesn't have nails, it will go away quickly. And it's true we have very few nails left. The USSR has been gone for 25 years. So what can the beast do? In this scenario we are talking about a fake invasion of a beach. You and I know it's a crock of shit. But to the public it's not. What the eyes see and the ears hear, the mind believes.

"The public is clueless of the writing on the wall. South Korea spends 35 billion a year just on their military. The *entire* GDP of North Korea is 40 billion.[1] Cuba is fucking richer than North Korea.

"The result is that South Korea is number 7 on the global firepower ranking compared with North Korea at 36.[2] North Korea is behind a country like Austria at number 34 on the list. Austria has 15 fighter aircraft to North Korea's 458 and has 56 tanks to North Korea's 4,200.[3] Why is that? In the twenty-first century, quality matters more than quantity. The South Korean F-15s and F-16s would hack hundreds of aging MiG-21s out of the sky while AH-64E Apaches and K-2 Black Panther tanks would shred the invading columns of aging T-55 Soviet tanks to pieces. That is if the North Koreans don't run out of gas first. Looked at Drudge lately?"

It takes me a few seconds to snap out of the trancelike state his thinking has forced me to and realized that yes, I have looked at Drudge lately. Just earlier that day, the headline was "Korea goes hot" with a picture of a Republic of Korea Marine in the prone position on a beach. I clicked on the link and it references something about the North firing shots over the De-Militarized Zone in response to our exercise. I remember thinking initially that this seems serious, but then a split second later, I came to my senses. I'm here off the coast and nothing like that is going on, we are more concerned with the camera angles of the AAV assault and making sure all non-essential personnel are cleared from the flight deck for photo ops then if the real North Koreans attack. I responded to V-Neck.

"Yeah, actually it was headlined with Korea going hot."

"You see? Are you scared one bit of this conflict going hot?"

"No, not really, if anything, us being here is almost a provocation. You could say well we are practicing for the real thing if it does go hot and we are deterring North Korean aggression. That's not an invalid point and deterrence is important, but consider this. We aren't doing a real exercise with a simulated enemy and if the war goes hot, we will play how we practice and do a circus show, when we should be doing a real invasion. Dudes will get schwacked trying to look cool and stay online with other AAVs and deconflict airspace for photo shoots rather than integrate fires. If we are truly here to do an amphibious assault if need be, we should practice it. Practice how we play. Add friction, launch from far away, have a thinking red cell."

He interrupted as he saw I was getting it.

"Now you're starting to see it. But who knows we are doing a circus show? No one except us. The public and North Korea don't see it. You know who is directing this parade right? Brigadier General Kennedy, no doubt a great American, but he was a man chosen for a specific reason. Before taking command of the Third Marine Expeditionary Brigade, he was the Director for Marine Corps Public Affairs.[4] He knows a thing or two about propaganda and information operations. We all know how strong the Marine Corps propaganda is.

"The average history student thinks Okinawa and Incheon were exclusive Marine Corps operations, but the army played a huge role too. And for this exercise we absolutely need a guy who knows how to 'sell' an operation. And by sell, I don't mean tactically, I mean literally financially. We have to keep the money flowing. We need to wow these Koreans and make them believe amphibious assault is awesome and relevant. Shit, the Koreans only built one amphibious assault ship, the *Dokdo*, when they were supposed to build three. Maybe they are catching on."

The anger just boiled my blood. How dare this monster take advantage of America. I don't let it burn me up though. I just allow it to fuel me. I could care less about Korean freedom, but then again Samsung big-screen televisions are awesome.

"Okay, I'm on board, so how do we fight this monster. I love America and its people. They deserve better. What can I do?"

"Nothing. This is actually good for the Marine Corps. You heard them in there. If we don't keep these shows up, we'll go away and I'll be on the street. Anyways, man, I gotta go call my wife and ask her about her new Samsung Galaxy S5. She already pre-ordered hers for the April 11 launch date. I heard it has a 16-megapixel camera. That's 3 megapixels higher than the S4. *And* it has a 29-hour-talk life. Had you heard that?"

"No, I hadn't heard that," as the wind fell out of my sails.

"I'll catch you later, man. Keep your head up. Just imagine if you had to still use a flip phone instead of a smartphone or owned just a few pairs of American-made New Balance shoes versus the dozens of pairs of imported shoes I'm sure you have. Life ain't so bad."

He slapped me on the shoulder and walked out.

The ship has been darkened and a Christmas-like red glow of light filled the empty hallway.

Calls to Families

After Dash and I ate our dinner of crab legs and baked potatoes, we made our way down to the chapel area phones to call our loved ones as directed by Secretary Kerry. In order to reach them, you must navigate several sets of nearly vertical stairs that descend approximately four levels down into the ship. We took our time eating so we were anticipating that not many people were using the four archaic phones. I was actually surprised to find every phone in use with another Marine patiently waiting in line behind them. Only one phone lacked a queue and so I solemnly assumed my position in line.

The Marine in front of me was one of the captains from the CH-53 Squadron. I was trying to think about what I'm going to say when I call my parents. In my head I'm reciting and memorizing all the things they have that are built or designed by the little Asians we protect.

An Apple computer for both parents, my sister, and both brothers.

Mom has an iPhone as well as both brothers and sister. Dad has a flip phone still but needs to upgrade.

Mom has an iPad.

We have a pretty bad-ass projector in the basement.

Mom has an Acura RDX, which is made in the USA.

Dad has a Toyota Tacoma, which is made in the USA.

Brother just traded in his truck for a Kia Optima, which is made in the USA.

Sister has a Honda Civic, which is made in the USA.

We have two Suzuki Quads.

Brother has a Kawasaki KX250.

I have a Dodge Dakota, which is made in USA, *but* I noticed the alternator and air-conditioning compressor are made in Japan.

I can't think of any clothing that is made in the USA other than some of my military boot socks and my Bellville boots. I did buy some New Balance made-in-USA running shoes though.

I snapped out of my recollection exercise because the Marine in front of me raised his voice significantly higher than when I went in my zen-like trance. I recognized him from his side profile as Hangman. He was actually my roommate on the ship. He got the call sign because his dog was in his car with him on a leash and tried to jump out. He held the leash and hung the dog, killing it deader than a doornail.

"What? It's made where?" He seemed incredulous.

"So the Pro Comp wheels on my Dakota were made in China? I never knew that. God, I love those wheels. Honey, go into the kids' rooms. Look at the 40-inch flat screens in each room. Where are they made?"

He saw that I'm staring at him and addressed me.

"Hey, man, I'll be done soon. My wife is just checking on the kids and all their toys and stuff. Did you know Pro Comp makes their wheels in China now? Apparently all the big names make them in China now. Dick Cepek, XD, Mickey Thompson. A lot of tire companies are going there too. You have a Dakota, right?"

"Yeah, but mine came with nice stock black wheels. I don't need to upgrade. After the factory Goodyear tires went bald, I had to order some tires from the mainland. Firestone told me they could put new tires on right away. I inspected the showroom tire they recommended and it was made in Mexico so I ordered some Dick Cepek Trail Countrys online."

"That's cool, man. Check out Hankook tires, they are made in China. I really like mine."

He turned back around as the receiving end of the phone cackled to life.

"Baby, oh my God, so their Samsung LCD 40-inch series 5 flat screens are made in Mexico? But it's a Korean company, right? Baby, God bless those South Koreans. They know their main business is consumers like our family in the USA and they are just making the televisions closer to the USA so they don't have to ship them across the ocean. That's why we get them at such a great price. God bless the North American Free Trade Agreement. I thought all their stuff was made in Korea, but they are racing to the bottom just like us. Aren't you proud of me that I'm protecting them so they can make their stuff in a country just to the south of ours and then import it for our consumers to enjoy?"

As he finished the last sentence, he glanced over to me and cracked a sly smile then returned to his conversation.

"What's that, baby, you just got the girls a cell phone plan? But they are only six and eight years old. Don't you think they are a little young to have an iPhone 4S? Maybe start them out with something simpler but still cool like a Motorola Razr? You got a plan from Verizon? For how much? Wait, you just added them to our plan for only 20 dollars more a month and you can upgrade the phone in two years?"

He was becoming visibly emotional at this point. I thought I could make out a little water in his eyes.

"Baby, I fought for that. I'm making sure those stay cheap. I'm protecting the little Asians who make those phones for pennies an hour. I, I just can't imagine our family if we didn't have those cheap electronics. I know we only have a few thousand dollars in our Roth IRA and we need to get out from our mortgage that is underwater, but I'm so glad we are happy in the here and now. If those girls didn't have those cheap phones, how could they talk to their friends or take pictures of stuff to send me?"

His last words were choked up and he couldn't even finish because he just started sobbing.

"Baby, I'm sorry I gotta go, this is just too sentimental for me."

He hung up and only made it a few yards from the phone and keeled over onto his knees. He was crying. Rather than call my folks, I decided to help him out. Dash was waiting in the background as well and came to help.

In the short period of time it took Dash to come to his aid, he had slumped over and was on the ground just convulsing in the fetal position. He was mumbling words we can't quite decipher but it had something to do with the cheap phone plans he was just speaking of moments before. I may not be recalling this correctly, but I also picked up a few tidbits about bicycles from Walmart, video game systems, and Ugg boots. Dash and I didn't want to cause a scene of drama, so we pleaded with him to suck it up and stand up, but he just kept crying.

After about a minute, his spasms had reduced in frequency and intensity and the crying had ended. We finally succeed in getting him to his feet, but he was still making those sucking sounds of someone who has just finished crying really hard, "*Heeeippp, hheeee, hheeeii, heeeippp, heeeiii, heeeii, heeeiipp.*"

No more tears, just massive gasps of air. The *heeiips* were interjected by a few short, robust sniffles. Dash and I each took an arm and assisted him up the stairs. As we finally lugged him into the stateroom we share, it was dark throughout the ship and the red lamps were lit. My other roommates were not in the room, likely continuing to plan for the show.

Luckily he was in one of the bottom racks and we helped him roll in after we pried his boots off. Flight suits are actually very comfortable to sleep in. His sniffles and sobs had subsided to a level that is professionally acceptable for a man who just had a traumatic experience.

I decided to be courteous and see if he needed anything.

"Hangman, can I get you anything, brother? We are gonna head back to the ready room to plan."

He slowly pointed up to the small desk that is two feet from the edge of his rack. It seemed there was some sort of tablet lying on it being charged.

"You want your tablet?" I asked.

He just nodded slowly and took another sniffle. I walked over and unplugged the thing and recognized it as a Samsung Galaxy Note 5.0. I have one myself. They are made in Vietnam. Good piece of gear. I handed it to him in bed. His tablet has an Otterbox protective case. He took the protective face plate off, which doubled as a stand for the tablet, and propped the tablet up for viewing.

He then motioned for something else on the desk. I squinted in the direction of his finger and spotted some Bose noise-cancelling head phones. I frowned then grabbed them. He hooked them up to his tablet and fired up an episode of *East Bound and Down* from late in the first season. Dash and I just stared for a few moments, drew the curtains on his rack, and made our way out into the dark hallway. As the door was closing, you could hear him laughing.

The Road to War

28 March 2014

It is one day away from the dog and pony show. I tossed and turned the night before. My heart was torn between all my cheap electronics, my job security, and the prosperity of the American people. Today we were having our Road to War brief. This brief basically lays down the historical context for conflict, who the main combatants are, the enemy situation, our assets, and how we will be attacking the problem. In a training environment, you obviously have to fabricate this stuff.

Our squadron back in Kaneohe Bay in Hawaii would usually tie the scenario to the island chain. Since we could only shoot on the Big Island, we would act like the bad guys were infiltrating the eastern port city of Hilo and moving their units uphill to the center of the island. The good guys were doing the same thing in the western port of Kona. We would meet in the center of the island full speed ahead, *Braveheart* style.

Once we became part of the 31st MEU in Okinawa, the scenarios were tailored to the island of Okinawa. The scenarios usually centered around a Communist insurgency that was growing in the northern part of the island. This insurgency was financially and materially backed by a foreign government. Although all the names of the opposing forces were fictitious, it was obvious we were assuming the foreign government was China.

The common denominator is that there is an enemy situation. We are operating to counter their threats and maximize our strengths. That is until Ssang Young 2014. As our XO mentioned and the speakers the night prior hammered home, there was no enemy situation for this exercise. No anti-ship missiles, no mechanized infantry battalions, no air defense.

I found out after the exercise that there was actually a small contingent of South Korean soldiers playing the role of the enemy on the beach. They dug some shallow holes about 50 meters from the water and waited to be run over. I don't know if they did their homework on that one, but even by the battle of Okinawa, the Japanese figured out it was more advantageous to move into the center of the island and wait. But then again that would make it hard if not downright impossible to get a picture of both the opposing force and the amphibious landing *at the same time*. Taking pictures is of course the main goal of the exercise. The pictures are then edited and reported on by the propaganda division of the Marine Corps, the Public Affairs Office.

Today the navy and Korean ships were practicing a photo op. Dozens of ships were joining the shoot. South Korean single-engine Hueys and Sikorsky Blackhawks flew from their Korean mother ship the *Dokdo* to do bounces on the BHR. The *Dokdo* was like the USS BHR but the Korean version. They were going to build three like it, but only built one because even they realized amphibious assault is a joke.

Several of us were hanging out in the ready room, essentially waiting for our marching orders. No one was allowed up top in the afternoon because they were doing a command-and-control mission with an Osprey to take pictures of the armada of ships as they zoomed about the ocean. I saw a few of the pictures after the event.

The ships were aligned beautifully, all following a parallel path with BHR flanked by the slightly smaller *Dokdo* as well as the USS *Denver* and the USS *Ashland*. The other ships from the 13th MEU join in with the USS *Boxer* being the equivalent to the BHR and the USS

New Orleans and USS *Germantown* being the equivalents of the other two ships, respectively. The MEU had just upgraded itself to become a Marine Expeditionary Brigade or MEB. The MEB, or circus show, is commanded by Brigadier General Kennedy. This parade required some serious planning.

Around 1500 V-Neck came in from an air-planning board meeting and described what was happening with the airspace. All of the Cobra and Huey pilots gathered around the map on one of the tables in the ready room, eager to learn the plan and itching for action.

You could tell V-Neck was about to drop some truth on us, he just had this look about him when he was about to lay it down. He began, "Okay, so a few things have changed, okay well a lot of things have changed."

He pointed to the map of the South Korean peninsula that was focused around the Pohang area. The map essentially contained a small slice of the southeastern corner of South Korea, the rest was blue ocean. The map had an overlay taped across it that had all the ship's operations boxes on it. The operations box, or op box for short, was a square of specified dimensions assigned to each specific ship in the exercise in order to have room to maneuver and simultaneously maintain safety with other ships.

Initially the Cobras and Hueys were on the USS *Denver* while the MV-22 and CH-53s were on the USS *BHR*. However, the smaller ships get thrashed by the waves a lot easier and it was an obstacle to training because if the ship rocks too much, you can't take off or land and hence practice landing on the ship. The ship's pitch and roll have to be within certain limits in order to fly.

After several days of cancelled training in early March, there was talk of moving all of us onto the *BHR*. Being the large ship she is, she hardly moved in the same type of waves that were tossing the Denver around. Think hitting turbulence in a Gulfstream versus a 747. Bleeder and V-Neck made that decision easy when they crashed Cobra 41 into the deck of the *Denver* while training at night.

Well, crash isn't the right word. Their skid tube failed on a landing and the aircraft almost rolled over. They are both badass pilots and luckily saved it. We had to sail back to White Beach and have the mess craned off. After that it was a no-brainer and we moved all our aircraft, people, and gear to the *BHR*. Back to V-Neck.

"First off, we were supposed to be on the *Denver* and it is operating in the southern op box." He pointed to the op box on the map. "From there, we would be able to do some shooting at the southern range near Pohang. We would not have been part of the dog and pony show, but it would be some good training.

"Since we are on the *BHR* to the north"—he pointed to the op box, which was significantly farther from Pohang than the southern box was—"we don't have the gas legs or airspace coordinated to shoot in the South. Then comes the airspace above Pohang. They were supposed to shut the Pohang airport down so we could notionally seize it. It was due for construction anyway. That has fallen through as well and Pohang airport will not give us any airspace to allow jets through its corridors. These corridors allow for large air traffic to step down altitudes as they pass through. So we can only go to the ranges to the north since we can't go through their airspace. The ranges up north are cold, not live ordnance."

If I didn't think this exercise was necessary to keeping electronics cheap and hence keep rotten materialistic American consumers happy, I might have become upset. But I now know in my heart I need to just subordinate myself to the task and do what my country asks to make this dog and pony show look good. What if people have to keep computers for more than two years before they buy a new one? Or clothes? What if people have to use hand-me-downs like I did? Just the thought of it made me sick.

I was vindicated almost immediately.

"But, after I just got out of the air planning board, I was able to volunteer us for a pivotal part of the dog and pony show. Turns out they need some Hueys and Cobras to escort the Ospreys as they carry a few VIPs from the *BHR* to Pohang. And, get this, we will be doing a fly-by of the reviewing stands. It's basically a set of bleachers near the beach that has good observation of the beach."

He paused for dramatic effect. I could see several of the guys in my peripherals just nodding confidently, taking in the plan. Good shit.

I asked a question.

"V-Neck, what is the deal with those reviewing stands? Who will be watching this show?"

"Good question, I can't say for sure, but I understand it to be mainly South Korean dignitaries and military leaders with American military advisors as well. Word is this dog-and-pony show they are calling Ssang Young may go down as the greatest piece of media smoke and mirror propaganda since Leni Riefenstahl's *Triumph of the Will.*"

After V-Neck gave us the lowdown on the show, we set to work. The younger pilots like myself get to work planning. Dash and I were assigned the crucial task of making a fuel diagram product. Products are just the generic name we give for the half sheets of paper we fly with called a smartpack. Smartpacks are comprised of products. We carry airport diagrams, frequency tables, digital map copies called chips, and other products as necessary.

For this operation since there was no tactical scenario and because we will be operating fairly far from the ship, our fuel planning needs to be spot on. Dash and I are well regarded for our planning prowess so we dig into the fuel diagram.

We used PowerPoint, the standard medium for communication in the military, and let the creative juices flow. Our vision for our product is a custom-made map chip that has the operations boxes on it as well as the routing checkpoints. In between these points will be arrows connecting them all together. We figured out how far it is between all the points, then used the average speed of our aircraft to figure out the time it takes to transit between the points. Distance equals speed multiplied by time. Knowing the distance and speed, we can solve for time. With this time and an average fuel flow, we can derive the amount of fuel needed between points. Sounds straightforward, but there are around two dozen checkpoints and all we have is a blank PowerPoint slide.

We divided the work priorities and I began a rough sketch of the operating area along with the points. I started cramming the numbers while Dash worked on the product. Since the operations boxes are secret, we cannot put any type of scale or coordinates on the product. As long as you know the points and how much fuel you need between them, you are good. Where you start and where you end isn't relevant, only the absolute distance is.

We ran into a few problems though. I felt that the outline of the boxes should be dashed, but Dash thought it should be solid. Some of the boxes were touching and I thought it showed the distinction better. Another issue was the arrows between the points. PowerPoint has so many different options for the type of arrows you can affix to a line. I prefer the kind that are totally filled in and look like a black triangle at the end of the line. Dash likes the ones that look like an arrow from a bow and arrow that a kid would draw. Simpler but not as professional looking.

Then came the points themselves. I felt they should be hollow black circles, but Dash wanted to use squares. We both knew what the superiors want. Something that looks good on paper and looks good when you brief it. It's just a matter of differences of opinion on how to make it look good. It's not what you say or what you do, but how you *look* when you do it. Leadership, both ground and especially aviation, is about looking good.

We put our arguments aside and finished the meat-and-potatoes planning then dove back into the presentation issues. Dash copied a digital map of the Pohang area and pasted it into the PowerPoint slide. He then used the freeform function to trace the outline of the South Korean coast in the vicinity of Pohang. Once the trace was done, he simply deleted the map chip and the freeform drawing remained.

I used our Joint Mission Planning Software or JMPS to figure out how far it is between the checkpoints. This software allows you to enter the check points in an overlay that you can save then turn on and off. You can save the overlay then use it for later. It is easy to clutter the screen with overlays of airspace, airports, and obstacles.

I couldn't seem to find the overlay so I went to find My Friend. My Friend is really good with JMPS stuff. My Friend wasn't far away, just in the other corner of the Ready Room trying to educate the Osprey pilots on how to actually fly an aircraft rather than push some buttons and watch what happens. The Osprey flies itself. I'm not kidding. My Friend came over and took the mouse from my hand and started exploring the folders within folders to find my checkpoint overlay. After about 10 seconds he found it.

"Here it is," My Friend said. "These fucking Osprey monkeys must have moved it. Hey!"

He spun around to face the room. He was genuinely mad.

"Which one of you monkeys moved the fucking overlay for the checkpoints into the airport diagram folder?"

None of the Osprey or CH-53 pilots said anything. My Friend is only a first lieutenant, but they were all captains. My Friend obviously commanded respect.

"Okay, well, whoever did it, go kill yourself. My friend—" as he pointed to me—"is trying to make a fuel product and the overlay wasn't where it was supposed to be. Don't let it happen again."

"Thanks, Friend."

I got up and we gave each other a hug. We average about 10 hugs a day.

"Anytime, Friend."

And he returned to educating Osprey pilots.

Dash and I settled our differences and came up with what was a very good product. When it was done, it became a one-stop shop for all the Huey and Cobra pilots to figure their fuel burn. It took us over three hours to finish. As with all products, version control is important. We named it Version 1.0 or V1.0 and put our names as the point of contact or POC in the bottom right of the slide. That way if someone has a question about the data, they know whom to contact. The date is included as well. A small change would be V1.1 and a large change would be V2.0.

Later that night when we went to print dozens of our products, we found that SWUD had gone in, without our knowledge, and made some change. We know this because the version was changed to V1.1 and it had SWUD's name as the new POC. We scanned the product and honestly can't find what was changed. I cleverly saved a version on my external hard drive in case the network crashed. When I opened our original, I discovered SWUD had changed the color of the text box for naming the points. It's a subtle change, but nonetheless a change and hence rated a new version number and a new POC.

It was beginning to get late by the time we finished. It was around 1900 local time. Operations had been working hard to synchronize the timing of the plan, maintenance had been working overtime to ensure all aircraft are up for tasking, and the dog and pony handlers had been combing, bathing, and clipping the animals to get them ready for the show.

Because I was working on the fuel product, I didn't even bother checking the schedule and just assumed I'd be told if I was flying. Around 1930 they assembled all the pilots and rolled through the air flow charts. The air flow is an Excel document that shows the time blocks that each aircraft is flying and from which ship. The type of mission is also included. The senior CH-53 pilot, a major, was briefing the flows.

He was using a retractable pointer and as he pointed to an event on the flow, he was reaching *across* his body. Basically he was on the left side of the audience and was using his right hand to point and hence had to slightly turn his back to us. This is a major no-no for briefing. Always stay open to the audience. Never turn your back to them. Rookie.

I slowly followed along with him. Looked like the aviation elements from the 13th MEU actually have a role to play in the show. They were conducting an air assault on an objective using CH-53s with support from AV-8B Harriers and Cobras and Hueys operating from the USS *New Orleans*. They will be lifting First Battalion, Fourth Marines, a unit permanently stationed on Okinawa. Scanning down to the line for the MV-22s for our ship the BHR, I saw that they had been assigned a mission of "Media Standby" as well as "Distinguished Visitor (DV) Standby." I guess that's for all the newspaper and media reporters to snap their pictures of the show. I expected this because V-Neck mentioned it previously.

One more line down was our Cobra and Huey detachment on the BHR. It didn't say anything. I sort of suspected this because our original ship was supposed to be the Denver, but we moved to the BHR. Just to be sure this was correct, I glanced behind me to the seat where V-Neck was sitting. I noticed he had fallen asleep so I just assumed his word about doing the stands fly by to be true even though we weren't on the flow. The CH-53 major finished the brief by stressing that the entire goal of the operation was the time on target or TOT on the beach. Everyone had to make the TOT in order for the show to go off right.

He elaborated, "I can't stress enough that this entire thing revolves around that TOT. Once the ground guys set it, we have to be able to make it. We want the first wave of tracks hitting the beach at the exact same time that the first CH-53s land with the air-assault Marines. The MV-22s carrying the media and the general need to be overhead at the exact TOT as well. And finally for the H-1s, you guys need to be overhead those reviewing stands at that TOT. Usually the enemy and intelligence drive operations, but since there is no real or simulated enemy, it is this holy TOT that drives us. It's gotta be good, gents. The general is holding us to a standard of plus and minus 20 seconds from the TOT. Do I have any questions?"

One of his fellow CH-53 pilots raised a hand and the major called on him.

"Yes, question right there."

"Sir, what about minimum weather for aviation? Have we decided what the minimum weather should be?"

"Good question, we will make the judgement call early tomorrow morning. As of right now it's not looking good for weather. In keeping with the wishes of the parade conductor of the MEB, General Kennedy, this show can't commence without aviation."

The schedule was finally published and I was not on it. I helped with what I could to make the final preparations.

I felt strongly that I should retake the ownership of my and Dash's fuel product from SWUD so I opened it. I was in the process of changing it back to our original formatting when another Cobra pilot, Highway, came up behind me.

"Hey, we are running late on that fuel product. Just print what ya got, okay?"

"Roger that."

I left it as is with SWUD's name on my product and began printing and stapling smartpacks as well as helping make a few more slides for the briefs. Around 2200 I overheard an argument in the ready room between Bleeder and another major who I believe to be the air officer for the 31st MEU. They were arguing over how the Cobras and Hueys should be used for the show.

Bleeder thought they should be armed and conduct live fire ranges. The MEU major maintained their role as unarmed assets to conduct a fly-by of the reviewing stands. You don't want to mess with Bleeder in attack mode. Dash and I have learned from many unpleasant firsthand encounters. The MEU major eventually won the argument only because he is a member of the staff and has the weight of the general and his wishes for a dog-and-pony show behind him. He was lucky. Bleeder fucks people up.

Finally around 2300, I took a break and read a few chapters in *They Were Counted*, an intriguing novel about pre-World War I Hungary. As I was reading, the sergeant major of our squadron as well as the master gunnery sergeant, or Master Guns for short, were having a meeting. Master Guns is essentially in charge of personnel in the maintenance department. Himself and the sergeant major couldn't be more different. Sergeant major has a high and tight haircut and does everything by the books. Master Guns, despite being an alcoholic that is in the early stages of Parkinson's, is much more pragmatic.

The attendees of the meeting were the staff non-commissioned officers of the aviation maintenance departments. An SNCO has the rank of staff sergeant or higher and they are the most experienced and seasoned of the enlisted ranks. Since our squadron is comprised of H-1s, CH-53s, and MV-22s, there are over two dozen Marines in the meeting. The topic of the meeting is whether or not Marines should be allowed to roll the sleeves of their coveralls. The Marines who work on our aircraft wear not flight suits but mechanic coveralls. Since it was fairly cold this time of year in Korea, many of them wore warming layers beneath their coveralls. I paid attention to the debate.

Sergeant major kicked it off.

"All right, ahhh, listen up, ahhh, so we don't have a policy right now ahhh for Marines rolling their sleeves in coveralls. Ahhh, I've seen lots of Marines with half-rolled sleeves, full rolls, quarter rolls, or no rolls at all."

The Marine Corps is huge on leading by example and sergeant major was showing them how it's done. He was wearing a tan flight suit even though he wasn't an aviator or crew chief by military occupational specialty. He was leading a discussion on how to properly wear a uniform.

Master Guns attacked, "I've never seen it to be a problem. We don't need a policy."

His head involuntarily twitched ever so slightly. The more he gets worked up the more it twitches. He continued, "Who is making a fuss about this, anyway? It's not the navy. I haven't heard shit from them. They have ridiculous uniforms. Green, purple, yellow, and red turtlenecks and khaki pants. They look like a bunch of fucking teletubbies. Why do we need to go around telling Marines that are working on aircraft how to roll their sleeves. What matters is the quality of their work."

Sergeant major was looking concerned and shot back.

"Well, ahh, we can't just not have a policy. Who here, ahh, wants to say let's vote on ahhh a policy for how maintainers should ahh, you know, roll their sleeves?"

Maybe three or four guys raised their hands. A few staff sergeants weighed in.

"I've never seen sleeves rolled. Everyone should just have them down at all times."

Another added, "Well, on the West Coast, we removed our buttons as soon as we got our coveralls and there is no way to roll them down without it looking shitty because you couldn't button the ends."

Sergeant major returned to the debate, "Well, ahhh . . ."

Dash tapped me on the shoulder and mentioned going to get some food during midnight rations or Midrats. I quietly packed up and left.

The weather was terrible on the 29 March so the show was postponed until the thirtieth.

The Dog and Pony Show

"Love your country and fight for your country.
Believe in truth, and that is enough."

-Johannes Steinhoff, Luftwaffe fighter ace

30 March 2014. 0530L.

D-Day. The show was happening today. Weather was shit on the twenty-ninth so we rolled the show to the thirtieth.

Once again I was not on the flight schedule and since all the products and planning had already been accomplished, I just ate chow and strolled to the ready room. On my way I took the catwalk route rather than stay inside the ship to check out the battlefield and get some fresh air. I could easily observe the beach that we will be "assaulting." It was maybe just two or three nautical miles away. Several Korean non-military vessels spotted the waters around us. Don't they know we are putting on a show to keep them safe? Show some respect, I thought.

Word was a rehearsal was taking place on the flight deck early in the morning before the launch. If there was one, I didn't hear it. The usual routines took place in the ready room. The pilots received their aircraft assignments, took a weather brief in English, and air traffic control procedures in ebonics.

GYCO was flying in the lead Cobra that was doing the fly-by of the stands. Part of me was jealous because I want to be part of the action, but I still feel like part of the team because I helped plan. I was ignorant and oblivious of the planning conducted by the ground guys in their amphibious assault vehicles. I assumed they loaded all the dogs and ponies properly along with at least one handler per assault vehicle. They must have rehearsed the parade once the animals disembarked.

There were television screens in the ready room focused on each of the spots on the flight deck. When GYCO and My Friend's Huey lifted off, I felt a swelling of patriotism. Go show those Koreans how good a parade we put on. Semper Fi!

I waited out the invasion in the ready room listening and observing everything I can.

About two hours passed and I saw the blur of whirring helicopter blades reappear on the television screen. They made it back. As soon as GYCO and My Friend returned to the ready room, I questioned them about how it all went down.

Overall the execution was excellent, they said. One of the AAVs lost power to a track and started just spinning in circles in the water like a sperm cell that has lost motor control. It didn't make the show but other than that, they said it was an impressive effort. The dogs left the AAVs first since they are faster and acted like "shock troops." Following them were the larger ponies and Clydesdales ferrying supplies like doggie treats, water, doggie poop bags, hay for the ponies, and extra camera batteries for the reporters already waiting on the beach.

My Friend said the AAVs threw out a really cool smoke screen prior to hitting the beach. There were also dozens of Marine public affairs officers or PAOs on the beach getting shots of the assault. GYCO said there was a large contingent of Marines already on deck on the beach just lounging around. None of us were sure where they came from.

GYCO said when they passed over the reviewing stands, all the Koreans and dignitaries looked really impressed. They said the fuel product Dash and I worked on that SWUD took credit for really helped them out. The ground guys asked them to remain overhead to do a few more fly-bys and they weren't sure if they had enough fuel. They just referenced the product and gave the ground guys an exact time for how much more overhead time they could provide.

We stood around for a few moments more as several other pilots filed in. They included the Osprey pilots who flew the media and General Kennedy, the lead parade conductor, over the reviewing stands. The general was slapping guys on the back and congratulating them on a job well done. Word was Korea might place a few orders for the Osprey and make it the first foreign sale of the aircraft.

I ducked out for just a second to use the restroom outside the ready room. One of the enlisted Huey crew chiefs that was on My Friends' flight was slumped in the corner of the end of the hallway. He was shaking uncontrollably and looked like he is in shock. I quickly stooped down and asked him if he was okay and what was wrong.

He mumbled something about how he saw one of the dogs accidentally crushed by a pony. I guess GYCO and My Friend didn't see it happen, but this crew chief did being in the back of the aircraft with a better vantage point.

Immediately after that he started reciting verbatim the difference between a restricted and unrestricted sexual assault report. He shivered but eked a recorded message.

"Restricted reporting allows a Marine who is sexually assaulted to confidentially report the assault and receive support, medical treatment, and counseling *without* a law enforcement investigation. For restricted reporting, you must only report to a uniform victim advocate, civilian victim advocate, sexual assault response coordinator, healthcare provider, or chaplain."

He paused for about a second and took a deep breath then continued, "Unrestricted reporting allows a Marine who is sexually assaulted to report the assault and receive support, advocacy, medical treatment, and counseling *with* a law enforcement investigation and the support of the chain of command. For unrestricted reporting, you can report to a uniform victim advocate, civilian victim advocate, sexual assault response coordinator, chain of command, or law enforcement."

Good shit, I thought. Despite being in shock and almost incoherent from the carnage, he fell back on his training. Just because of morbid fascination, I let him start the recording over which he does without even being told. However, after he began the third one, I was convinced he was actually in trouble so I ordered him to stop. He didn't so I smacked him with an open palm followed by a backhand.

"Get ahold of yourself man," I shouted.

He ceased and started to cry. I told him to hang on and quickly summoned the closest navy corpsman. They escorted him away and he ended up making a full recovery.

After having an assplosion in the toilet, I gleefully returned to the ready room. In the short time I was away, GYCO had somehow taken command of the room and everyone, General Kennedy included, was formed up around him as he held the place of authority at the front of the ready room. There were about 30 Marines, mostly pilots, assembled, awaiting what looked like a speech. General Kennedy was beaming ear to ear with pride and silenced the crowd, which was still fairly rowdy.

"Gentlemen, quiet down, one of our Cobra pilots, call sign GYCO, has something he wants to say. Listen up! GYCO, the floor is yours."

GYCO grinned and pulled a small piece of paper from his pocket that looked like a sheet from his kneeboard. The kneeboard is simply a board we strap to our leg that has a clip for holding a writing pad and other important aviation documents. GYCO held the sheet with both hands and began, "Thank you, General. Gentlemen, I just took part in the fly-by of those reviewing stands. What an experience!"

"Ooorah!" yelled one of the younger Marines in the front row.

GYCO continued.

"From the air I was able to see things that guys on the ground couldn't. Just as Francis Scott Key was inspired when he saw the British bombard Fort McHenry and wrote our national anthem, I was also inspired by what I just witnessed. I'm not anywhere close to being on par with Francis Scott Key, but I wrote a poem on the flight back to the ship and I'd like to share it with you so here it is.

"Once upon a time, in a land far, far away
A defense lay, while dogs and ponies all play
Sand castles, bleachers, smoke screens and glee
News articles were written, but we took a knee

Public affairs officers all danced and smiled in their merry way
While Marines ate chow and filled ashtrays
The dogs and ponies were kenneled after the fact
Mission accomplished, an American act."

As he finished and looked back up to the crowd the general took the reins again.

"Motivating! Thanks GYCO. That was an awesome poem. Give 'em one!"

"Kill!" The Marines responded in unison.

"Marines, this dog and pony show means a Marine Corps for the next eight months until the Treasury reaches another borrowing limit. And my, how quickly does the word of our work spread out here. I just heard from one of the Korean dignitaries that the Samsung Galaxy S5 due to launch in early April will retail around $199.99 with a two-year contract from Verizon, Sprint, or AT&T. That is 10 dollars less than what was anticipated before our fake invasion. Gentlemen, this why we fight, for cheap electronics for American consumers. And we did it without firing a single shot. Talk about a one-sided victory. Everyone, three cheers for our dog and pony show. It was a resounding success."

"Hip Hip."

"Hooray!" The crowd answered.

"Hip Hip."

"Hooray!"

"Hip Hip."

"Hooray!"

"We have ice cream set up in the wardroom for all. Come join us."

The general led a lively procession down the hallways of the ship. Everyone he passed got a high-five.

As I strutted down the hall, I wondered if this is what it was like for the Marines on the ships in World War II when they learned Japan surrendered. Eugene Sledge in his memoirs *With the Old Breed* said some men on his ship cried when they learned they would live through the war and not die invading mainland Japan.

While I wasn't in tears, I was damn close. No 8-year-old American girl will be without a Samsung Galaxy S5 for more than $200 dollars (with a 2-year plan, of course) or a San Francisco hipster without their iPad for a penny over $300. Not while I'm in the military. It is hard to put words behind the feelings of American idealism I felt during our victory wagon to the wardroom. Oooorah!

I've included several choice pictures that the public affairs officers took during the exercise. For the reader who wants to see more, simply Google "Ssang Young 2014 Marines" and you'll find plenty of good shots.

With the exercise over, the 13th MEU ships set sail for California. They were at the tail end of their deployment and ready to return home. The 31st MEU remained in the vicinity of Korea for a few more weeks to execute several smaller training scenarios before sailing back to Okinawa in mid-April.

Despite not flying in the show, I did participate in several training evolutions in Korea afterward. The training was surprisingly good and relevant. I began to lose track of how many rockets and gun rounds I was shooting. I decided to tally my weapons expenditure totals before Ssang Young and also tally my weapons expenditure for the entire deployment. Those interested in how much ordnance I shot during my time in Korean waters can simply subtract the first column from the second.

My personal weapons expenditure *before* Ssang Young during my deployment to Okinawa:

MJU-32 Flare (Decoy Flare)	0
MJU-49 Flare (Decoy Flare)	0
SM-875 (Practice Flare)	0
AGM-114 Hellfire Missile (K, M, and N models)	0
2.75" Rockets (all warhead types)	0
2.75" Mk 149 Mod 0 Flechette Rockets	0
Advanced Precision Kill Weapon System (2.75" Laser Guided Rocket)	0
2.75" Smoke Rockets	0
5" Rockets (all warhead types)	0
20MM Gatling Gun	300 rounds
AIM-9M Sidewinder	0
M257 Illumination Rockets	0
M278 Covert Illumination Rockets	0

Weapons expenditure totals for the *entire* deployment:

MJU-32 Flare (Decoy Flare)	0
MJU-49 Flare (Decoy Flare)	0

SM-875 (Practice Flare)	0
AGM-114 Hellfire Missile (K, M, and N models)	0
2.75" Rockets (all warhead types)	0
2.75" Mk 149 Mod 0 Flechette Rockets	0
Advanced Precision Kill Weapon System (2.75" Laser Guided Rocket)	0
2.75" Smoke Rockets	0
5" Rockets (all warhead types)	0
20MM Gatling Gun	300 rounds
AIM-9M Sidewinder	0
M257 Illumination Rockets	0
M278 Covert Illumination Rockets	0

LCD Sound System and a Wardroom Poem

5 April 2014

After many weeks of hard work, the Marines and sailors of BHR were pleasantly surprised with a concert on the flight deck. It was kept ultra-top secret until the last minute. Almost no one knew about it until the day of. After a frustrating week of Ssang Young games, fake invasions, dozens of VIP lifts and media talking about how great the Osprey is, the crews were ready for a break.

There was only one problem, the band didn't get their gear on board. The lead Osprey brought James Murphy and his current band cast on board, but the Dash 2 Osprey that was supposed to bring their gear on board was diverted to take a VIP to Seoul for negotiations to sell it to the Koreans. Being the innovators that they are, LCD Sound System gathered all the night crew Marines on the flight deck and started an inventory of what gear they had on hand. Here is an account of the gear actually present:

300 sets of tie down chains
400 feet of fuel hoses
15 red fuel cans used for fuel samples
20 glass jars with lids for sampling other fluids
25 Rubber Mallet Hammers

20 PFK each consisting of a mirror, a crescent wrench, a flat head screwdriver, a Maglite flashlight, and SPIRE wrenches to zip tie things together
5 Tug carts to move aircraft in and out of their spots
A P-25 Fire cart with its associated crew members in their firefighting spacesuit ensemble
8 Sets of Ground Handling Wheels
Each Marine and sailor also had a cranial helmet and float coat.

LCD lead quickly took control of flight deck control or FDC, getting a crash course from the integrity watch officer in the operation of the various phones, cameras, screens, and PA systems needed to control such an epic operation. The IWO is responsible for the security and condition of the aircraft after flight quarters. He makes sure they are chained up, aren't leaking, and coordinates with the bridge if an alternate power unit or APU needed to be started to conduct maintenance.

With his cameras, he could see almost all parts of the flight deck, forward, mid, aft, the slashes where they store aircraft, even in the hangar bay one floor below where a MH-60S was undergoing maintenance. His phones could connect to all parts of the ship, but most importantly he would need to communicate with the bridge and the officer of the day (OOD).

The OOD gives permission to move aircraft around the flight deck, start an APU, or conduct major maintenance. They steer the ship and give us winds. LCD lead did his best to get a zero wind condition but still maintained a zigzag to avoid North Korean subs. And always being safety minded, LCD lead was shown how to use the P-25 phone to position the fire cart as he saw fit in case someone just jammed out too hard and started a fire.

While James Murphy was setting up in Flight Deck Control, Pat Mahoney, a venerable member of the band specializing in percussion, was furiously organizing the Marines and sailors on the flight deck. His job was made easier by the color coding system the navy uses. He took all the fuelers, who wear purple, and had them lay out their hoses. Each length of hose was about 30 feet long and made of a highly flexible rubberized plastic material. Each end had metal fittings, one for the pump side and the other for the aircraft. One sailor was on either end and their job, when ordered by LCD lead, was to make sinusoidal waves.

The brown coats were the mechanics, or flightline Marines; they had the biggest part to play. They were the percussion instruments, utilizing their PFK screwdrivers and the rubber mallets to drum on the fuel cans, which gave a lower-pitched sound as well as the glass sampling jars, which had higher frequencies. They were arranged like a xylophone. Being by far the most numerous, the extra flight mechanics also picked up the crescent wrenches and were arrayed in a circle to use the flight deck as their percussion surface.

The red shirts were manning the P-25 crash truck and stayed put to monitor possible fires. The white shirts are the combat cargo Marines and sailors, and are responsible for moving cargo from the hangar bay to the flight deck and vice versa. They got some pallets out to slide around on the deck to make a sort of washboard stroking sound of the old school. The avionics Marines, wearing green, take up positions in the flight deck control to ensure the PA system is working throughout the entire ship. The blue shirts, also known as chain monkeys, were given the dozens of sets of chains and chalks to make scraping and percussion. The entire evolution only took about one hour to fully set up and by about 0300 they were ready.

We spoke about centralized control, but we need to talk to the individual leaders, because without them LCD head wouldn't be able to carry out his intent. The yellow shirts are the flight deck handlers and landing signal enlisted members; they signal aircraft to land and when flight ops aren't in session, they direct the towing and placement of aircraft. LCD lead gathers them in FDC for a brief rundown of the songs to be played. They wear an intercom system in their cranials so they can hear FDC for orders too. Right at 0330, the first cords are struck. Looking out on the flight deck at everyone organized by color, in their respective positions, ready and willing to jam out is a sight to see.

The first song is "Someone Great." A good choice, it is slow and builds layer upon layer in complexity and sophistication. Avioinics began it with what almost sounds like a siren but not as shrill or loud, like a dull throbbing with a slight scratchy feedback. They rigged something up in the intercom system; we heard it throughout the entire ship. At first we dismissed it as another weird navy ship sound, but as we continued to toss and turn at :13 seconds, about a dozen flight mechanics began their drumming routine on their glass bottles. *Da da da dat da da da da dat*, simultaneously an almost imperceptible bass note began with a flight deck handler cupping his hand on the intercom system microphone.

You might think on a ship out in the ocean you wouldn't transmit much sound through the hull, but it is actually very easy to hear it, almost like it's right in your rack there with you. The officers were on the second level, one below the flight deck. Back to the music, at 30 seconds in, with the three combined melodies building, a deep dub sound began a slow *bong bong . . . bong . . . bong bong bong bong . . . bong*. This sound is the result of white shirts slamming the hull of the ship with large rubber mallets. Each one has just one hit to make, then just times it so when it comes back around to them, they are in sync. The first couple were rough, but by about one minute, the LSE has them in line and they are in unison. As the song buildt toward a minute, a sharp feedback was inserted, almost sounding like a DJ twisting his tables.

Fire up YouTube right now and listen along.

At approximately 1:07 the siren sounds became higher in pitch and what resembles an electronic keyboard began a quickly changing melody of notes. This was the one instrument LCD brought with them. LCD added things in pairs, as you have seen, and the vocals are no different. At 1:37 the vocals began with the addition of what sounded like Christmas season bells but is really a flight liner on a smaller bottle creating a high pitch.

"I wish that we could talk about it . . . but there . . . lies the problem . . . With someone new I couldn't start it . . . too late . . . for beginning . . . The little things that made me nervous . . . are gone . . . in a mooooment . . . I miss the way we used to argue . . . locked . . . in the basement."

The vocals were just the last delicious layer in this musical masterpiece. One level beneath the flight deck in the officer berthing, you can hear all of this. Even if you have to sleep in for a night flight, you will be awoken to this electronic synergy. It was so scintillating it even permeated foamy ear protection.

The next song they kicked it up a few notches with "Get Innocuous." It dropped with some heavy bass notes from the mechs drumming accentuated with a raspy sound of fuelers rapping on empty trash cans. The complexity just builds from there and when it really gets going at 1:39 the volume just kicks up a notch and another layer of percussion comes in. The mechs were working their asses off. James Murphy, once comfortable with his base layers, began the vocals.

"Hooomeee . . . home in the late night . . . and away . . . away in the half life . . ."

They found a few girls who had vocal experience and got them up top to flight deck control. After a few minutes of the lyrics, they chimed in with a beautiful refrain, "You will normalize. Don't it make you feel alive."

All the sleeping officers and sailors just gave up at this point and came out onto the flight deck and started jamming out right alongside the band. This went on until breakfast started at 0430 and several key players had to get the fires stoked to make us some bacon.

The next morning, I sat down for a breakfast in the wardroom and was trying to wake up while humming "Someone Great" under my breath. Lost a decent amount of sleep, but man, what a performance. The girl working the griddle was very nice but quite blunt.

"Good morning, sir, what would you like?" in a very loud tone.

"I'll have egg whites scrambled with everything but cheese and ham."

"WHAT, SIR?"

I almost started she is so loud. I repeated it, keeping in mind she meant well.

"Yes, sir."

She was wearing just her boots and utes and a paper chef-type hat. Her upper arms were pure Jell-O.

Last week during midnight rations at 2300 when I was dumping my trash, I picked up an opening into the kitchen with my peripherals. It was a view into one of the prep rooms and she was just sitting on the ground slumped over sleeping. Her back was up against a stainless table and her head was slumped, parallel to the floor. The chef hat was still on though.

As I sat down I picked up *The Almanac,* a one-sheet front-and-back newspaper for the *BHR*. I flipped over to the back side and there was a poetry winner. Apparently there was a contest. It's called *A Poem*, by ABH3 Robert Burns. I read it once and was speechless. Absolutely brilliant, fucking amazing. So moving. I was joined by the air boss, a navy commander. He picked up another copy of the poem. His mood was marginally brightened by what appeared to be some good journalism by *The Almanac.*

"Oh, look, a poem," he smirked slightly and began reading it under his breath but still loud enough that I could hear.

"I sit and think about you and everything that I did wrong.
You died before I could make it right, so I am writing you this song.
I remember being kids hungry with no money stealing from the gas station.

Blink my eyes once and you were gone, incarcerated."

"Hmmm." He grunted slightly as the confusion set in.

"Blink my eyes twice and you were lying on the pavement.
Glad God has you in the attic now for you were living in the basement.
Life was dark, it was cold and all you needed was a little light.
Sadly I was too immature so I never did what was right."

His eyes squinted for a millisecond and he shook it off with a quick shake of his head. The original optimistic countenance vanished and he continued. It's too good to not keep reading. Think of a scene of a car wreck with brain matter all over the road.

"I recall getting mad and you and I would fight.
I wish every fist I ever threw as an opportunity to hug you.
All my pride aside I hope you truly know I love you.
So does the rest of our family and does my son too.
By the way you are my uncle and my son will have your middle name."

The boss was frozen.

"I pray that God has eased you pain; you are the reason why I changed.
God only knows why I never picked up the phone to call.
I guess I got so used to you not being around at all.
I wrote a letter to you explaining everything that I was feeling.
A multitude of scripts with the intent of give us some sort of healing.
Promises of us starting over and how I planned for us to go far.
Work schedules and minor distractions resulted in me losing it in my car.
Those bullets didn't just end your life but they propelled you to the stars.
I'd give blood and bone to hear your laugh and the loud music you blasted.
We didn't just bury your body but a piece of me went with you in that casket.
I sit and think about you and everything I did wrong.

You died before I could make it right, so I am writing you this song."[1]

The air boss paused for a few seconds and said, "Man, that's some heavy stuff."

I love breakfast on the *BHR*.

The 31ˢᵗ MEU's Response to a Korean Ferry Sinking

16 April 2014

The mighty USS *BHR* was sailing back to White Beach in Okinawa. By the next morning MCAS Futenma will have been in range of the MV-22 Osprey and most of the aviation elements will have departed.

Dash and I were engaging in some light conversation.

"Dash, how are we going to bang these girls?"

We were in our usual spots in the ready room after eating a scrumptious breakfast. Here we bullshit and read books until lunch. Dash basically has a girlfriend at this point but can't close the deal because we are on the ship. We are scheming on how to get laid when we get off the ship and back onto Okinawa.

The girls I was referencing were from the Search and Rescue or SAR detachment on the boat. They were based in Guam but get attached to the ship for the float. Their squadron was HSC-25. Helicopter Sea Combat. They fly an amazing machine. The MH-60S. Basically a naval version of the Blackhawk. Unfortunately, all they do on the boat is fly around in circles off the starboard side of the ship for four hours at a time waiting for a helicopter to crash into the water.

The girls from the squadron were pretty fun, although I did see one of them cry back in flight school when she failed a flight. She was overreacting. Little did she know that in advanced flight training, short of crashing a helicopter, she was going to get her wings. As a female she had nothing to fear. It becomes too politically risky to hold women to the same standards as men in advanced flight training. I speak from experience.

The idea on the boat is to get what is known as a "boat girlfriend." She is just your high-school crush that you hang out with in a genuine friendship sort of way because legally, physical intimacy is not allowed on the ship. A joke one of our senior pilots told me was you can't talk to your boat girlfriend. As soon as you do, you have to find a new one. Keep it like grade school, afraid to talk to girls.

The *abovementioned* girl who cried in flight school was my boat girlfriend. Kat was her call sign. I decided to write her a grade school love note and passed it to her without talking. It was clutch. She didn't write back. I eventually had to talk to her because we planned a mission together.

"Well, I invited them out to the Kadena Officer Club on Friday and we'll invite them back to the barracks after the club."

Dash was getting wild eyed.

I countered.

"That's good, but what game plan should I roll with, things are already awkward. I wrote my boat girlfriend a note and didn't talk to her for two-thirds of the float. Plus, she doesn't seem like a one-night-stand type of girl. I guess I have to go with a frontal assault, just put it all out there."

"We have to use alcohol, no doubt about it. One weekend isn't long enough; we have to accelerate things."

Dash was a forward-thinking man. I responded.

"Naturally, of course, naturally. You aren't going to last but a few seconds; we have been away from the Internet for a while."

"No, I'm just going to be natural. Eat the box for a while, then finger blast, then jerk off while I'm eating to get the first round done. Then back to eat, blast, fuck. I think it should work. The first time I see the pussy, I need my face to be in it. That's how I know if I can date a girl. I have to eat the box like the first or second date. Even before sex. Looking back the only girls I got along with were the ones whose box I ate before I had sex for the first time. Bottom line, if I don't enjoy eating her box, I can't date the girl."

I know he doesn't always do this with his girls, so I called him out.

"Oh yeah, but what about that local piece of trash you picked up at O'Kelly's Pub in Honolulu before we left for the deployment. I doubt you ate that girl out. She was gross."

"No, you are right about that. You have to draw the line sometimes. No eating for her, just finger blasting. I basically made a porno. I wouldn't fuck her, but just did a three-finger ultra-blast with water squirting out everywhere."

"Jesus! You are fucking sick, Dash. If Senator Gillibrand heard you talking, she would faint. You need to teach me that three-finger ultra move. I only know the middle finger and I go gentle. Well, you are only gonna get one night with these girls, so better go for it all. I say if you are drunk enough, you might not have to jerk off, but we'll see. It's gonna be awkward either way."

As we were talking, we get word that there might be a situation developing. Ssang Young was over and we were steaming back to White Beach in Okinawa to unload. What could be happening, I thought? Did they leave behind a few ponies on the beach?

Word was there was a Korean vessel sinking about 100 nautical miles away. There were around 500 passengers on board. We were Cobra attack helicopter gunship pilots and hence could give a shit less about helping anyone. We walked to chow and overheard more rumblings in the chow line.

The PA system blared to life.

"Assemble the crisis action team in the conference room."

I looked across the wardroom to Dash and lip synch, "This is it, we're going to war," in my best impersonation of Major Powers from *Heartbreak Ridge*.

The Crisis Action Team, or CAT, is the standard rapid action planning cell for the 31st MEU. They gathered all the representatives from each discipline. Ground, air, logistics, and navy counterparts sat at a conference table and debated about how to solve a problem.

River City was launched shortly afterward. No communications were allowed out.

V-Neck was chosen as the representative for the Cobras and Hueys. As he was leaving the wardroom to attend the CAT, he grabbed me and said I should come just for the experience of seeing a CAT in action. The commodore, a navy captain O-6, is in charge of the Amphibious Ready Group or ARG. It consists of three ships. The USS *Bonhomme Richard* (BHR), the USS *Denver*, and the USS *Ashland*. She is ultimately in charge and she lives on the *Bonhomme Richard*. She will chair the CAT. As we took our seats in a massive conference room, the XO of the BHR lays down the facts. I paraphrase them here.

At 0900L a South Korean passenger ferry transmitted a distress signal from approximately 12 degrees west of Byungpoong Island. The ship was listing and taking on water. Approximately 471 passengers on board, 320 are students along with their teachers. There were 20 crew members. A total of 34 naval, coast guard, and civilian ships, and 18 helicopters were involved. As of 1300L, 165 passengers had been rescued by the Mokpo Coast Guard. All other passengers were told to jump into the water. The water temperature was approximately 55 degrees. At this temperature you survive for

1.4 hours without an exposure suit and at 8.4 hours there is a 50 percent survival estimate. Yonhap news agency reported that the ship had run aground. One passenger was quoted, "We heard a big thumping sound and the boat stopped."

The clock was ticking, as long as a temperature differential exists, heat will transfer. From the hot to the cold, from the body to the sea, until it reaches 55 degrees.

The ARG captain then initiated the meeting with a trite saying. She lacked command presence.

"First off, I want to thank everyone for assembling here on such short notice. You have been doing great work. Keep your heads on a swivel. Now, I know there isn't a lot of information to go off of here. We could just as easily turn on the news like CNN or Fox and they would increase our situational awareness fivefold but we just declared River City so no communications are allowed in or out.

"The big unknown variable is the South Korean response. As professionals we have to resist the tendency to assume that since they are Asians, they are incapable of helping their own country. Korea has the thirteenth-largest economy in the world.[1] Our guttural and natural response when we see Asian natural disasters is to force our way to the front of the line and demand they allow us to help them for their own damn good. I can't stress it enough, our natural reaction might not be right here. It's always true with the brown people, but not always with the Asians. Yellow is closer to white than brown. So let's hear the courses of action (COA). Amphibious assault vehicles, let's hear your thoughts."

The Marine captain representing the AAVs spoke up.

"Ma'am, I've spoken with my Marines and we are in concurrence that unless we get within 10 to 15 nautical miles of the wreckage, we will be of little use. Right now we are 120 nautical miles out and with the clock ticking, I can only submit the tracks should not be a COA. Once we approach the 65 nautical miles of EF 21, we could launch just to see what honoring anti-ship missiles would look like.

That's never been done so we're rolling the dice and I'm not sure how we would fuel up en route or on our return. Definitely suicidal even without an enemy opposing us on the beach. I vote no for using AAVs."

She looked deep in thought, as if she was trying to grab another buzz word or acronym but couldn't. She quickly recovered and moved onto the boat platoon, "Very well, boat Marine guys, the ones with the little rubber boat thingys, what say you?"

Barely keeping his composure, Captain Kuskewski, the company commander of the reconnaissance Marines, answered, "Ma'am, we could definitely pluck survivors with our boats, but like the AAVs, we can only troll at 8 knots, not nearly fast enough to get there to make any sort of appreciable difference."

"Uhh okay, so we can use the dingy rubber boat things, but we need to get them there faster. Double-check me on the math here," as she began the math aloud.

"Distance is rate multiplied by time. We have a fixed distance to the wreckage site. Actually, let me just illustrate this for the Marines in the room."

She rose out of her seat with gusto, beaming with pride, and waddled over to the dry erase board. She wrote the equation $d=rt$ and continued her explanation.

"So since the distance to the ship is fixed and we want to minimize the time we have to increase our rate. Does that make sense to everyone?"

Inwardly she beamed with pride and thought, "You show 'em, Beth. All these men doubted you. They never thought they'd work for a woman. Now I'm in charge."

Capt Kuskewski slipped, however, and rolled his eyes. I was staring at him to gauge his reaction. His reaction seems to say, "Oh God, here we go again."

The commodore was watching him too and didn't like what she saw.

"Capt Kuskewski, is there anything you want to add?"

"No, ma'am," he said with a gentle shaking of his head.

She pointed a crooked finger at him and yelled, "Well, I saw you just rolled your eyes at me. Don't you ever fucking roll your eyes at me again, you Polish perogi-eating piece of shit! I went to Annapolis, for Christ's sake, and I'll be damned if some hotshot Marine thinks he is smarter than me. They don't make anyone navy captains. Do you understand me?"

"Yes, ma'am."

He regained his bearing.

Her hand was quivering and her eyes were scanning from man to man to ensure her point was made. She took a deep breath and resumed.

"Now, that unfortunate event is behind us, let's continue with the equation. We need some way to get there faster. The Irish workers down in the boiler room can only shovel coal at a maximum rate of 2,000 pounds per hour. 1,000 pounds per hour gives us our normal cruise speed of 15 knots, and if we get 1 knot per each increase of 100 pounds per hour above 1,000, we can go 25 knots max. Still not enough for us to make it to the crash site in the next half hour."

The timid hand of the senior surface warfare officer went up. The surface warfare officer or SWO is a navy person who specializes in a particular discipline regarding the ship. Some work in propulsion, others navigation, and others weapon systems.

"Yes, Commander Axelson, what do you have to say?"

She was visibly vexed because he was stealing her thunder.

"Ma'am, the boilers don't run off shoveled coal any longer. The last coal-fired boiler was decommissioned shortly after World War II. All our boilers now run off a petroleum fuel similar to jet fuel called F76."

She pondered his statement for about a half second then exploded.

"Don't you think I already knew that, you smart ass. Who asked you for your opinion, anyway? I did the conversion in my head of F76 flow into pounds of coal per hour. I was teaching the least common denominator. Marines don't know what F76 is. If you can't handle hearing it in coal in pounds per hour, then you shouldn't be here. How you got your surface warfare pin I'll never know. Take your chair and go face the corner of the room, you dunce. Expect to stay there the rest of the meeting."

Commander Axelson gathered himself, and with the humble air of a man going to bury his faithful dog of many years, he went and faced the corner of the room.

"Does anyone here have any ideas for increasing the rate at which we can reach them? What about our aircraft, they have to be able to help out somehow. What about the Osprey, it's the rockstar piece of equipment on the MEU, what can it do? It has to be able to do something. Also if we use it and save the day, surely Korea will want to buy dozens of them for future use. Somebody give me an idea, damn it."

"We coulda use dey Ospreys and putta dey Duckys insride dem wit da Maweens aready roaded in da rafts. Da Osprey canna come to a row hawere and kick dem outta da back."

Everyone looked over to the Osprey representative toward the end of the table. It was Ngrsh. The Ospreys, especially their commanding officer, are known for their general aversion to anything risky or outside the box so it came as a surprise when he piped up.

"What is a Ducky?" the commodore asked.

"It's the rubber boat thingys, ma'am, they are actually technically called combat rubber raiding craft or CRRCs. Commonly called cricks."

Everyone turned to see Commander Axelson who had decided to chime in. The commodore threw a dry erase marker at him and he winced involuntarily as it missed his head.

"No one asked, you dunce. Turn back around."

The commodore scolds as she held another dry erase marker in the throwing position. The commander turned back around.

"Okay, fly boys, you have exactly 15 minutes to figure out how to make this plan work. Get with the dirty butt Earth men and figure out many you are going to take. I don't really like this plan, but we have to justify our existence. In all likelihood the Koreans have assets on station that can deal with this issue. If we don't show our value to them, they might kick us out of the country and defend themselves. I have stock options in Huntington Ingalls Shipbuilding, the makers of this ship. Their stock might go down if we stop protecting Korean waters."

Everyone let out a forced chuckle and began filing out of the room. Since the Hueys or Cobras weren't tasked, I just headed back to the ready room and stood by to help if necessary.

On my way I heard over the PA, "Assemble all MV-22 crew chiefs in the ready room."

By the time I arrived I am almost run over by a half dozen crew chiefs. They had a determined look in their eyes, like they finally have something solid to operate around instead of just make-believe. They must be tasked to go and get their boats from the ground guys. As I squirmed and ducked around, this burst of energy entered the ready room I saw all the Osprey pilots assembled at the front of the room. The commanding officer was standing with Ngrsh and by the look on the CO's face, he knew the plan. He was distraught.

(Okay, tactical pause here. The astute reader at this point knows the majority of the material in this book is based on truth and a small fraction is truth exaggerated for satirical effect or to fill in gaps of memory or storyline. I just wanted to state for the record the remainder of this chapter, including missing required critical skills training over a civilian sexual assault response coordinator, is 100 percent true.)

"All right, everyone, right now the COA is to drop cricks from the back of the Ospreys to the survivors. I know most of you haven't done this, I have only done it once. It is pretty dang dangerous. When you get into ground effect, the salt spray can degrade these engines real fast. You have to be hawking your engine gas temperature the entire time."

After reading the operating manual for the Osprey a few days later, I discovered the engines will shut themselves down in order to avoid burning themselves up. In other words, the engine will override the pilots' commands for more power and shut down.

Seems reasonable, shut it down so you don't damage or destroy it. Once it's off, the airframe simply falls gently from whatever altitude it was holding and smokes itself into a crater. Good design if you ask me, protect the engine, fuck the pilots and Marines being transported. That way Rolls-Royce can say the engine didn't "fail."

He continued, "We wouldn't usually take this much risk, but people are dying so we are gonna press with it. Ngrsh is going to give a quick class before everyone steps to prepare you for launching the cricks. Okay, I gotta go."

He quickly dismissed himself to go brief the MEU CO about how he was about to sacrifice his aircraft.

As soon as he left, the worker bees get down to business. The operations duty officer working the flight desk was issuing order after order. We needed a quick brief from the enlisted personnel working for the navy to tell us some pertinent information.

First up was a representative from the Meteorology and Oceanography Office (METOC). The sailor that walked up before us was a man by the name of AW2 Tuggs. He meant well, you can tell, but he was just a fucking space cadet. He got up in front of everyone with his few papers in hand and seemed lost in the sauce. He seemed almost frightened. His demeanor was that of a dog that has been hit a few times for no good reason. I felt like if someone dropped their pen he would flinch.

"Afternoon, gentlemen, AW2 Tuggs with METOC brief. Prevailing winds will be northeasterly with visibility unrestricted. Ceilings will be around 030 scattered . . ."

Everyone taking the brief just looked at each other. They all knew visibility was pretty shitty, but they just humored the poor guy. After his brief he just nodded his head around aimlessly for a few seconds and sauntered back down the aisle between the ready room chairs.

Next up was traffic control. They briefed the type of departure and arrival based on weather, the ship's current position, nearest dry land in direction and distance. Lastly was Tactical Control, or TACRON. They give the frequencies and order in which to contact each agency in and outbound. If we should lose communication, we have a way to prove we aren't an enemy trying to attack the boat. We use what is called a RAMROD, or a word that has 10 letters and each one corresponds to the numbers 0 through 9. An example would be MARINES FLY. If we can't authenticate with our transponder, they pass us three letters like R, N, and S, and we add them together and give the reply. The TACRON rep stood up. She has some trouble pronouncing the RAMROD some days.

"Outbound will be center, greencrown, icepack. Today's RAMROD will be BLACKSMIFT. That's just what it is today, uh yeah eh BLACKSMIFT. B . . . L . . . A . . . C . . . K . . . S . . . M . . . I . . . F. . . T. BLACKSMIFT. Any questions for TACRON?"

"Yes, understand the RAMROD is BLACKSMIFT or BLACKSMITH?" a mid-grade captain asked.

"Oh, yes sir, it's BLACKSMITH," still sounding like BLACKSMIFT.

While all this is going on, more scrambling was occurring behind the scenes to get everything ready. A half dozen Osprey pilots were pulled to get pre-flights of the aircraft done. The aircraft were already spotted for takeoff on the port side of the ship in anticipation of the fly-off the next day. The mood was optimistic; we finally have a concrete mission.

Rescue some drowning people. Ngrsh prepared his brief straight from an Osprey publication. The large projecting screen that we brief off of was now displaying warnings and cautions from the Osprey Naval Tactics Techniques and Procedures or NTTP.

"Okay, we a gonna go oder quickry hero casting operaytion. Everyone risten up. Besides da CO and myself, none of us ha done any hero casting operaytions."

The first slide was just the general overview of helo casting. The CO was back, obviously still worried, and stole the thunder from Ngrsh for the first few slides.

"Okay. Helo casting approaches are conducted at altitudes of less than 20 feet and 20 kts or less of ground speed. We are gonna be low and slow. Expect the Earth men to deflate the boats so they can be jammed into the Osprey. The Recon bubbas are working their walk-throughs as we speak down in the hangar bay. They will work all the strapping, loading, and unloading once we are on site. Don't worry about that shit. We need to focus on flying at 20 feet 20 knots over the unforgiving ocean."

Ngrsh scrollseddown a bit on the page.

"When we get out to the aircraft we'll do a walk-through with the crew chiefs for the internal talkies that are going to happen. For now, I want to focus on the notes, cautions, and warnings that are in the NTTP."

For those not intimate with naval aviation, all the publications pushed out for every type of aircraft contain notes, cautions, and warnings embedded within the chapters. To be specific:

Note: An operating procedure, practice, or condition that is essential to emphasize.

Caution: An operating procedure, practice, or condition that may result to damage to equipment if not carefully observed or followed.

Warning: An operating procedure, practice, or condition that may result in injury or death if not carefully observed or followed.

Back to the story.

The CO put his last words in then handed it back to Ngrsh.

"First, when we come into the area, it will likely be a few miles from the crash site, 150 feet, 50 knots ground speed until we reach .6 to .8 nautical miles from the insert point."

Ngrsh then began rolling through the notes, cautions, and warnings as I read along in my head.

Note:
Expect the waterfall effect, or the movement of water up through the rotor system then misting back down, to occur around 35 feet. All outside visual reference will be lost. At around 13 to 18 feet normal vision will be resumed.

Warning:
A controlled approach is essential to maintain outside visual scan and avoid spatial disorientation.

Caution:
Landing gear should remain up to give maximum clearance.

A few heads in the room deftly glanced from side to side with a look of disbelief, but the notes, cautions, warnings just kept on coming.

Caution:
Weight loading in the CRCC is crucial to avoid flip over. Due to the downwash of the MV-22 the CRCC may flip or fly away when exiting the aircraft. Ensure the motor, gear, and tie downs are secure before takeoff.

Note:
The aircrew should configure the aircraft in the event the raiding force become casualties. This includes but is not limited to crane hoist and stretcher basket.

Caution:
Depending on the sea state, altitudes below 10 feet may result in the aircraft striking the water and damaging antennas or ejecting crew members.

Note:
As swimmers and CRCCs exit the aircraft the decrease in gross weight will result in a climb and airspeed increase without a corresponding reduction on the Power Control Lever(throttle).

Note:
Upon publication of this NTTP there is no agreed upon operating procedure for conducting helo casting operations. The units to be supported will guide operating procedures.

Caution:
The fast rope shall not be jettisoned as the swimmer will have no way to retrieve it.

Warning:
Forward motion must be maintained at all times. Lateral and rearward is to be avoided at all costs.

Warning:
Due to the complex nature of helo casting, it is encouraged to practice the maneuvers in a simulator or low chop water such as a lake or river or even dry land before moving to the open ocean.

Warning:
The presence of high salt spray engine deterioration will be indicated by the relationship between MGT (measured gas temperature) and torque. If MGT decreases 40-50 degrees for a given torque that represents the limit on deterioration. In a heavy salt spray condition this may happen in 3 to 5 minutes.

"Allrite, I know dat's down and derty, but do enreone have enyee questions? We needa to walk in 15 minute."

A quick look around the room revealed the gaunt faces of men who knew they have just been condemned to death. No one objected.

"Allrite, I see you on da radios, requencee 340.05, time 45, ret's frex!"

Immediately after the brief, I rolled one level below the flight deck to inspect the worker bees. Dozens of Marines were furiously deflating the CRCCs in order to fit them inside the Ospreys. Once partially deflated, others were using ratchet strap tie downs to bundle them up in order to be shoved inside an aircraft.

By the time they get into their aircraft and load the boats, however, the weather had degraded to just a couple hundred feet, the visibility is shit, and the water is choppy, causing the ship to pitch violently from side to side. The waves alone will preclude dropping the boats. But the showstopper is the revelation that Korea already has dozens of helicopters and rescue ships in the area. We finally turned on the news a few hours later and saw dozens of Korean helicopters and ships around the now overturned ferry. I still think we could have helped.

Over the next few days, the morbid details emerged of how the children of the ship were told to stay in their rooms rather than abandon ship. The death toll slowly began to rise. A few dozen corpses here, another few there. As noted previously, after 8.4 hours, half of the people in water will not be alive. The BHR stayed on station for moral support over the next few days and launched several aircraft to work "search and rescue."

The area we were assigned is fairly far away from the crash site and the altitudes do not allow for good observation with our onboard sensors. I saw some of the footage from one of the Blackhawks from the HSC detachment. Reminded me of the footage of the buildup to one of the great amphibious landings of World War II. Dozens of helicopters and even more vessels dotting the ocean in a large diameter outside the crash site.

During our diversion for the disaster, life on the ship settled back to its old routines. They had a game show–type event with the civilian activities coordinator over the ship's audiovisual system. She positioned herself in the ship's recording room and had a few sailors help her out with drawing little strips of paper from a tumbling basket. The topic was sexual assault.

They asked a question and you could grab a nearby phone and call to answer them. I was lucky enough to get through on the question concerning restricted and unrestricted reporting. She then called me down to the room and I got a sweet BHR gym towel. I was in need for one after battling ringworm on the upper inner thighs for a few weeks.

The Korean Defense medal is awarded when you operate on Korea or in Korean waters for 30 days or more. Some scuttlebutt, or rumor, began circulating on the ship that we were only four days away from reaching the 30-day mark and hence receiving the medal. Most guys reasonably wanted to stay on station to see the mission through and recover all the corpses.

If we've stayed on station this long, what is a little longer? At the same time another piece of scuttlebutt was circulating that we would leave the following night in order to be able to make some scheduled training for the sailors of the BHR in Sasebo, Japan, after dropping the Marines off at White Beach in Okinawa. Sasebo is the home port of the BHR, which is in mainland Japan. Okinawa is several hundred miles to the south of mainland Japan. Without our delay for the ferry disaster, it would have been no problem, but now the situation was looking critical.

Armed with this scuttlebutt, I decided to dive into one of my favorite underground networks: the Surface Warfare Officer lounge. The SWO lounge was right across from the wardroom and was technically a place for the surface officers to study and get work done in a quiet place. However, after we got our boat girlfriends, they gave us the code and we chilled in there. I would propose that the SWO lounge network is a corollary of the Junior Officer's Protection Agency, or JOPA.

The Marines and sailors aboard the BHR were made aware by the captain of the ship that we would indeed be returning in time to make the training in Sasebo. The evening of the departure from the ship's patrolling box, I strolled into the SWO lounge after a lovely dinner of crab legs in the wardroom. As it turned out the ship couldn't depart because one of its MH-60S helicopters was on deck in Korea to pick up a special guest. Miss Sarah ▇▇▇. She was a civilian Sexual Assault Prevention Response Coordinator or SARC. This made sense to me, as I mentioned in the FROlough chapter the SARC is usually a civilian.

I was told this by a young female ensign. She knew because she just came from the bridge. The young ensign tried to unload a lot more anger and despair at the state of the navy, but I politely held her back. The bridge was where they steer the ship and monitor its defenses. She clearly overhead the conversation being had between the more senior members of the crew.

The ensign said Miss ▇▇▇ was coming aboard to do some training for the ship. She said Miss ▇▇▇ was late in getting her bags out of the airport. The MH-60S the ship sent to pick her up decided to shut their aircraft down to save fuel since she was delayed. When they went to start back up, they sheared a pin in one of their starters. The ship couldn't leave without its helicopters back on board. If we started steaming for White Beach, we would be too far from Korea for the helicopters to make the flight back.

The ensign said the plan was to fly the part and maintainers out and fix it. Me and Dash immediately raced to the ready room to inform our fellow Marines of the situation. We obviously weren't concerned with the Sasebo training, but we needed to get guys on planes to send them back to Hawaii very soon after disembarking in Okinawa. As we ran there, I was moved and saddened by the plight of Miss Sarah ■.

She obviously was just trying to get us some good training and get the word out about restricted versus unrestricted reporting. I almost stumbled a few times I was so shaken up. We were only able to cough up about half the story before the captain came on and informed the BHR of the delay minus the reason why. Sasebo training was cancelled. Six hours later, the broken helicopter was repaired and we were on our way back to White Beach. The first waves of MV-22s launched early the next morning and by sunset all the Marines were back on land in Okinawa.

As for the girls, well, let's just say what happened will be declassified in 2035. SWUD will be 100 years old then.

The Commisery

Early June 2014

In late May I returned to Hawaii from the deployment and lived with Dash in Kailua. GYCO moved to Honolulu to take cooking classes and see the "city scene."

Sunday morning, another dawn on the island. Always stirs feelings of wonder, awe, and gratitude. The cool sea breeze of the ocean a few blocks down the road kept me comfortable all night long. No need for air-conditioning, just a ceiling fan. The curtains facing the ocean whipped back and forth gently and sometimes in a backdraft phenomenon, they are sucked violently into the screens with an accompanying howling noise. They then dropped harmlessly back in a pendulum-like fashion, dampening out within a second or two to their static position.

The howling wasn't disturbing but soothing and almost reminded me of a winter wind whipping across the snow back in the Midwest. In between the ebbing and flowing of the curtains, I could sense the sun's rays peeking out over the houses that are only a few meters away from mine. I say sense because my eyes were not yet open. I opened them.

Beautiful vertical streaks of red, yellow, and orange heralded the beginning of another day on God's earth. A few dynamic cloud formations have risen up like steep mountains and tower well over the tallest structure for miles around. Although one couldn't hear the waves, you could definitely smell a trace of the fresh, salty wetness of the ocean.

I usually wake up naturally a few minutes before my alarm goes off and this day was no exception even on a Sunday. As I shook off the grogginess of sleep, my alarm went off. I had been using my wristwatch as an alarm even though I should revert to the soothing alarm I had on my tablet. I only used my wristwatch while on the ship since cell phones didn't work and my tablet was uncomfortable in my rack. Habits tend to linger, so this morning was no different.

It was 0730 and I liked running in the morning before traffic and other people cramp my style. I did a leisurely three miles and finished in a modest 16:55, a little slower than normal but still under 17:00. I strapped my sandals to my camelback prior to the run and hit the beach park to take a quick dip to cool off. After a few playful wave dodging maneuvers, I was satisfied and headed back in. My signature move is the "Normandy." I held my breath and fell face first into the water where it is about 12 inches deep and the waves were just gently cascading rather than crashing. Usually I'm simulating a sniper bullet head shot, but if I'm feeling good I'll simulate a lethal mortar round impact and do a facetious back flip with under rotation to land on my stomach.

As I floated back up, I do a dead man's float and slowly drifted to shore. The whole process could take anywhere from 30 seconds to over a minute if the waves are weak and spaced far apart. It took some training to push through the 2-minute mark for holding my breath but running helps. As I skid onto the beach, I just let the surf move my lifeless body this way and that, only digging in my arms and legs if I feel like I'm going to roll over. Eventually I either have to come up for air or someone intervenes because they think I'm dead. That day a dog running on the beach with its owner happened to lick my head and I got up. I gathered my belongings and commenced a leisurely walk back to my house.

The walk let the perspiration stop because nothing upsets me more than still sweating *after* you get out of the shower. After showering and shaving, it was about 0830 and I still had a few items to add to my shopping list at the commissary or supermarket for the civilian reader. It is subsidized heavily and always a target for closing during budget crises. Due to the outrageous prices in town for food, the commissary naturally attracts a lot of customers.

They open at 1000 and I'm always careful to be there on time to avoid the crowds. I've never really experienced a huge crowd at the commissary, but I've heard stories. I devised a system where I methodically list what things I need to cook through the week based on the recipes I've selected. I utilize a small top spiral bound notebook. I cleverly organize the page into three rows with the top row going to produce and meats, which are on the left and right side of the page. The middle row is non-perishables in the aisles, and the last one the dairy and frozen section. It gives me a logical flow of when I start to when I end. It is proven that people who go to the store hungry and with no list buy more junk food.

Anyways I got a little carried away reading an article on my tablet from David Stockman's Contra Corner about the causes of World War I. I looked up a few names and dates I am unfamiliar with on Wikipedia and got lost in endless links of interesting stuff. I fell into a trancelike frenzied state of knowledge hunger and when I snapped out of it, my wristwatch read 1100. Dang. Oh, well, one hour late isn't that bad, I think.

I filled up my Nalgene with bottled spring water, added my daily three drops of echinacea supplement, and I was off. I listened to "Pacific" by Goldroom on the short drive in. Amazing ambient track that stirred a sense in the soul of infinity and epic. I especially loved to pair the audio and visual of the bay as the trees fade away along the roadway. I snagged a decent spot under the shade, maybe 150 meters from the front door of the commissary. It is 1115 exactly. List, check, pen, check, water bottle, check, reusable bags times three, check.

Strolling in, I glanced over my shoulder at some more amazing cloud formations. Never ceases to amaze me what those pockets of moisture come up with. The Kaneohe Bay commissary has a drive-through in front of the store that is covered, like a hotel check-in. For the senior retired citizens or disabled to pull up to get help loading their groceries. Oftentimes they have displays of stuff that is on sale or steeply discounted. Usually it is bulk items like double-pack cereals, toilet paper, grilling stuff, or detergent. Think like Sam's Club or Costco but actually useful-sized stuff that won't be around for years if you buy it.

Today there was some double packs of lighter fluid, bags of charcoal, long wand lighters, toilet paper, and detergent. I scored a small detergent, lighter fluid, and toilet paper. Little did I know just half an hour later those choices would save my life.

I strutted into the entrance, two automatic doors, and flashed my military ID to the friendly young woman working the podium to check IDs. For some reason she had a few sandbags around the podium. They rose about halfway up the podium. A small Vietnamese-looking child slid past my leg and added another bag that she was carrying on her shoulder. Hmm, I think, must be one of the bagging lady's kids or something.

The podium worker encouraged her, "Phuong, you have to add them faster, go fill another one up. Go along now!" and gestured her back outside.

The girl obeyed without question and bolted back out. It struck me as odd so I observed her leave and through the windows I picked up another anomaly I failed to catch on the way in.

There were the usual baggage workers lined up in a loosely spaced row just behind the displays of charcoal and toilet paper. They stood at parade rest with their arms behind their backs and wrists crossed, scanning left to right in a rhythmic pattern. As their faces panned to the extremes, I was struck by the tension on their faces. They were expecting something. What are the hell were they waiting for, I wonder? This isn't Best Buy on Black Friday at 0430. *They* lived life and death. This was just a medium-sized supermarket on a lazy Sunday morning.

I dismissed my spidey sense and wheeled around to start my shopping. As I made the turn, I instinctively scanned my peripherals for an exit in case of an active shooter situation like I learned about in the Violence Prevention Program Awareness Marine Net yearly training online module. I've gotten damn good at it with practice and in that split second turn, I identified the exit doors as a potential exit. Nice. Great training.

To my right they usually have some more deal items but of smaller nature like chips or juicebox packages. Today they had erected an amazing fortress of the long-style twelve-pack of pop cans that are shaped like a stadium with a small-scaled green field in the middle, made up of 7 Up twelve packs. Pretty slick, I thought. It's modeled after the University of Hawaii's stadium. Taking just a few seconds to scan the smaller deals, I picked up nothing of interest. I redirected my scan to the list that sat vertically oriented and slightly canted toward me in the position of the child seat so I could look down at it with ease. First things first, some Golden delicious apples. My favorite.

On my way to the apples, I passed a stand that was set up offering samples of dehydrated apple chips. I didn't recognize the brand so I slowed my cart to investigate. The woman working the stand was trying, God bless her. All black clad with yoga pants, stud nose ring, early thirties, decent body, and curly mid-length black hair. She just looked like she has seen better days though, looked like she has seen more wieners than the urinals at Yankee stadium. I felt pity and decided to take a sample. Not bad but not good, I was expecting them to be semi-soft but they are indeed hard chips. Pity wins, so I choose a few small bags to complement packing my lunches.

The commissary's layout is fairly standard. Produce first, then as you keep to the outer wall, they have a stellar poke salad deli, which is sushi tuna but mixed with all sorts of goodness with rice on the side. Then the meat case, milk and dairy, and finally meat deli and bakery. In between all that is flyover country for the paleo lover, just your typical store aisles. I approached the apples and selected about a half dozen. Crossed it off the list. A few feet away strawberries were stacked in the typical medium-sized plastic cartons. I loved these in oatmeal and as I retracted them I continued the motion up to my chin and inhaled deeply while simultaneously closing my eyes to null my visual sense and augment the olfactory. What a smell, what a great day to be alive and enjoy what God . . .

"Nathan, Nathan, get your ass back here, right fucking now!"

I squinted to make out what appeared to be a large mammal entering the store, her child, this Nathan, had gotten away from her and was admiring the can stadium. As my eyes refocused I don't have reason to alarm, just another dependapottamus. They were a common sight in today's military. For the civilian reader, a dependapottamus is a military-dependent spouse, usually female, that has grown to such a size they rival a hippopotamus. They lead sedentary lifestyles in free air-conditioned base housing, rarely moving more than a few hundred meters, inside their home, mind you, every day. Some Marines will call them a dependasaurus, but I prefer the mammal comparison.

The child sulked back over to his sow mother and she jerked his arm toward herself when he got close enough while scolding him, "What did I tell you? Stay near the cart and don't touch nothin'."

She slapped him on the butt once and they moved into the store.

I proceeded with my shopping and moved a few more meters into the produce to get some bananas. Before I could select a bunch, I hears commotion at the front of the store. I glanced back again, actually feeling somewhat perturbed this time, and what I see shocked me. The woman checking IDs was trying to reason with an older woman in a motorized wheelchair whose calves have swollen immensely and was wearing what appeared to be hospital scrubs to hide her corpulent body. I couldn't hear what they were talking about, but the expression on the wheelchair bound woman showed confrontation.

Behind her I just saw masses of people. Dozens upon dozens of dependents attempting to enter the commissary. Well out into the parking lot, the mob could be seen and they were beginning to funnel in. Almost like zombies. Two of the workers that were standing post out front had moved inside and both were holding their hands erect in front of them in the universal sign to keep your distance. What were all these people doing here? I double-checked the time, it was 1130. Are the crowds that different between 1030 and 1130, I thought? I've seen a few crowds before but nothing like this.

I have a habit of overreacting, so I pared down my initial shock and decided to just shop a little quicker to head off the rush. No sooner had this decision been effected in my head than I noticed a young girl, maybe six years old, in her mother's cart a few feet away. She bore an uncanny resemblance to the young blonde girl in *Poltergeist*. She looked me straight in the eye and said, "They're here!"

A chill ran down my spine and simultaneously I heard the cacophony of the motorized wheelchair Type II diabetes retiree dependent ram through the sand bags that had been emplaced around the podium. The worker manning the podium went stumbling backward to avoid being run over, tripped, and fell into a display of assorted Hawaiian fruit punch jugs. She disappeared between them as the jugs rolled into the void she just created.

Little Phuong, who was standing beside the podium, instinctively jumped like a little lemur. She aimed easily for the humongous lower calf of the wheelchair pig and attached like an Alabama tick. However, the sow jerked the handlebars of her cart with such snapping force that Phuong was flung, tangentially, luckily, into a display of diapers. The workers attempting to hold the crowd back saw her predicament and rushed to extract her. Their departure from their post just opened the floodgates and dependents began pouring into the store. To hell with checking IDs.

My quick estimate was about 150 people, not including small children, were soon in the store. You'd think I would be shocked and shaken up but being a Ssang Young veteran I've seen the carnage of the battlefield and so am numbed and unfazed by this display of violence. It actually makes me calmer and more zen like.

The first couple I encountered had three children, all under the age of 5. The dad was the Marine, about 22 years old. He pushed their cart and on his back in a baby carriage backpack is one of his kids and *on that* child's back was the smallest child. Each level of person is about 6 inches higher than the previous they are latched onto so the youngest child was towering around 7 feet above the ground, holding a commanding view of the commissary. The mom was walking hand in hand with the oldest child. She was wearing tight-fitting beach-type shorts that her sausage thighs protruded out of delineated by a ring of cellulite and craters where the pale flesh meets the bottom line of the shorts. One leg has about 6 different tattoos with the most prominent being a tiger shark profile view swishing in an aggressive pose around her knee. They neglected any fruits or vegetables and immediately pressed onward toward the meat case around the corner.

Right on their heels was a young couple, they weren't married. The typical case of a lance corporal falling in love with a girl too young. He looked no older than 19 years old and she was likely the same age, maybe even 18. She was holding a tablet device that I'm not sure if it was a phone or a tablet. She was frantically texting or dialing for all I know. A large tattoo adorned her barren upper chest and once she was done with her tablet device, she wedged it between her outer boob and shirt. Half of the device still protruded in a sick manner from the paltry flesh.

Behind them was a group of local Hawaiians. Surely if the podium girl hadn't been trampled senselessly, they wouldn't have been allowed in. I know they weren't in the military. It's hard to describe them using continental American terms. It was a mom, a dad, and two kids. The kids struck me as being in their teens but they were both over six feet tall. They all sported large frames that seemed to defy nature. I would stop short of calling them fat because they weren't fat in the American sense of fat. American fat is rolls and cellulite and double chins. They were just big boned. The speed with which they moved was downright deceptive.

Peeling off the to the left of the Hawaiians were two overweight but not obese women wearing unnaturally tight-fitting business-casual-type black slacks and collared shirts likely strolling over from the chapel across the parking lot. They struck me as the type that think they are in shape but are really just a few years away from a peaceful dirt nap. I can pick out individual lumps in their heinous butts and the lead one has an impressive life preserver ring of fat while her companion sported a large fat upper pussy area or FUPA. They were both married, each had their own cart and were talking on their cell phones to what I assume were their husbands but I can't hear over the percussion of hundreds of clattering feet.

Another dependent that stuck out causes me to do a double take. I thought by their definition dependents are female wives. What I see proves me wrong. He was a white male, about 6'2" tall with long, wavy brown hair. Long meaning it reached about 4 inches *below* his shoulders. If I had to guess, the last time he shaved was two weeks ago. He was wearing a white Puma track suit whose construction appears to be some sort of shiny, short-haired fleece. The jacket was unzipped down to his belly button and lay bare his soft body that hasn't seen weight training in years. Not fat, but very flabby. He walked with a slight pimp saunter and in his own mind I know he thinks he is looking fresh to death. His son is with him as well and they are in a hurry. By his bearing I guess he was not prior military.

Behind that it just blurred. All I saw was dozens and dozens of shapes pushing their way into the store with a few motorized retirees surging between the blurs as well as children without leashes darting through openings in the mass. As I said previously I kept it cool and continued my shopping.

I acquired a few more items from the vegetable section, crossed them off the list, and shifted into the potato and onion section. The sounds emanating from behind me were hard to describe. Babies were crying, children that can walk were complaining, being beaten by their parents or single moms for attempting to sneak things into the cart. I started to think I'm now at a place of communal misery, or the commisery.

I glanced behind me to sneak a glimpse while holding my bearing. Is this Walmart? The people looked the same. With my head start and planning I figured I will be fine to make it out of there. Just to be safe, I starred a few items on the list, indicating they were my minimum for leaving the store. No matter what happened, I had to purchase these things to just eat tonight.

As I made a ninety-degree right hand turn at the end of the produce, I squinted to make out what I was sure cannot be true. At the other end of the store, where the dairy was located, and where you make the final turn to enter the checkout line assuming you hit dairy last, I could see carts lined up. Patrons, in a seemingly drugged trance state, were slouched over their carts brimming with purchases. The fact that the line stretched so far back can only mean there were at least thirty people in line.

I could feel the world narrowing around me or so it seems. I decided to execute my minimum grocery list option. I sprinted to the meat section, which was already swarming with fat dependents (I guess they made a beeline for the meat upon entering) who were busily buying what seems like every last fucking package of ground chuck. Luckily they left the leaner sirloin alone and I scored a pound. One of them had a hospital patient bracelet, likely from a recent visit, as she looked deathly pale and wore a muumuu-type dress, no doubt to hide her hideous figure. I glanced at her cart. Looked like her diet consisted of diet Pepsi, frozen pizzas, hamburger helper, iceberg lettuce, ground chuck, and Doritos.

I decided to leave my cart for a moment to move quicker and do a spin move around a woman pushing an oxygen bottle cart and whose every step sends her soft upper arms in a torsion twisting-type motion whose amplitude dies off within a few seconds. The larger dependents have stayed closer to the heavy meats like steaks and ribs while the leaner poultry was relatively untouched. No sooner did I slide a tray of chicken breast into a plastic bag than I came eye to eye with a couple that seemed out of place.

Like me they were frantically jamming chicken products into salmonella-safe bags. The husband I would judge to be mid-twenties, dressed nicely in a collared polo and jeans. His wife was wearing a sensible paisley-flowered mid-knee-length dress. Both of them looked like they take care of themselves and held a standard of self-respect. I don't know if it was because all of us were angry and scared but the look we traded basically said, "What are *you* doing in a place like this?"

With the clock ticking, I rushed back to my cart, which was now sandwiched among throngs of entitled shoppers. I was not scared at this point just furious. Furious first at myself for fucking up my timing. Furious second at the dependents.

I arrived in time to see a middle aged African-American man wearing athletic shorts and a wife-beater and sandals trade his small shopping basket for my cart. I guess he needed more items and didn't want to fight the crowds for his own. He had even placed his toddler into the baby seat, carelessly smashing my beloved list. I let him do the dirty work of extracting *my* cart from the twisted mess of carts. I politely headed him off and stated, in the most salesmanlike manner I could muster, "Sir, we are having a one-day sale of Purple Drink, buy 10 get 10 free. Right down aisle 7."

I gestured with my hand. Aisle 7 was far enough away for me to launch my plan.

"Hurry while supplies last."

Without pausing to question my credentials, he bolted toward aisle 7, leaving my cart and his toddler before me. Initially I was going to toss the kid into someone else's cart, but I felt bad for him, not his fault his dad was an asshole. I tenderly removed him from the cart and stuffed him at the back of a shelf, safely behind a few bags of dog food. He should be safe there until this assault passes and daddy Deshaun finds him.

With my cart now rightfully repossessed, I wove into the international foods section. My goal was to get stir-fry sauce and taco materials to compliment the ground sirloin and chicken I just acquired. My quick scan noticed the basket items that the inconsiderate bum put into my cart. I swiftly tossed cornbread mix, bacon, collard greens, and dry mix Kool-Aid from the cart carelessly to the ground. I decided to keep the watermelon because I love watermelon personally and it looked like he chose a good one. I know this because when I thumped it with my thumb while holding it close to my ear, it made a dull but resonant sound. Nothing worse than pithy watermelon!

The amount of cart collisions in the aisle began to worry me. Averaging about 3 collisions every 10 seconds. The dependents were pouring into the aisle from both ends. I tried to stay polite but have had it. I cooled down because the ordeal was almost over. I could see the self-checkout for 15 items or less 25 meters away. The glow of the sign above the line emanated like a heavenly calling card for salvation. As I stretched for the taco shells I felt a sharp, point source pain in my right Achilles tendon. I instinctively rolled to my right as my ankle gave out. As I fell I turned to see that the original sow that overran the podium had just claimed her second victim, me, with her cart. I reached for my ankle but refrained from swearing, "Ma'am, you just ran into my ankle. That really hurt."

She paid no attention and zoomed past me, indifferent to my pain or her carelessness. My fury turned to rage, I got back up, bracing myself on the cart. With hate in my heart, I slung the taco kit like a Frisbee down the aisle. It hit a troll-looking woman in the back of the head who was comparing two different types of General Tso's sauce in each arm. Her dumb head tilted forward then mindlessly snapped back to its original position and continued comparing labels. Zombies!

I placed my bad ankle on the cross bar between the two rear wheels and started pushing with my left. Skateboard shopping cart battering ram! I didn't know how it will end, just that I needed to escape this aisle. A few dependents were pushed aside and as I approached the end of the aisle, I realized my rage went too far. I couldn't slow down. I collided with the wall of the 12-pack stadium and flipped over the cart, landing safely in the end zone of the mock field.

I wasn't the only one to take refuge here. A lovely young African-American girl, with a sweet Southern accent, was tending to a middle-aged woman with a head wound. She had wrapped it with some toilet paper the best she can. I recognized the older woman as the one who ran the sample table for new products or promos right in front of the 12-pack stadium.

I raised my head up enough to see over the wall and drew on my memory to imagine where her table would be. Sure enough, it was turned over. The George Foreman Lean Green Grilling Machine she used for cooking was lying on the ground and grease streaked the tiles in a small radius around the appliance. Toothpicks, plastic sampling cups, coupons, napkins and small bits of the sample sausage were on the ground too. A blind seeing eye dog, undoubtedly having escaped from its master in the mayhem, was nonchalantly lapping up the grease and eating what's left of the sausage.

"What happened?" I asked.

"I was just doing my normal routine of preparing a promotional product for today. Chicken breakfast sausages. When they overran the podium, they smelled it and I couldn't handle all the requests, the foreman wouldn't cook fast enough. One woman asked if she could use her woman and infant children food credits and I said it wasn't covered by WIC but was covered by the Supplemental Nutrition Assistance Program. She got mad and said, 'Well, not *all* of us get food stamps, bitch!' and swung her purse and hit me in the head. Dazed and bleeding, I retreated back here. A few moments later the dependents tore apart the table."

"Fucking savages! I'm sorry I shouldn't talk like that in front of women. We are all getting out of here. Honey, get her ready to move."

I instructed the Southern bell to ready the casualty.

Despite my instinct to lead in a crisis, I was struck by disappointment as well. How did things go so poorly so quickly? I showed my ass today. I pulled it together. I told myself under my breath, "I'm a fucking millennial, and no matter how I perform, I'll still feel good about myself. Doesn't matter how awful I am, I'll still think highly of myself, my capabilities, and my sense of self-worth."

I got my Motorola Moto G out, took a quick selfie, posted it to Facebook with an appropriate status update, and tended to the situation at hand.

The announcement system came to life.

"Attention, shoppers, if you are using food stamps, the debit option is not working in checkout counters 1 and 2. Please refrain from entering those lines."

I thought to myself, how is it that the military rates food stamps? An idea came to me on how to get out. I stealthily reached into the cart and grabbed the laundry detergent, opened the cap, and tossed the jug onto the floor in front of the aisle I just came from. I crawled out of the opposite side of the stadium and got the attention of one of a few dozen Southeast-Asian baggers who were stoically standing with their tip jars and bag dispensers.

I told a young man, the only one not bagging or begging, there had been a detergent spill at the end of aisle 1. The announcement system flared to life again and within a minute, a mop bucket crew had arrived. The detergent deterred more dependents from exiting the aisle *or* trying to cross the store to other aisles. This gave me the lull I need to escape. As I picked up the old woman to hit the self-checkout, I noticed an untouched box of the chicken sausage on the ground and I needed breakfast calories so I picked them up.

We had to shout to hear one another as the awful din of the store being eviscerated was too loud to hear over. Since I only had six items, I got through the checkout quickly. I gave them both rides home. The younger girl lived on base, just happened to get separated from her mom in the initial panic. The older woman lived in a humble one-bedroom off base. Her husband recently passed away and she was doing the promotional gig stand just to stay busy. I methodically drove home, thankful to have escaped with nothing more than a bruised Achilles. The sausages were indeed good.

The Sickness of Mankind or Counter 23 Measures

In the final analysis, machine power is never enough. It is the man on two feet with hand grenades, rifle, and bayonet-backed up by all that modern science can devise-the man with fear in his stomach but a fighting heart, that must secure beachheads. He it is who wins the glory and pays the price, who changes the course of history. Man is still supreme in a mechanistic war.

-Hanson Baldwin, after observing Marine amphibious assault in World War II

Late June 2014

After multiple futile attempts to shoot a live Hellfire during the deployment, the cards finally fell into place. In June I was scheduled to make the trek out to Kauai to fire a live Hellfire at a crescent-shaped rock to the southwest of Nihauu called Ka'ula Island, but since it is so small we just call it K Rock. It was an all-day event and three helicopters participated.

To check that my laser designator was working properly, I lased about 10 kilometers out focusing the sensor on the middle of rock. The symbology in the cockpit indicated the missile's seeker was tracking correctly. In other words, the return of the laser striking the rock was strong enough for the missile seeker to acquire and lock onto it. As we turned inbound on the only final attack heading allowed, 270 due west, I let loose an AGM-114Q (Hellfire with a dummy warhead; the usual combination is a shaped charge) from about 5 kilometers out. The time seemed like an eternity, but when the missile slammed directly where I was aiming, it was impressive.

Impressive in that the technology I had my fingertips was even physically possible. Not even a hundred years ago aircraft were not being used in warfare. And now we can destroy the heaviest armored tanks from 8 kilometers away. Well, as long as the tank is just sitting there in the open with no air defense whatsoever, which is how we train. But that's another story. The Hellfire countered tanks but tanks at one point countered something. And another weapon system now counters helicopters carrying Hellfire. Appreciating the context of how this came about is important.

The machine gun, in its current recognizable configuration, made its combat debut in the Russo-Japanese war of 1905 in which the Japanese used them to devastating effect on the Russians. The Japanese were on a roll until they fought the Marines in the Pacific ruh. The Europeans took notice but especially the Germans. The Germans more so than the other European powers incorporated the machine gun squad as integral to the infantry platoon. At the start of World War I, they had 16 Maxim-type machine guns per infantry battalion while the British only had 2.[1] An excellent read on this subject is *The Gun* by C.J. Chivers. Mainly about the AK-47, it nonetheless has an outstanding historical account of the rise of the machine gun.

The average history student knows this weapon transformed World War I into killing fields. The result was static, trench warfare. It turned the battlefield into a place where the bravery of charging the enemy was turned on its head to be suicidal. The fortified position had taken on a new meaning. How could the stalemate be broken? The pressure and urgency of the stalemated trenches of World War I produced an answer and on 16 January 1916 that answer rolled off the assembly line.[2]

As they were shipped to the slaughter fields, the British attempted to hide their true nature by describing them as "water tanks." The second half of the name stuck and from thereafter the metal crawling machines were known as tanks. The American Holt Manufacturing Co. in 1906 produced the first one from a steam agricultural tractor. The aim wasn't initially for warfare, just welfare, for the farmers of America. In 1911 and 1912 several Austrian engineers drew up specifications for tracked vehicles to be utilized for martial matters. No armament was specified and no prototypes produced.

In October of 1914, just a few months after the initiation of hostilities, a British lieutenant colonel by the name of Ernest Swinton put forth the notion of using armored caterpillar-type tractors to punch through trenchlines. He was aware of the American Holt tractors and hence used them as inspiration.

Soon after in November a Frenchman by the name of Breton proposed attaching mechanical wire cutters to the American Holt tractor and aptly calling it a "Baby Holt." After a short development and feasibility assessment by both the British and Russians, the British pushed forward with a tracked vehicle concept. Lieutenant Colonel Swinton was the tactician specifying what the machine should be capable of. Designers William Tritton and Walter Wilson then set to work on the design.[3]

After a few trial runs, it was clear the tank could be a game changer so in March of 1916 Swinton set to organizing a tank force. Just as the tank itself had to be shrouded with a judicious layer of secrecy, so did its operators. The first operators were known as Heavy Section, Machine Gun Corps. The first tank action was seen at the Battle of Flers Courcellete in September of 1916. This battle was an intermission show for the main attraction of the Somne, fought between 1 July and 18 November, and in which over 1 million men from the British, French, and German armies were killed or wounded. Many of the tanks broke down and of the 49 that found their way to the battlefield, only 25 joined the assault.[4]

For every punch there is a counter, and to every counter there is a counter, and to that counter there is a counter. With respect to tanks the focus will be on armor since Hellfire is the ultimate goal of our study, but the other two factors of tanks are mobility and firepower. I include discussions of firepower to give context for why the armor kept getting thicker. What good is a heavily armored tank if its mobility is poor? And what good is firepower if your own armor is thin?

Beginning with the Mark I tank, it took a rhomboidal shape for the track mounts and welded those to a square housing. On the side of each rhomboid were attached two sponsons, basically a square-shaped outcropping where machine guns or larger diameter weapons were attached. The design was necessary to cross the deep trenches of the scared battle landscape of World War I. The Mark I had male and female versions with the male holding two 6-pounder guns and four 8mm Hotchkiss machine guns and the female holding four .303 in machine guns and one 8mm Hotchkiss. The male/female distinction occurred mid-production run because it was feared that massing infantry could overwhelm the male and hence an all-machine-gun version was adopted for the second half of the first production run. Armor varied in thickness from .23 to .47 inches. [5]

The French experimented with using the American Holt tractor as a chassis for their Schneider Assault Tank, which featured boatlike rivet construction and a front-mounted wire cutter. The St. Chamond shared the same Holt chassis but had an electric drive, unique for its day.[6] The British Mark IV featured many improvements especially with respect to its engine, but my perspective notes the addition of improved armor, not thicker, still .47 inches, but stronger.

Imagine what the Germans naturally did when they saw these behemoths lumbering toward them? They shot at them, likely hundreds of men shooting at one tank. That added to the roar of the uncovered engine in the middle. I wonder if they wore ear protection? After realizing their bullets bounced off, the Germans went back to the drawing board and came up with tungsten-cored anti-tank bullets. As soon as this punch was swung, the Brits counter with the new armor. The Germans countered this counter by developing a 37 mm anti-tank gun which could penetrate 1.6 inches of armor.[7]

The Renault FT-17 appeared in 1917 from France. It had the look of what we think of when we imagine a tank. Armor was .87 inches maximum. Developed in large numbers, many were snatched by the Germans as they rolled into France for the third time in a century in World War II and utilized them supporting roles in the occupation.[8] The Germans were ahead of the game with Maxim machine guns and infantry tactics but lagged in tank development.

Rushing to get something into the fight, they fabricated what resembled a large, rolling machine gun bunker. The Sturmpanzerwagen A7V was absurdly large, had a crew of 18 men, 7 machine guns, armor 1.18 inches thick, and could only move at 5 mph.[9] The tanks of World War I were crude, using prior technology of boat building to rivet them together. Their goal wasn't yet anti-tank warfare or smashing through enemy lines then driving deep to the rear but the support of the infantrymen.

Following World War I, the thinking was slow to change and the Russians, with influence from the FT-17, created the T-26 with .98 inch armor. When engaged by the Japanese in the Far East, they realized the riveted hull was easy prey for anti-tank fire. A welded hull and turret soon followed designated the T-26S.[10] Following this, a stolen British design designated T-28 rolled out with 3.15 inch armor.[11] Several nations delved into making reconnaissance-type tanks with light machine guns that were small in size and fairly quick but low on armor. The most notable, for comedies' sake, is the Type 92 Tankette from Japan. Looking at a picture of them is comical due to their miniature size and the yellow assholes driving them. Being penetrated by ordinary rifle bullets they were quickly relegated to rear area operations like towing ammo and the like.[12]

As previously mentioned the Germans were a little late to the game with tank design. The first French mechanized division was formed in 1934 with 220 tanks. Germany followed soon after with their first Panzer, or armored division in 1935.[13] Their first Panzerkampfwagen (PzKpfw) I had minimal armor at .51 inches and was used primarily to train tank crews after Germany began rearming while another solution could be found. The PzKpfw II was rushed into production to again fill a gap until bigger and badder tanks arrived. The PzKpfw

II had 1.38 inches of armor. The PzKpfw III and IV complemented one another.

The III was meant to be a tank killer and the IV was meant to protect the tank killer with HE shells to defeat infantry and artillery.[14] Both tanks had maximum armor of 3.54 inches. The armor and guns proved inadequate. The 37 mm on the III, which was borrowed from the previously mentioned World War I anti-tank gun, had trouble knocking out enemy tanks during the Battle of France. Despite the French having more heavily armed and better tanks such as the SOMUA S-35 with its 47mm gun and 2.2-inch armor, the Germans won using a classic movement to contact approach they had been honing since the end of World War I.[16]

The Western Europeans and hence Americans learned slowly but surely and moved away from machine guns as main tank armaments and bought into the fact that in order to beat other tanks, you need bigger guns. Physical proof of this lapse was obvious in the design of the M3 Grant/Lee American tank, which had a 75mm gun added late in production in a sponson to the right side of the hull beneath the center mounted 37mm gun.[17]

The Russians actually had a leg up with their heavy KV-1 with 3.94 inches of armor followed shortly thereafter by the legendary T-34. The sloping armor was a great leap forward in that it deflected incoming rounds from a 90-degree striking angle. The pattern is beginning to emerge now. After getting their PzKpfw III and IV whipped by T-34s, the Germans rushed back to the drawing board. The fearsome Tiger I had the legendary "88" mm anti-aircraft gun as its main weapon, along with 4.33 inches of armor. In fact in an engagement in 1944 a single Tiger halted a *division* in France taking down 25 tanks before it was finally destroyed.[18] The Panther increased to 4.72 inches(291) followed by the Tiger II 7.28 inches.[19]

The infamous tank battle at Kursk in 1943 involving 6,000 Russian and German tanks, which ended with tanks ramming one another after all shells were expended, saw the Russians prevail more due to numbers than quality of tanks. The Tigers and Panthers present at the battle set the Russians to designing a counter tank. Their answer was the IS series of tank, named after the initials of their leader Joseph Stalin. Technically a successor to the KV series, the IS series had several iterations, with the IS-2 being the most produced just shy of 4,000 units. The goal was to counter the German 88 with armor and also defeat the Tiger and Panther armor with its main gun. The result was 4.7 inches of armor and a 122 mm gun. After the war in 1948 the Russians kept the iterations going and built prototypes of the IS-7. Taking the idea for using anti-aircraft guns on tanks from the Germans, it had the S-70 130mm flak gun and weighed around 68 tons and due to this burden of weight never entered mass production. Keep in mind the current American M1 Abrams weighs 62 tons. From here things started downsizing a bit for the Russians.

The Germans in their love of making things extra big even took a trip to the absurd with the PzKpfw VIII Maus, a humongous vehicle with the comical name Mouse, with a 128mm gun and 13.78 inches of armor.[20] With the ubiquity of tanks roaming the World War II battlefields, some thought was given to producing Self-Propelled Anti-Tank guns or SPAT. Commonly called tank destroyers, these vehicles usually used existing track systems and several didn't even have turrets. Just a tank-killing gun slapped onto some tracks. A good example is the German Jagdpanther with the same 88 gun as the Tiger. The Russian SU-100 looks similar but with a 100mm gun.

Although good at killing tanks, they suffered from poor visibility and lack of secondary armaments like machine guns. Many times after smashing tanks and advancing, they would be swarmed by infantry using grenades, Molotov cocktails, or anti-tank mines. One counter was to put Zimmerit anti-magnetic paste over the entire hull of the tank. It prevented magnetic mines placed by infantry from holding to the hull. Many Tigers used this counter and can be seen in most historical photos along with the sharp looking black uniforms of the crews. SPAT use has fallen off and few remain in service today.

The trend of bigger gun, thicker armor, bigger gun and so on begs the question, what is the limiting factor on the caliber of the main gun? As seen above with the IS-7, sporting a 130mm gun, why not just go to 150mm, 170mm, or put a German rail gun like Schwerer Gustav at 80 cm, 10 times that of the Tiger 88, onto some huge tracks? The Americans did this in one respect by putting the British 17pdr, or 76mm anti-tank gun, onto their mass produced Sherman tanks and called it the Firefly. It could lock horns with and destroy almost all the German heavy tanks. Needless to say guns getting exponentially bigger would be impractical from a production and tactical standpoint.

Another consideration is ammunition. A short discussion of tank gun rounds is in order. There are two ways to defeat thicker and thicker armor, make the killer round bigger or make it faster. From physics recall kinetic energy is $\frac{1}{2}mv^2$. To make the round have more energy and hence more punching power, either increase its mass or increase its speed. Mass simply means a bigger round, which at some point becomes impractical. For the high-school educated reader that missed the square above the v, you can see that increasing mass only increases energy in a linear fashion. However, if you double speed, you then quadruple energy so it pays to have a faster round rather than a bigger round.

Enter the Armor Piercing Discarding Sabot, or APDS. French engineers initially developed the idea in 1940, but after the German victory over France, they packed up and moved shop to England where they were further assisted with development. Steel armor piercing (AP) rounds would shatter when they impacted at velocities greater than 850 m/s. Tungsten carbide, having a density double that of steel and the ability to withstand the shock of greater velocities, was selected. The round itself looks like a long dart and to accelerate it required a traditional round but with a slight modification to allow for the smaller weight.

The solution was placing a sabot, the French word for shoe, around the dart. The end of the round looks like a small bowl with the pointy end of the round sticking out of the center. The bowl is the sabot. It basically held the round into the metal casing and once expelled from the gun would catch the air stream and be pulled off, leaving the graceful dart on its way to death dealing. Eventually a spin stabilized round was developed to allow for greater length to diameter ratios and they are known as Armor-Piercing Fin Stabilized Discarding Sabot or APFSDS. Modern tanks use these.

Stepping back to our present discussion, the APDS round was first introduced to the British 6pdr or 57mm in 1944 and to the 17pdr in September of 1944.[21] At the onset of the war the British 2pdr could penetrate 2 inches of armor at 1,000 yards. By war's end the abovementioned 17pdr with APDS could penetrate 8 inches at 1,000 yards. Factor of 4 increase there. The German 88 with an AP round could penetrate 5 inches at 2,200 yards and their APDS could penetrate 6 inches at the same distance.[22]

In addition to APDS technology, another fascinating weapon found its way onto the World War II anti-tank battlefield. Its arrival would mark an epoch in the quest to kill tanks, a truly revolutionary, non-linear jump forward. This technology was the shaped charge. More often than not, civilian technology had a predecessor in the military world. However, the shape charge belonged first to the civilian world before making a nascent entry into the world of killing tanks.

Miners clearing rock discovered a conical cavity cut into a block of explosive would increase its effectiveness and hence save gunpowder. A man by the name of Charles Munroe, a chemist working for the U.S. Naval Torpedo Station in 1888, discovered the focused energy effect of a void on the surface of an explosive. Being the good observant scientist, he noted that the stamped manufacturer's name on a piece of explosive was cut into a metal plate that it was detonated next to. His results were published in 1900 in *Popular Science Monthly*, but the military utility of such a device lay dormant as tanks had yet to rumble into battle.[23]

The physics of shaped charges are complex but a rudimentary explanation will go a long ways. A shaped charge is a hollowed-out cavity in the shape of a triangle or smoothed cone. The mad scientists have tweaked and refined the shape, size, and liner material to maximize its potential over the years. The usual liner is made of copper. On the pointy or convex side resides the explosive, packed all around. On the opposite end is some type of cap that seals the cavity and uses various fuses to initiate the explosive behind the shaped charge. This whole shebang is enclosed in a container of some sort. This cute little package rides on a rocket assist or in today's versions inside a missile. As this device strikes a metal target the explosive charge detonates and the cone collapses.

Visualize by making two knife hands and then touching left and right fingertips in front of your body. The explosive is on the back side of your hands. As it goes off, move your hands toward yourself while keeping the fingertips touching. Do this until your finger*nails* touch. This process forms a high-velocity jet of linear material with the focal point your fingertips. The tip of this jet is on the order of 8,500 meters per second, while the aft end is around 1,500 meters per second. As the forward end moves quicker than the aft end, it gets strung out and a metal slug of material in the aft end comprises around 80 percent of the total mass. The slug plods along at only 600 meters per second.

As this jet strikes the armor of a tank it produces stresses that far exceed the yield, or give, strength of the material. The armor simply flows away from the point of contact like water moving out from a drop in a pond. Don't forget about Mr. Slug behind this jet that enters the hole and immobilizes or kills the crew. However, the primary damage is done by target armor picked up by the jet as it enters, called spalling. The abovementioned miracle is called hydrodynamic penetration.[24]

Another noteworthy attribute of these weapons is the fact that striking velocity is irrelevant to effectiveness. The charge can be screaming in at a few hundred meters per second or just a few meters per second. As long as the cone goes off against the metal, the effect will take place. A 90-degree impact angle is optimal.[25] A modern-shaped charge can penetrate armor to a depth of 7 or more times the diameter of the charge.[26]

In fact at the Lawrence Livermore laboratory in 1997 a shaped charge penetrated 3.4 meters of steel. That's 133 inches, or just over

11 feet. Granted this was the largest shape charge ever built, but you get the point.[27] Good luck, tank designers. Shape charge rounds for use in anti-tank weapons came to be called High Explosive Anti Tank or HEAT. A common misperception with the acronym is that the killing effect somehow uses thermal or heat energy. Not true, as described above; the effect is kinetic.

The development timeline is filled with arcane details that I have refused to dig into and instead have chosen to focus on the important first then subsequent weapons themselves. The Americans had the first significant weapon with the well-known Bazooka in 1942. The launcher was built around the existing 60mm M10 shaped charge and was the conception of Army Lieutenant Edward Uhl working in the Ordnance Corps.[28] Although an original idea, it suffered from several design flaws. The resourceful Germans, after capturing a few batches, reverse engineered it with a bigger warhead of 80mm and German precision and called it the Panzerschrek or Tank Terror. Later models with a larger warhead could penetrate just over 6 inches of armor.[29]

The Americans got their hands on this weapon and also copied the copy, making the M20 Super Bazooka with a 90mm round.[30] In an interesting historical aside, the American general public knew of the Bazooka but were ignorant of shaped charges. In 1945 the U.S. Army got with *Popular Science* magazine to expose the secret in an article titled "It makes the steel flow like mud."[31] From there marginal improvements in warheads, range, and penetration were made but the premise of slinging a shaped charge out of a tube stayed the same.

Replacing the Bazooka were various recoilless rifles firing the HEAT round like the American M67 or the Swedish 84mm Carl Gustav. The Carl Gustav is back in use with the U.S. Army, only because of its utility in blowing up the bunkers of our latest patients of democratic idealism in Afghanistan. Finally shoulder-fired missiles came along with the 66mm M72 Light Anti-Tank Weapon or LAW. The FGR-17 Viper was slated to replace the LAW but failed due to public outrage over safety concerns and cost overruns. The M136

AT4 was then selected and is currently fielded by many militaries around the world.

The Germans in 1943 came out with their Panzerfaust, or Tank Fist. It was a handheld, man portable, one-time-use anti-tank weapon. The shaped charge was propelled on a small rocket that was fin stabilized. Shaped charges don't like spinning because it contorts the jet of metal when it detonates. They didn't look too intimidating. Just a large conical shape on the end of a thin long tube. Its range was fairly low but increased with successive iterations from 30 to 150 meters and a simple sighting system was attached to the tube.

Over 6 million were produced and could penetrate 200 mm or almost 8 inches of armor. So the combatants of World War II spent tremendous resources and time to develop bigger and better tanks with thicker armor and better guns, only to be neutralized by a lowly soldier cowering in a foxhole waiting for the lumbering giant to get within 150 meters. Epochal times indeed. It was succeeded by the Russian-made Rocket Propelled Grenade.[32]

The RPG isn't really a grenade, although some of the warheads are fragmentation types like a grenade. Its original conception was a copy of the Panzerfaust and it has seen never-ending improvement since the RPG-2's introduction in 1949. The RPG-7 goes hand in hand with the AK-47 as the weapon of choice for the Communist insurgent. It is the most widely fielded anti-tank weapon in the world. In a tandem warhead configuration (covered shortly), the RPG-7 can penetrate over 23 inches of armor.[33] The RPG-18 and 22 look similar to the LAW and the 26, 27, 28, and 32 all look similar to the AT4 with the last one, the 32 being circa 2008 and capable of penetrating 30 inches of rolled homogenous armor with a 105mm tandem HEAT warhead.[34]

The cheap, effective lethality of shaped charges were addressed in many ways but never totally solved, especially considering the cost of the technology needed to effectively parry them. Just look up a few videos of rag tag Free Syrian Army fighters, dressed in blue jeans and sandals, destroying Russian-made tanks with shoulder-fired shaped charge weapons.

A short discussion on the futile attempts of tanks to protect themselves will be helpful. As you should have already inferred, tank designers found ways to counter the shape charge. In somewhat clever fashion, they began adding pieces to the tanks after production that would increase the standoff between the shape charge detonation and the main armor of the vehicle. Marines in Vietnam, for example, would affix sections of chain link fence to their Armored Personnel Carriers with a few feet of standoff between the hull and the fence. This was done in reaction to losing many APCs to Charlie's RPGs.

If the molten jet is ignited a few feet away, it loses its kinetic energy quickly and as it contacts the hull lacks the punch to make its way through. So the idea was to detonate the charge a few feet away from the hull. Simple but it worked. Even on today's tanks like the Israeli Merkava, which find themselves in dense urban environments and hence susceptible to sneak RPG shots, they have small sections of chains hanging from the rear of the turret to protect the vulnerable seam where the turret mates to the hull. The Merkava engine is in the front of the tank to add additional protection. The Jews are cheap on lots of stuff but chose wisely to not skimp on crew protection. Nice job.

Another counter utilized that originated more from the drawing board than field expediency is Explosive Reactive Armor or ERA. Designers added small flat squares of explosive to the most critical areas of the hull. The instant the shape charge contacts the ERA it explodes outward, effectively deflecting the shape charge from getting an optimal angle to let loose its molten madness. This was the primary driver of adding another shaped charge to warheads like the modern RPG-32. The first charge sacrifices its life to detonate the ERA, once that's gone, the second charge, which is usually larger, has an unobstructed path to the main armor of the tank.

The Israelis were the first to outfit their tanks with ERA during the 1982 invasion of Lebanon. The decision was a wise one following heavy armor losses to shape charge weapons in the 1973 war with Egypt and saved many tanks from loss when struck by RPGs and AT-3 Sagger anti-tank missiles from mother Russia.[35] Shortly after Russia took note and added ERA of their own to their tanks. I understand there has been research into offsetting the second charge behind the first, because its effectiveness is decreased when in line with the sacrificial charge. I am unaware of any fielded system using an offset tandem warhead.

Jumping back to tank designs briefly, after World War II they form began to coalesce around the idea of a Main Battle Tank or MBT. Prior to this, as can be seen from the tanks of World War II, there was small, medium, and heavy. Many iterations of MBT occurred, but there is nothing cosmic or nonlinear from the post-World War II era until today that concerns tanks ability to defend themselves against mankind.

The allies and NATO settled on a 120mm main gun, which is used in the M1 Abrams, British Challenger, French Leclerc, and German Leopard. The Russians modern MBTs use a 125mm main gun.[36] Armor on the tanks has become classified and I don't have access to it, but the trend has been to use composite materials sandwiched between conventional metals. The composites drastically reduce the effect of spalling, the effect of the shape charge jet pulling the tanks metal along with it as it enters the cabin. The bottom: line it's not possible to protect the tank in all areas.

The next development was in range and accuracy for the shape charge payload. Note that 6 million Panzerfausts were produced. Range and accuracy were inversely proportional for these first shape charge weapons. The further your target, the less likely you were to hit it. In fact, an evaluation conducted by the U.S. Army on a moving target at 9 miles per hour and dimensions 15 feet wide by 7.5 feet tall was fairly damning of unguided munitions. For the RPG-7, at ranges of 50, 100, 200, 300, 400, and 500 meters the probability of a hit was 100, 96, 51, 22, 9, and 4 percent, respectively.[37]

Doesn't inspire much confidence.

The solution was to put the round into an accurate missile. It started on the ground with classics like the Tube Launched Optically Tracked Wire Guided or TOW missile. This was a classic in the later stages of Vietnam and was just recently phased out of use in the Marine Cobras. After I shot mine from the Cobra, I got to keep the used tube but being the entrepreneur I am I sold it on Ebay for $2,000 as "one of the last TOW missiles to be shot from a Cobra! This deal won't last!"

The Soviets obviously had similar missiles in their AT family. Guidance was one of several forms of command to line of sight or CLOS. Manual CLOS is literally steering the missile by radio or wire link with a joystick and some aiming device. Semi-automatic command to line of sight or SACLOS is where the operator holds his sight on the target and the missile interacts with the sight to align the two. The TOW is like this. With a max range of close to 4,000 meters and a probability of hit breaking well over 50 percent, it was a vast improvement over man-launched RPGs.

Soon enough these weapons found their way attached to aircraft. Tank killing from the air can be traced to the Germans when they attached the venerable 37mm anti-tank gun to the Stuka diver bomber and called it Kanonenvogel or cannon bird. Germany's ultimate ace with 519 tank kills was Hans-Ulrich Rudel. His memoirs, *Stuka Pilot*, are well worth the read. In fact it was required reading for the designers of the most badass tank killer aircraft of all time. The A-10 Warthog. In April of 1972 some Warrant Officer types became the first helicopter crews to destroy enemy armor using 2.75" HEAT round rockets flying Cobra helicopters.[38]

The TOW was used one month later after being rushed to the front. I am ashamed to say the first TOW kills came off of a UH-1B Huey and not a Cobra. Huey pilots go ahead and gloat. But your brand-new UH-1Ys can't fly in the rain and don't shoot TOW anymore and you are back to the weapons you used in Vietnam. Rockets and guns. Booyah.

The Soviets could also shoot their ATGMs like the abovementioned AT-3 as well as numerous other iterations off their helicopters. From here the Americans took a different approach to precision bombing.

Early 1960s research into Precision Avionics Vectoring Equipment was used to increase accuracy of conventional bombs. Paveway sought to use laser energy to guide a general purpose bomb during the terminal phase of its fall. Early in 1968 the first Laser Guided Bombs (LGB) were dropped in Vietnam.

One notable example of their utility was the Thanh Hoa bridge. American planes flew 870 bombing raids on this single target and were unable to knock it out. Not until 1972 did F-4 Phantoms loaded with Paveway I did they knock it out. Today's LGBs like the GBU-12 are amazing pieces of gear utilizing BANG BANG guidance. Bear with me for the next few paragraphs as I dig into the history of laser seekers used in Hellfire.

First a definition. A semi-active laser seeker is one that has a receptor that is sensitive to laser energy. It picks up on reflected laser energy and homes in on it. The semi part of the name comes from the fact that the weapon that contains the seeker has no laser of its own. It only receives the energy. The laser has to be from another source, like the aircraft or a ground based designator. This is contrasted with active homing where the designator and seeker are both in the weapon.

In November 1966, as the war in Vietnam was raging, the Laser Missile Systems Branch was established to develop a tactical weapon system that utilized lasers. Research in this field had been ongoing since 1963 undoubtedly borrowing from the PAVE work. In 1967 Hughes Aircraft Company and Martin Marietta finished a feasibility study for a laser semi active missile (LASAM). The pocket protector nerds gave it a thumbs up.

With the thumbs-up, the Combat Developments Command approved the program for Missile System, Target Illuminator Controlled. MISTIC would replace LASAM. The program was to specify what type of role the weapon would need to fill and additionally advance the existing laser technology to weapons grade shit. The project was neglected for a few years with little to no funding. After being pulled from the back burner and thrown some money, there was a back and forth about what type of missile to develop as an anti-tank weapon, including a tower-mounted fixed missile. The assistant secretary of the army for research and development said fuck, we'll do it live and started a new initiative for terminal homing for fiscal 1972.

First named Heliborne, Laser, Fire and Forget Missile, its name subsequently changed to Helicopter Launched, Fire and Forget Missile or HELLFIRE. Its main warhead design would be none other than our friend, the shaped charge. In February 1972 HELLFIRE was officially funded and a Ground Laser Locator Designator (GLLD) contract was awarded to Hughes and International Laser Systems, Inc. Contracts were also awarded for an Airborne Laser Locator Designator (ALLD) to Philco Ford Corporation and Bell Aerospace. The Bell product was cancelled due to cost overruns and Philco won for the ALLD while Hughes' GLLD won its contract.

Rockwell International was awarded development of the laser seeker in March 1975. In June of 1976 Rockwell and Hughes delivered their HELLFIRE prototypes. The remainder of 1976 was occupied with boring internal reorganization but the important takeaways were the requirement to the development lightweight laser designators. These would be used on the ground and were given the title Modular Universal Laser Equipment or MULE and the Light Weight Laser Designator LWLD, which became known as the Laser Target Designator or LTD. Hughes Aircraft Company won the development contract for the MULE and got their first units into operational testing in February of 1980 while the parallel LTD ended up being cancelled. Martin Marietta in 1978 received two new contracts to develop a low-cost alternative laser seeker (LOCALS), which was selected in February of 1982.

The first HELLFIRE shot occurred on 25 September 1978 at Redstone Arsenal. After a few more years of testing and validation HELLFIRE was approved for full scale production in March of 1982 with Rockwell making the missiles and launchers and Marietta making the seekers. On 28 August 1984 a joint firing of a HELLFIRE was conducted at the Yuma Proving Ground. An OH-58D Kiowa Warrior located the target and lased for an AH-64A Apache which fired a direct hit with a HELLFIRE. In mid-1986 the Apache and

Marine Corps AH-1W were approved to use the HELLFIRE system. On December 20 1989 Apaches fired seven Hellfire during Operation Just Cause in Panama with all being direct hits. Desert Storm kicked off with Hellfire on 15 January 1991, with Apaches taking out SAM sites. The Marines were actually tasked with the mission but Cobras of the era didn't have auxiliary fuel tanks and thus couldn't make the journey. Our HMLA Squadrons deployed four of six active squadrons during Desert Storm. 48 Cobras schwacked 97 tanks, 104 apcs, 16 bunkers without a single loss of an aircraft. Desert Storm also ended with Hellfire on the Highway of Death.

In June of 1993 the Fox model of Hellfire was released. It featured a tandem warhead to defeat current ERA. HELLFIRE II began its development in fiscal 1992 with changes occurring to the flight profile of the missile as well as better electronics and launch motors. Hellfire defeats armor by using a top down flight profile to strike where armor is thinnest. I can't say how much armor Hellfire can penetrate but let's just say it's on the order of how tall teenagers are. The Cobra was given the go ahead for HELLFIRE II in 1996.

Tank designers once again went back to drawing board with futile results. They came up with Active Protective Systems or APS. The focus of APS is to "intercept, destroy, or confuse attacking enemy munitions" and can be broken down into hard kill and soft kill. From my source, "Anti-Tank Guided Missile (ATGM) production, lethality and proliferation has far outpaced armor protection. This, coupled with advances in top attack ATGMs and munitions launched by aerial platforms at ranges that far exceed that of direct support (DS) air defense systems, have multiplied the threat to the armor force."

A hard-kill APS is a close-in defense counter that destroys the enemy munition prior to impact. Literally shooting shotgun-type fragmentation in a small area around the tank prior to missile impact. Ghetto as hell if you ask me. The soft-kill systems try to decoy, jam, or confuse the missile. Modern Soviet can tell if they are being targeted by a laser and then pop smoke to scatter the laser return. The most advanced systems have their own lasers to cause a false target spot.[39] Hellfire countered with some upgrades of their own that are secret.

Many other variants of HELLFIRE were introduced, the main difference being the type of warhead. All you need to know is that none of them are tank killers and hence can't turn the tide of a battle. In fact, the Americans took a step back and were tired of firing six-figure-price-tag HELLFIRE missiles at IED emplacers and so developed a laser guided rocket to be a cheaper alternative. Known as Advanced Precision Kill Weapon System or APKWS, it was introduced too late to make any difference in the COIN campaigns in Afghanistan and now is the envy of every wannabe warrior flying helicopters.

An armor-piercing rocket is in the works for use with the M282 Multipurpose Penetrator in conjunction with APKWS, but is nothing more than a cheaper, less effective, redundant, armor-piercing round. As noted 2.75-inch HEAT rockets were used in Vietnam prior to TOW. APKWS can't hold a candle to Hellfire; just look at the development timeline and resources. Why APKWS is being developed, I don't know maybe to make Huey guys feel good about themselves. I've never personally shot the stuff, but I've briefed that I *would* carry it on a mission. You see, in the Marine Corps we have no money for ordnance to train with, so we just play make-believe most times. I've personally shot over 100 APKWS rockets, simulated, of course. On an average deployment for training, our squadron took around four rockets to "split" among dozens of pilots. In reality, just some senior guys went and shot all four.

The bottom line is the Hellfire in its current configuration for tank killing, the K-2, can defeat *every* known modern main battle tank. As mentioned previously, the shaped charge was a game changer. Tank designers found small things here and there to improve survivability but shaped charge technology was running right beside them. Tanks countered, then shape charge countered, then tanks countered the counter, and so forth. Tanks add spaced armor, then shape charge got bigger to make a longer jet of molten metal and bridge the gap, tanks add explosive reactive armor, shape charge adds two of himself to each warhead, tanks add active protective systems to spoof lasers, laser trackers tighten up the window in which they receive laser energy. You get the picture. Shape charge wins in the end.

The discussion up to this point has focused on tanks and not aircraft. The inductive reader should see what comes next. The huge flak batteries of World War II soon became obsolete with the speed of jet aircraft. The Americans first developed what would be the epochal cousin to the shape charge. The Man Portable Air Defense System or MANPAD. This is the weapon helicopters fear most. Rather than shoot thousands of rounds of flak or machine gun at aircraft the design of the MANPADS used the aircraft itself as part of the targeting system. MANPADS use passive targeting, meaning they rely solely on the aircraft to feed targeting information to the missile. This information is the heat energy coming from the exhaust of the aircraft.

Looking similar in appearance to man-portable ATGMs, MANPADS can be fired by a single soldier. The first iteration, the American Redeye, entered service in the mid-1960s along with its competitor from the Soviet Union the SA-7 Grail. Both could only attack from a rear aspect due to their seeker technology. These were effectively countered with flares such as the MJU-32. The flare simulates aircraft exhaust and decoys the missile. We carry them on our aircraft on the side of each wing stub. Each wing stub has pods that you load the flares in. We have a system called an ALE-47 that senses the exhaust plume of an attacking missile and in theory kicks off flares.

There is a lot of great detail I'd love to share, but it's considered secret so I have to hit the wave tops and keep it short. MANPAD designers countered with cooled seeker heads and a new type of guidance logic. The American Stinger and Russian SA-14 and SA-16 are examples. These were countered by more advanced flares like the MJU-49 that don't "burn" in the visual sense, but they burn pyrophorically. They instantly rust once they hit the air and that reaction creates heat energy.

The next generation of MANPADS then introduced Counter Counter Measures or CCM such as the SA-18. CCM allowed the MANPAD seeker to decipher, in hundredths of a second, what was a flare and what was the actual target. It can then reject the flare and track the aircraft. Flare and aircraft defensive designers then countered with programming cocktails of different flares in conjunction with one another and precise timing between the firing to defeat the CCM. The next generation of MANPADS then added CCMs that could be reprogrammed to deal with certain flare combinations.

Along the way MANPADS have increased in maximum range and altitude as well larger more lethal warheads with laser and proximity fuses. Jets can overfly MANPADS but helicopters can't. Maximum range is now approaching 8 kilometers. What is more alarming is who makes them. It used to be just the USA and USSR; now more than 30 countries produce the entire system.[40] State actors like Russia deploy MANPADS with their armored units, riding in armored personnel carriers to defend against helicopter attack. Non-state actors obviously can shoot them from anywhere and have.

The next generation of MANPADS I understand have imaging seekers. So instead of looking for heat energy in the infrared spectrum, they are literally looking in the same spectrum our eyeballs look at. It's basically a camera in the seeker.

How to counter this I'm not sure, but if I were a designer I'd make a blow-up life-size helicopter replica to tow behind the actual aircraft like a banner plane does. That way you at least have a 50/50 shot the seeker bites off on the tow decoy rather than your decoy. I'd fly with it.

Sike!

I'll try to add up the counters, finally starting with the machine gun. Each sentence is a counter. Machine gun defeats the charge. Tanks defeat the machine gun. Anti-tank gun defeats the first tanks. Thicker armor defeats the first anti-tank guns. Bigger tank guns defeat thicker armor. Sloping armor and reinforcing weak points defeats bigger tank guns. APDS defeats sloping armor. From here we leap to shaped charge. Shaped charge HEAT rounds defeat the best armor. ERA defeats the first shaped charges. Tandem-shaped charges defeat ERA. Classified armor composites defeat legacy shaped charge weapons. Top down attack HEAT missiles defeat classified armor composites. APS defeats laser trackers with soft kill systems. Upgraded electronics defeats soft kill systems. MANPAD I defeats the helicopter. Flares defeat the MANPAD I. MANPAD II defeats the early flares. New pyrophoric flares defeat the MANPAD II. MANPAD III defeats the pyrophoric flares. Flare cocktails defeat MANPAD III. MANPAD IV defeats the cocktail with reprogramming. That's 22 and I'm being conservative. So the newest MANPADS with imaging seekers really should be called Counter x 23 or Counter 23 Measures.

The constant factor is man. Man wielding his shoulder-fired weapon, whether it be a shaped charge or MANPAD, still rules the battlefield and causes the win or loss.

The Marine Net Violence Prevention Program Awareness Online Training Module and Coming Clean

Following my return from post-deployment leave in early June, I had a little time on my hands and so I decided to knock out some Marine Net yearly training. Marine Net is an online catalog of military instruction courses. Each year we have to do the *same* training modules all over again in order to make sure rosters are filled out properly.

A new course I knew I had to knock out was the Violence Prevention Program Awareness. Note the title: it's not just violence prevention awareness nor is it a violence prevention program. It is a course to make you aware that there is a program in existence that prevents violence. Marine Net courses are laid out in a similar fashion to a Windows Media Player screen with volume, play, glossary, and navigation tools at the bottom with a white box on the lowest portion of the screen for text.

The opening screen for the program is a Quantico-type building with grand-looking reddish brick, somewhat aged, but still properly maintained. Slide one hooks your attention with a quick violence vignette. A corporal storms into an office and demands to see his Staff Sornt. Dialogue plays at the bottom that is paired with the audio. The visuals give the impression of motion video but are nothing more than several pictures played quickly in slideshow fashion. Think of a crude cartoon, you have different poses of a character on successive pages and as you flip the pages, the illusion of motion is created.

The corporal is livid and storms past the receptionist in search of Staff Sornt. He weaves and turns into a maze of office cubicles and interrupts the conversation between a crater-faced civilian and Staff Sornt about what appears to be a commanding general's readiness inspection and deficiency that was found. (see my chapter on CGRI for more info)

Staff Sornt confronts the corporal as he brandishes what appears to be a Kimber .45 caliber handgun. The cinematography is amazing, multiple different angle shots of the corporal's gun and zoom panning of the Staff Sornt as he intervenes to add dramatic effect. If you watch closely, the acne civilian just ducks out and leaves the situation entirely. He obviously did his VPP training because step 1 in an active shooter situation is escape. After demanding the corporal stand down there is a 5-second climax of pointing gun, pointing fingers of Staff Sornt, jump zoom to the corporal's angry face, Staff Sornt, pointing gun, Staff Sornt, then bang!

The next few slides detail in a pie chart the types of workplace violence citing the Department of Justice and Department of Labor 2009. I was interested by the fact that 51,000 rapes took place in the workplace. Why isn't Senator Gillibrand all over that? The next slide has a timeline of attacks across the U.S. military. Included are the 2003 attacks at Camp Pennsylvania in Kuwait by Sgt. Asan Akbar killing two and the 2009 Fort Hood shootings by Major Nidal Hassan that killed thirteen. The program stops short of labeling them terrorists or Islamic extremists, which would be insensitive, but instead generalizes their condition to radicalization. The Fort Hood tragic sequence of events was the impetus behind the Marine Corps Violence Prevention Program Awareness. The program doesn't mention it, but it should be noted that the day of the shooting, Hassan told his neighbor he was "going to do good work for God" and bestowed on her his Koran.[1] Surely not Islamic terrorism.

Police can only react whereas on a day-to-day basis, we the co-workers of a potentially violent person can have our radar up for behavioral concerns that lead to violence. One of the hallmarks of Marine training, both classroom and online, is painting the overall picture of the instruction you are about to receive. The awareness course is just the bottom of the pyramid of knowledge. Above that sits the recognition course for NCOs and first line supervisors. Above that the team course for commanders, appointed Force Preservation Council members, company grade, and civilian mid-level managers. One more step up is the Violence Prevention Officer (VPO) Course for battalion and squadron commanders. Finally, the ultimate ninja of violence prevention (who is actually allowed, per MCO 5580.3, to kill people whom they deem potentially violent) is the appointed installation program representative who undertakes the Violence Prevention Representative (VPR) Course.

The course makes clear that predicting violence is hard and any ideations should be brought to the unit's violence prevention officer or representative. They outline the different risk levels: moderate, high, and extreme. Moderate risk includes social withdrawal and loss of interest in work. Similar to those contemplating offing themselves. Other moderate signs are mood swings, being a member of a fringe group like Black Lives Matter, the Animal Liberation Front, Tea Partiers, or Occupy Wall Street, and being interested with incidents of violence. The tutorial shows a man's cubicle with warning signs like a shooting range target with bullet holes and a *Scarface* picture with his own face pasted over Al Pacino's while he is in his floral shirt waving a 9 mm. A moderate risk vignette staring the corporal is played showing his lack of interest in working out and marital problems.

High-risk shifts into the more confrontational like threatening or intimidating behavior and angry outbursts. An indicator differentiating this category from the medium-risk category is the obsession with violence. The manifestations of which could be personally created artwork that is morbid or grisly, writing about death and destruction, or being sympathetic to violence promoting organizations. Lastly there is anger toward the U.S.

The tutorial ties in with how Major Hassani made statements prior to the shooting concerning the right of Muslims to conduct terrorist attacks against the U.S., fought orders sending him to Afghanistan, and even had email correspondence with a radical Muslim cleric, Anwar al-Awlaki, querying whether it was okay to kill bystanders in a suicide attack. With a little reflection, the average student of the Violence Prevention Program Awareness can realize the similarity between a radicalization attack and every red-blooded Marine who gets off seeing things blow up. The two are almost identical. The high-risk vignette morphs the corporal into becoming more confrontational. He fights with his worthless do-nothing wife at a barbeque and his home life is beginning to unravel. He becomes a local fixture at bars and comes home drunk and strolls right into work soused. His attitude changes from apathy to confrontation and his bride thinks he may smack her.

Finally, the last category is the extreme risk. These behaviors are grievous indeed: physical abuse of spouse or children, toting your guns to work, talking about guns too much, and "exhibiting a fascination with weapons or destructive power that is out of the ordinary."

They don't really define ordinary, but I assume it means any erotic feelings after seeing explosions that last more than 30 seconds. A link within the screen lists over a dozen red flags for potential terrorist support such as expressing allegiance to terrorist ideologies and traveling outside the U.S. to train with terrorists. The last storyline following the corporal portrays a beaten man. His wife has left him and he won't make sergeant. He mopes in his cubicle with the visuals showing alternate faces of confusion, rage, and depression. His Staff Sornt has written him a Page 11, a disciplinary measure that stays in your records, and the corporal says he'll get even with Staff Sornt at the range next week. The module makes clear that is a threat and should be labeled extreme risk.

The last quarter of the training shifts into survival strategies for those involved in an actual shooting in the workplace. The training highlights that this situation is highly unpredictable, will happen very quickly, and take a deadly toll, reinforcing the need for training to predict when such attacks will occur. Regardless the order of actions is escape, hide, or confront the shooter. If you are confronted, "fight to live!"

So to summarize, the VPPA draws on numerous topics ranging from no-shit radicalization attacks and subtly pairs and equates them with 90 percent of the Marine Corps, which deals with alcohol, anger, divorce (77 percent rate since 2001), and obsession with watching things go boom. With the recent spike in Marines intentionally shooting other Marines in the office and battlefield, I felt the training was relevant and illuminating.

After leave I finally got a chance to shoot a Hellfire in mid-June. The Hellfire I shot was at a rock in the middle of the ocean that was a SAM site, I remember when I heard the *whoosh* as it left the rail of the missile launcher. Staring at my screen as I was lasing the target and the missile was locked up the seconds seemed like an eternity.

I became conscious that I was getting an erection. Not a full-on morning woody, but definitely not limp either. As the missile slammed into the rock, I went from slightly aroused to fully erect. I quickly calmed down because I had to focus for rocket and gun shooting afterward, but I didn't forget that it happened.

Now, with this training in mind, I wonder, did my reaction put me in the extreme risk category? Did getting aroused by shooting a Hellfire fall into the category of "fascination with weapons or destructive power that is out of the ordinary"? Or was it just the high-risk category?

I'm a member of a violence promoting organization, the Marine Corps, and hence supportive of it. That's definitely in the medium-risk category. I've definitely created some pretty violent artwork too. But an erection over a Hellfire? That *has* to be wrong and in the extreme risk. I'm a Marine in the extreme risk category for violence. I'm self-diagnosed.

After I realized what's going on, I was devastated. I hung my head in the halls and only rarely engage in conversation with other guys in the squadron. How did I become this way? Is it my fault? Was it something I did to transform me or is it just the way I am? Was it something I failed to do? Paranoia starts occupying my mind. Do other people see it? Are they going to report me? I would if I were in their shoes.

But the commercials! They have guys swinging swords at lava monsters and climbing these crazy cliffs and shit. Shouldn't that arouse some chauvinistic fervor in the young men of our country? After a week of moping, I was so depressed when I got home on Friday and crawled into bed, I reached into my nightstand for my Springfield XDM .40 handgun.

I pulled the magazine and ejected the round in the chamber. I then laid the gun in the top drawer and the magazine and ejected live round in the lower drawer just in case. Putting a conscious step between reaching for the weapon and shooting myself is a good operational risk management step. I've used this technique during bad days in the past. Losing relationships, getting home after sitting through hours of Sexual Assault Training, and the like.

What's really alarming is the fact that I've been this way for so long. As I reflected on how far back I had this affliction, it stretches all the way back to grade school at Saint Catherine. Me and my buddy Onye Mora, a quirky kid with a huge Catholic family, would spend hours just drawing these clash battles in our notebooks from around the fourth grade all the way through eighth.

Onye started drawing them first and I just naturally followed, mesmerized with the process. The usual scene was cliffs, a half dozen of them. Think turning a piece of paper to landscape mode then drawing fairly steep mountains, like a zigzag whose peaks hit the middle of the page. Do that to the other side with the peaks interjecting the first ones drawn, then turn the page back to portrait. Upon these "cliffs" some of the goriest, cruelest, and sickening scenes of humanity were consecrated.

Onye was literally from Africa and so his drawings were focused on the Africans defending their homes against the white man.

Hence all his drawings have stick figures with black heads and white heads. I thought this was a worthy cause to portray and so my early drawings look similar. The Africans always have the home field advantage but less effective weapons, mainly bow and arrow, spear, knife, and axe. White man has his guns, planes, jeeps, automatic weapons, flamethrowers, rocket launchers, and assorted ATVs. I think in one of my drawings the whiteys have an open semi-trailer filled with armed men being pulled into battle. The white men have to be on the offense though. And as any good Marine officer will tell you, defense is the stronger form of combat.

I've included several of my original, unaltered drawings. Onye's were better, but I no longer know his whereabouts. The observer has to understand that these pictures represent a split second in the battle, that's the best I could do. Obviously the battles were pitched and decisive, but I just capture a split second of the carnage. As our drawings evolved, I took a liking to the SWAT-type raids and drew large, multi-level buildings. The bad guys were some druggie-type thugs. For whatever reason I include some Marvel superheroes like Venom and Spider Man getting in on the raid.

Onye continued to evolve his original drawings and started to become obsessed with the notion of total death. He would have a regular battle developing then the whiteys drop an atom bomb or some other Mother of All Bombs (MOAB) equivalent at the bottom of the canyon. I would literally watch him draw this bomb onto a complete drawing then make dozens of strokes with his pencil centered on the bomb and moving outward. Sound effects were paired with each stroke of the pencil and it soon became a lustful frenzy of killing everyone on the page. I just sat there and cracked up.

This is how we got caught. The teacher heard his sickening sound samples and nabbed us both. I didn't have time to hide my drawings because I was one mesmerized by the scene unfolding and two doubled over with laughter. We were at attention outside the principal's office while the teacher showed Mrs. Crabtree our devious drawings.

Eventually she called us in and left us to the justice of the principal. She asked us if we knew that based on the way schools are going, 10 years from now, drawings like this would get us suspended or even expelled. We said we didn't know that. She asked what compelled us to express such violent artwork.

We said we didn't know. We only felt it was the normal thing for us. She breathed heavily and gave us an ultimatum, either you promise to join the Marine Corps after high school or college in order to have an outlet for your bloodlust or I give these drawings to your parents and they deal with you. Onye chose to roll the dice with his parents, and here I am a Marine telling you this story.

Anyways, back to the present. Myopic vision, the problem is just right there in front of me, clear as day and I could see it with perfect 20/20 vision. Right there it never triggered anything. It was recognizable but my far vision, the concept of the big picture, wasn't. I've been on the wrong path for a while and a heavy weight begins to pull toward earth in my stomach. I begin to wonder if it's plausible to have a martial dichotomy in the Marine Corps. Can I train to kill but not have feelings of joy and pride when things explode? I'm confused. I don't know where I stand.

I begin rationalizing. I use the tool of confirmation bias to aid me. I begin with the conclusion that I'm innocent of any wrongdoing. From there I just start searching for evidence to prove my conclusion. It's bad science, not science at all really. It's a common tactic used by the global warming leftists.

No, I'm not this way. I *can't* be this way. That wasn't an erection or even a chub, not even a quarter chub. It's something else going on, not any desire to see things explode. It was just a hormone imbalance; I do recall not sleeping very well that night prior to the flight. You weren't yourself, it doesn't count. This for the time satisfies me and I ride the depression sine wave from the trough back up to the crest and I am feeling downright splendid a few days later.

It's behind me, my head moves to level as I strut through the halls. Feels so good to be at peace. Only lasts for a week. The weight in my gut starts at night as I calm myself down from the day and only have to deal with my own thoughts as I struggle to fall asleep. A few times I turn on some "Hydrophonic Garden" by Carbon Based Life Forms, Global Communication tracks, or fire up some 30-minute ambient tracks by Brian Eno in the darkness of my room.

I even buy a window air conditioner, not because I need to be cooler, but because I need to be calmer. The buzz of the fan adds ambient noise to pierce the silence. The silence allows my baneful mind to attack me. What am I feeling? One night I force myself to remove the confirmation bias filter I've been leaning on to feel good. As soon as it's gone the feeling is clear. Denial. I'm in denial that I habitually love the thought and practice of destruction. Everything about it.

Within a minute or two of the acceptance of the denial, another emotion creeps in. Anger. I'm angry at myself for pretending I didn't have a problem. To a lesser extent I'm mad at the corps for not conditioning me to repress my love of martial matters. Denial led to anger. It would have been better to just accept it. Thank God for the Violence Prevention Program Awareness module. At least they alerted me before it was too late and I threatened someone or the enemy. When it dawns on me that denial led to anger, I recall the works of Kubler-Ross. Her work focused on the stages of mourning or loss. They follow the pattern of denial, anger, bargaining, depression, then acceptance.

Sure enough I unconsciously try to bargain it away. I run more than usual, pray a lot, and do more good deeds than normal in some hope that my habits will change my life and God will change the man. None of it really works. I feel the same and fall into some depression. Not as bad as the initial shock's downers but still bad. Hard to sleep, zero sex drive, and disinterest in the gym or cooking. Luckily it doesn't last long and I just accept my fate like real men should. I admit I have a fascination with things exploding. I then seek help.

I head to the chaplain. We have a chaplain at the MAG, or Marine Aircraft Group, that is the unit above our squadron. I generally try to avoid the place as it is manned with heinous creatures and reject Marines. As usual the chaplain isn't doing much, just reading some news on his computer. There is a shelf inside his office stocked with the Our Daily Bread series, a daily meditation and prayer book that I have tried without effect. There are also many pocket Bibles and copies of Rick Warren's *The Purpose-Driven Life*. He looks up from the screen and just as about I'm to say hi, he beats me to it.

"Hi there, Captain, what's going on?" He is in a good mood. By the tone of his second statement I guess he can see I'm not.

"Hey, Chaps, well, I kind of had a personal problem I needed to talk about something going on in my life that has been bugging me really bad."

He becomes empathetically more serious in a split second and without saying another word just nods, gets up, and locks the door to his office.

"Sit down. You can talk to me about anything. What's going on? Just so you know if this is about sexual assault I am considered a privileged reporter, meaning what you tell me I will keep confidential."

I take a seat as he is finishing the sentence.

"No, no," I say casually, "nothing that serious, at least I don't think."

"Okay, well, let's hear it. No reason to keep it pent up, that's why you are here."

"You're right, I . . .," I don't choke up, but take a deep breath.

I feel a burning sensation deep in the middle of my brain that seems to emanate throughout my body. I feel paralysis. I somehow find the strength to confess.

"I think I might be at risk for violence chaps, I think I might be at an extreme risk for violence."

My voice is low but steady, and I gaze at the floor as I say it. Then I raise my eyes to his to see his reaction, fearing the worst. He's confused.

"Uh well, you mean like you want to hurt someone or hurt yourself? Are you suicidal? I have a Marine Net course I could prescribe for that, or some handouts. Actually right behind you is a poster for suicide prevention. You remember the acronym right? ACT. Ask. Care. Treat."

"Isn't the new one Recognize, Act, Care, Escort? I thought Ask. Care. Treat is old."

"Actually, you are right, Captain. I need to get a new poster."

I continue with the confession.

"No, nothing like that. I recently took that Marine Net Violence Prevention Program Awareness Course and it detailed all the symptoms of someone who might be at risk for violence. One of the symptoms is a fascination with destructive power and weapons that is out of the ordinary."

"Go on." He was beginning to look concerned.

"Well, I after I shot my Hellfire, I, well, I sort of got an erection after the explosion. I got off on an explosion. I love things exploding. I could watch things exploding all day. I also have drawn dozens of extremely violent pictures of battle between men. Here."

I produced the drawings, all separated into sleeve protectors.

He graciously reached across the spasm between his desk and myself and took the drawings, still looking at me the entire time. His eyes stayed on me for a few fractions of a second after his corpulent body had settled back into his chair then looked down. His eyes widened. I guess I shouldn't have led with the SWAT drawing. He started sifting through them, mortified. After about a minute of examining the carnage he spoke, still looking at the drawings.

"Sweet baby Jesus. Holy shit." He looked up. "Captain, this is disturbing. How long have you been intrigued by violence? Please don't tell me these drawings are recent."

He subtly reached with his free hand below his main desk drawer. Was he reaching for an alarm, I thought? A weapon to defend himself in case I spring on him? I'm not an animal, I'm just a misunderstood Marine.

"No, they are from grade school, around fifth grade or so. I was around 10 or 11 I think."

"Okay, that's a little *less* disturbing I guess. I'm still worried, I did that training too. Based on what you just told me, you are without a doubt at risk for violence. Definitely in the extreme category. You did the right thing by coming in. Feels good to get that off your chest, right? I'm sorry I swore a minute ago, that's not like me. I've just never seen such violent drawings before. That's the goriest stuff I've seen since *The Passion of the Christ* and *Dead Alive*."

"Yes, it feels like a weight has been lifted. But what can I do from here? Do I just live with it or can I be cured? I just want to stop feeling bad about being obsessed with violence."

"Hmm, I don't have experience with this, but I do have an idea. We need something to cultivate your empathy and compassion, something to soften that callous heart of yours."

"Jesus? I want to know more about Jesus. Wasn't there a song about that, breaking hearts of stone and giving hearts for love alone?"

"No, heavens, no. You are way too far gone for Jesus to help you. Maybe we'll get you on a Jesus program once we bring you back from the brink. If I was a betting man instead of a drinker, I'd say you had about a month or two left before you came to work and shot everyone and planted a few pipe bombs."

"Well, I wasn't really afraid of that, I just didn't know what I was becoming. Or what I am for that matter. As Patrick Bateman said, is evil something you are or something you do?"

"Interesting question, anyways, the idea I have in mind is actually a course. A recent course that the Marine Corps decided it wanted to start."

I saw where it was going and tried to cut him off.

"A course for potentially violent people? Are you serious? No, that would ruin my career. I came here in confidence, remember? There has got to be another way to help me."

"Absolutely. Calm down, Mr. Violent, and let me finish. Your secret is safe with me and mum is the word. The course is the Humanitarian Assistance and Disaster Relief course or HA/DR Course. With all the tsunamis and typhoons and earthquakes and stuff happening in Asia, the Marine Corps has been eager to prove itself in the region. It's part of the pivot to the Pacific. The corps can't just be full of violent people like you who desire combat. The military should be used for more than just a political force tool of last resort. We need compassionate Marines who want to help and not hurt people. The Marine Corps is wisely changing its image from a tough derelict breed of savages into people who help others. People helping people, you know all that stuff."

"So you think if I go through a course about handing out boxes of rice and pallets of water I'll get better?"

"Absolutely. I happened to go through the pilot course a year ago when I was in Camp Pendleton. The images of the brown and yellow people just ravaged and starving will melt your stone cold heart. Promise."

"Okay, whatever you say I need to do to get better. I trust you. But how do we sell the squadron on sending me to this course without them knowing the true purpose? I'm a Cobra pilot. Justifying a Huey pilot maybe, a 53 pilot for sure, and if I was an Osprey pilot they'd have to give me a reason to *not* go. The Osprey is the quintessential humanitarian assistance and VIP flight aircraft. Did you see the work they did during that tsunami relief in the Philippines? But a Cobra pilot? I'll never be involved flying the HA/DR missions. What can we do?"

"I think we can sneak you in, I just got word each squadron needs to have an HA/DR representative. I saw you are heading to Tactical Air Control Party school soon right? I saw it on a recent email for jobs in the squadrons."

"Yeah, I actually just learned last week I'll be doing a Forward Air Controller tour with 2nd Battalion, 3rd Marines and I'm going to the school right after Rim of the Pacific exercise. I leave in late July."

"Well, it would be easy to justify sending you because the HA/DR course is in Coronado where your TACP school will be. It's getting close to the end of the fiscal year in October and you and I both know how tight money gets until October 1 hits and the Treasury prints more money to put in our accounts. If we are already sending you to Coronado for a school lets just keep you there and knock out the HA/DR course. I'll mention it at the next training meeting. The squadron is so busy with other things we'll just slip you in there and they get their HA/DR representative."

"All right, sounds like a plan, I won't let you down and I feel like I'm already on the road to healing. Thanks Chaps, keep me posted about the dates."

"I will. Here are your drawings back."

I gathered my drawings and headed out the door. A few weeks later with Rim of the Pacific behind me and the paperwork all squared away, I was on my way to Coronado, California. The first course went fine. I stuck around for the HA/DR course.

I showed up on the appointed morning. They have a nice little sign on an artist pedestal outside the classroom that shows some Marines carrying a USAID box off of a CH-53 and it says, "Welcome to the Humanitarian Assistance/Disaster Relief (HA/DR) Course."

The one bald Marine was looking super moto and grunting as he heaved that box of supplies. I entered and took a seat in the middle of the classroom. There were about 10 other Marines, some officer, some enlisted. I was early and hence soaked in my surroundings. Looked like decent Marines around me. I wondered how many were here for the same reason I am? I took a wild guess it might be a few and break the ice with the Gunny sitting next to me.

"Hey, Gunny, why are you taking this course?"

"Hey sir, well, uh, it's a long story, but I got caught laughing when a 500 lb bomb blew up an IED emplacer. I was watching a video feed of the aircraft back at the Forward Operating Base and when the bomb hit the dude flew out of the screen like a bottle rocket. I mean he was there and then he wasn't, it's as simple as that."

I chuckled a little, imagining a terrorist asshole taking off like a bottle rocket. I assumed he is like me and thinks destruction is cool so I pushed it more.

"So they sent you to soften you up a bit? Like to make you more generous or whatever?"

"That's right sir, they thought my penance should be to become the unit's HA/DR representative. What about you, why are you here?"

"I got a mild erection when I shot a Hellfire and saw it explode."

He winced slightly, "Eww, that'll do it, sir. But how did they know?"

"Well, I carried it around for a while and after doing the Marine Net Violence Prevention Program Awareness Course I realized I might be at risk for violence and it just started to gnaw at my soul and I had to get it off my chest."

Our conversation was the sole one in the classroom and attracted the interest of the other Marines. Before I knew it, almost everyone was talking and about the same thing. Why they were sent to this course. It basically turned into an AA meeting. Each guy took his turn to introduce himself, the rest of the room simultaneously said, "Hi, [insert rank and name]," and they proceeded to detail the reason they were sent. The reasons were fairly consistent. The thing everyone had in common was that they were somehow excited by the violent nature of their jobs and were either turned in or confessed like I did.

The class lasted about a week and while I can't go into specifics because most of it was secret, let's just say that I had a change of heart. Some of the videos of disaster areas were just touching with hundreds of wind-whipped brown people almost overrunning the Ospreys and CH-53s. As the crew chiefs passed out rice and water, you could almost see the look in the Marines' faces that said, "Please keep making my running shoes and gym shorts. This AID is from the U.S. people who like their consumerism."

Leaving the course and Coronado, I had a desire in my heart to use taxpayer money to give food to other countries. As any good leader inspects what he expects, upon my return to Hawaii I fired up some videos from Live Leak of Apache gunships ambushing some Taliban. It's a night attack and the footage is from a Forward Looking Infrared or FLIR so it shows heat. After about 20 minutes, there is just white goo all over the screen from them shredding dozens of towelheads. Now before the HA/DR course I probably would have been fully aroused, but now I look down and I'm flaccid. I have been cured of my disease. Great training.

Ebola Scare and the Bushmeat of Waikiki According to GYCO

Mid November 2014

There is an Ebola scare across the USA. Would it reach the shores of Hawaii and if it spread, would the island be doomed? And the bushmeat, that meat from the bush of Africa that is sold at street markets and causing the spread, what exactly is it?

It was a distant memory. The thriving businesses, the exotic landscapes, and of course, the bushmeat. People travel from all over the globe to Hawaii for many reasons. Maybe to attend an island "gathering" in an effort to get a picture with a man in a thong and a woman with leaves, vines, and other corroding matter on her head. So, what is bushmeat, you ask? It is whatever you want. Seriously. Let's examine it. Done.

Upon further examination into "Aloha" we find it means affection, peace, compassion, and mercy. Not to mention "hello" and "goodbye." Hawaii is also nicknamed the "Aloha State." The "Merciful State"? Let's be honest, the only "Aloha" James Cook felt on 14 February 1779 was a compassionate blade. Then, "After his death, we all wailed. His bones were separated--the flesh was seared off and burnt, as was the practice in regard to our own chiefs when they died."

Definition 1: Exploratory Stinkrape

Here's another. You see, back in the day when a man loved a woman, he would club her on the head and drag her to a cave to unveil her bush. Today, it's pretty similar except the club is money and drink offers and the cave is a stank forgotten condo-wasteland barely visible through the layers of stained bedsheets drying in the wind and powerline spider webs. The term "clubbing" was born, but it has been transformed from "Let's go clubbing" into "Let's go to the club."

The modern male is unaware of these origins. The cavemen from hundreds of thousands of years ago would be very disappointed. Today, because we are in essence smarter than the cavemen, we feel the need to become intoxicated in order to understand the barbaric roots of our heritage. Jesse Ventura makes sense of this with his baby seal protection efforts.

Definition 2: Jurassic Matrimony

Here's the most common explanation. "No shoes, no shirt, no service" is a standard most respectable businesses uphold. In Hawaii, though, how is one to live "Aloha" if he or she is worried about putting their damn clothes on in the morning? I mean shit, it's ludicrous to think that garments are required at a meal, right? Well, this is the story of how the bushmeat was born.

The luau is a traditional Hawaiian party or feast that is usually accompanied by Hawaiian music, entertainment, and hula hoopin'. It may feature food such as shit-poi, crapalau pig, poke'mon, lomi salmon-ela, po-opihi, haupi-assmeat, and beer.

James Cook once said, "Ambition leads me not only farther than any other man has been before me, but as far as I think it is possible for man to go." Of course, he was referring to the combustion of Hawaiian food in his gut and the distance he was willing to go to try and appease the tribal nudes.

Definition 3: Firepit Butcrust

I have arrived at only one true definition. Once you have been inside the slums, I mean the deep slums, your nostrils peel from the inside and you are reduced to four senses. One does not know how he arrived or why he even left his 300-square-foot island sanctuary. I relate "slumming" to something you're all familiar with. Okinawa.

Crammed into an elongated phallic land mass, many people of the Orient live and smell each other. They constantly create new cute signage and fluffy shallow idols to pull their minds from the truth of the matter. They're stuck in the middle of the ocean on an island that 99 percent of the world couldn't care less about.

Within a slum, I mean a dank one, you'll find Hello Kitty dolls blaring incoherent battery-drained life lessons, pee-stained rainbow concrete graffiti facades, and dusty, barren cosmetology offices filled with dying dreams. The only hope you have of getting out is following the trail of oily tears that fall from the makeup laden faces of the forgotten bushmeat on their way to their part-time jobs.

The slums of Waikiki were built on the graves of young professionals.

Definition Finale: Slum Dame.

This leads me to an old poem, "There once was a slum, a slum so glum, that no slummer ever had a bummer. The drummers, the thumbers, the Jamaican rum runners. All were so beautiful, in the summers where from. Never again will this bum be so dumb."

Why We Fight or the Development of Heathenry

Take up the White Man's burden, The savage wars of peace—
Fill full the mouth of Famine And bid the sickness cease;
And when your goal is nearest The end for others sought,
Watch sloth and heathen Folly Bring all your hopes to nought.[1]

- Rudyard Kipling, third stanza of "The White Man's Burden"

Last week of November 2014

Arriving home somewhat late from one of my last days in the squadron before I depart for my Forward Air Controller tour with 2nd Battalion, 3rd Marines, I stepped into the house to the sound of a movie playing. Dash was on his computer looking up a drone on Amazon. A DJI Phantom quadcopter, to be exact.

He had *It's a Wonderful Life* playing on his Vizio with the sound coming from his Bose surround system. The movie was drawing to a close. We were watching it the night prior but it was pretty long and while it was a heartwarming and engaging movie, we just decided to put it off until the next day.

When I looked at the Vizio, George Bailey is about to commit suicide by jumping off a bridge into an icy river and his angel saves him. I sat down at the dinner table with Dash. He seemed to be more interested in what type of features he can add to his drone before making the purchase. He was eating a frozen pizza for dinner.

I alternated between watching the movie and reviewing the day's news on my tablet. I felt the need to be alone, so before I even glanced at the news, I went into my room and turned my computer on. My computer is connected to my Samsung 40-inch LED inch flat screen by an HDMI cable so I can see the monitor on a large screen.

Before I could begin perusing, I get a call from my girlfriend Laura. I was feeling pretty blue about work and was in general just having a down day. Stressed about starting a new job and everything. Plus during the holiday season, I think of Ohio, the snow, family, and friends. She has been incredible. Sweet as pie, attractive, smart, Catholic.

My heart was lifted when I see the caller ID and all my blues fade away. As soon as she said hello, I could tell something was amiss. She had been fairly aloof, but I chalked it up to her being busy. She was planning to fly home to Los Angeles soon to tie up some loose ends then move entirely to Hawaii to work as a nurse.

"Laura!" I was excited.

"Hey, Jeff." Her volume was quiet and unassuming.

"Hey, what's going on?" I refused to believe that disaster could be coming.

"What are you up to?"

"Just got back from work, about to eat dinner. Want to come over?"

"That sounds awesome but I already ate. We need to talk about something."

My heart sank. I didn't respond so she continued.

"I don't think I can do long distance when I go back to L.A. Just thinking about it has been hard. I think we should call it off for now."

Tears involuntarily welled up in my eyes as a burning, tingling sensation grew in my chest, branching out through all the limbs of my body. I could actually *feel* my heart breaking. No, no, this can't be happening. Please God, no. I attempted to reply but almost break down. I composed myself and try the pathetic tactic of reasoning and logic.

"Sweetheart, I don't understand you. You said I'm amazing. You said you never thought you'd meet someone like me. You said I'm perfect for you . . . I thought you were on board with being apart for a while. I told you that I'm getting deployed *before* we started dating, but I'll be back in six months. I'm just so confused why . . ."

She gently cut me off.

"You *are* amazing. I just think it's best for now. I've always respected you and you've been on my mind a lot lately. I'm sorry."

The burning sensation held its intensity. Was I having a heart attack? At this point, I could only pray that what's left of my heart stopped beating to end the pain.

We said our goodbyes and I hung up. I stared at the wall in front of my desk for about 30 seconds. No need to blink, my eyes had been lubricated by the tears, which slightly distorted my vision.

Dash yelled from the living room,

"Hey, with this drone I can get a camera that links to my tablet and record the video feed. Fucking awesome!"

I didn't respond and just let the pain sink in.

I've lost hope and I was in searing pain and I want the pain to stop. Since I was the source of the pain, I needed to go away. I calmly walked over to my nightstand and grabbed my Springfield XDM .40 handgun which was made in Croatia.

I slowly racked the slide to chamber a bullet so Dash won't hear me. I grabbed a small bath towel as well and returned to my chair. I fired up the Internet with the thought of playing Johnny Cash's "Hurt" for this occasion and while it opened I make the morbid preparations. I turned the gun around so my thumb was on the trigger with my fingers on the backside of the handgrip. I placed the barrel in my mouth, taking care to aim up and through my brain rather than through the back of my mouth, which might not be fatal. This is with my right hand.

With my left I placed the towel behind my head to catch the brain matter so Dash and Naval Criminal Investigative Service don't have to clean up so much and to muffle the shot. My bedroom window was open for the sea breeze and through it you can hear the ubiquitous roosters of Hawaii. They crow at all times of the day it seems and one had wandered down our street. He had been crowing periodically and so I tried to time my shot with the rooster crowing to cover the sound of the blast. I applied a slow, steady pressure to the trigger and began wincing in anticipation of the blast.

One last involuntary blink purged the tears from my eyes and they streaked freely down both cheeks. They charted a random path down the sides of my face, indifferent to my pain, obeying only the laws of gravity and fluid mechanics. This cleared my vision and I notice the Internet has loaded my home page of Yahoo news. I forgot about playing "Hurt" and looked at the page in front of me.

The top right of the page displayed in numerical order what was trending at the moment. I noticed the number one trend is about some young kids playing Led Zeppelin songs on a xylophone. The videos have apparently gone viral. I put the gun down for a second and watch the videos. They were amusing indeed.

I signed into my You Tube account and gave it a thumbs-up. I scanned an article about the president's immigration executive actions and read the comments section to gauge public reactions. Chucky Hagel had resigned as secretary of defense.

Justin Bieber sold out another concert. Some more of Bill Cosby's accusers have come forward to expose his apparently indecent past.

Iggy Azalea won an American Music Award for her latest album. Pierce Brosnan took his 17-year-old son Dylan out for lunch in Malibu. Dylan will soon be doing modeling work for Saint Laurent.

I wiped the tears off my face with my brain matter towel and then patted the rest out my eyes. I continued perusing.

A former Real World cast member from the New Orleans season was found dead of an apparent overdose in Wisconsin. Adrian Peterson is fighting the NFL's ban on him for apparent child abuse and the DEA is visiting several teams to investigate drug use.

A few tears had found their way into the drainage ducts in my eyes. I sniffled a few times and I was cleared up.

I could hear our next door neighbors telling their dogs to be quiet. They are Hawaiians and must have good stay-at-home jobs since I never see any of their five vehicles any place other than their yard during the week or weekend. I instinctively moved over to the Drudge Report.

After reading a few stories about the NFL's scandals and the riots in Ferguson, Missouri, I scrolled down to "the List" link on the website for the fallen soldiers. Looks like three guys died this month.

On 24 November SPC Joseph Riley, 27, of Grove City, Ohio and Sergeant Maj Wardell Turner, 48, of Nanticoke, Maryland, were killed by wounds sustained by an improvised explosive device in Kabul.

On 14 November, Army Sergeant First Class Michael Cathcart, 31, of Bay City, Michigan, died of wounds from small arms fire while on a dismounted patrol in Kunduz province. He was a Green Beret with a family heritage of service.

Then I found a story that heals my hurting heart. It's a story complete with dozens of pictures of protestors in Berkeley, California, who are raging in the name of Michael Brown. It's a parallel protest of the Ferguson riots after the grand jury did not indict Darren Wilson. There were over 1,000 protestors and some of them blocked Interstate 80 by forming human barricades. Traffic was backed up for hours. The text of the document isn't what gets me, it's the pictures of the protestors.

They are so well dressed and equipped. Nothing like the rag tag army of their Vietnam predecessors. A few are toting Hydroflask water bottles of all different sizes. As they march, numerous protestors film their act of righteousness with their smartphones in hand. Smartphones I helped keep cheap. Many of them are utilizing the "Hands up, don't shoot" defense that Brown used before being shot in cold blood.

I saw a few one-speed bikes, super-tight jeans, beards, and what appears to be bags of freshly ground free trade coffee among the throngs of young people. I am filled with patriotic fervor at the sight of these fellow Americans. And the final pang of emotion comes when I scroll to a picture of a human chain of protestors lying on the ground in Interstate 80 and one of them has an iPad and is holding it above his chest to film what is going on around him.

I fought for that iPad.

If it wasn't for me and my fellow Marines hooking and jabbing out in the Pacific putting on dog and pony shows to control those working masses at the Foxconn factories in China, he woulda paid $3,000 instead of $300. I finally felt like part of something.

After going back and forth between the material and immaterial, I realized it's the material that matters. I joined for the intangibles, but got the tangibles. I joined for a sense of purpose and job satisfaction, but I got a fat paycheck and benefits instead. The Marine Corps was more concerned with my happiness than my readiness.

These people are who I am fighting for. To know that the actions of myself and my comrades let these Americans film themselves while blocking a street to combat racism moves me beyond description. My sacrifice was *not* in vain.

I snapped out of my suicidal malaise instantly. I came to realize what's important. I just lost the woman I love, the one relationship besides God that gave my life meaning, I have very few friends, no family within thousands of miles, and I haven't shot a rocket in seven months.

Yes, what you don't have is great, but what you do have is immense, I told myself. I have six figures in the bank, I have no debt, I can call the DSTRESS hotline counselors at any time of the day to get help, or if they aren't available I can all my squadron's Military and Family Life Counselor, in a few days I'll get my bi-monthly direct deposit from Uncle Sam for $4,200 in my checking account, and last but not least, I helped make electronics cheap for America. And for me too. It's time to appreciate that.

I took all my electronics. Samsung flat screen, HP computer, Samsung tablet, Motorola Moto G, Tom Tom GPS, wireless printer, GoPro, Iron man watches, a few assorted memory sticks and external hard drives, and my recently purchased Kurzweil SP5-8 Keyboard and put them all into my bed.

I even headed out into the living room with the cold seriousness of a serial killer and unplugged my Cisco router. Dash complained.

"What the fuck, man, I was just about to order my drone. I need the Internet. You can fly it when it gets here. I got free shipping with Amazon Prime. It will be here in three days."

I didn't reply and made sure to lock my door when I returned to my room.

I added the router to the pile of electronics in my bed. I then organized them so I can get in as well.

I specifically positioned the keyboard in the spot where Laura used to sleep. I imagine the way I used to cuddle with her and fall asleep to the intoxicating flowery smell of her hair. But that was spiritual, the material I have now. I prop the one end of the keyboard up with a pillow.

I cuddled with the keyboard. I was happy.

Dash was knocking on my door and pleading with me to turn the router back on.

I could faintly hear the ending of *It's a Wonderful Life* out in the living room. George Bailey figures out what matters to him and has reunited with his family and all the people of the town have come by to open their wallets to dig him out of his predicament as they begin singing the joyous words of "Hark! The Herald Angels Sing."

"Peace on earth and mercy mild, God and sinners reconciled! Joyful all ye nations rise . . ."

Oh, George Bailey, I think, if he was only in my shoes here with all these great electronics, he would be even happier. Let him have his wife and family and friends if that's what does it for him. Me, I have these *things*. I drifted away into a peaceful slumber.

Notes

Chapter 1: A Dog and Pony Show: Origins

1. AH-1W Combat Aircraft Fundamentals. (March 2013). P 1-1
2. Ibid. P 1-9

Chapter 2: Joining the Marines

1. Hitler, A. (1971) Mein Kampf. Boston: Houghton Mifflin Company. P 280
2. Montgomery, D. (2004) Amid ruckus of 'Get Motivated!" convention, Jessica Lynch offers quiet inspiration, advice. [Electronic version]. *The Daily Herald*, D3. Retrieved May 17, 2015 from *http://www.heraldextra.com/lifestyles/amid-ruckus-of-get-motivated-convention-jessica-lynch-offers-quiet/article_cf41e743-a328-528b-9d15-424a07a5c606.html*

Chapter 4: The FROlough

1. Burns, R. (2013, October 5) *Pentagon: Most Furloughed Civilians Ordered Back* Retrieved from *http://news.yahoo.com/pentagon-most-furloughed-civilians-ordered-back-175149741--politics.html*
2. Beard, S. (2013). Pentagon's Chief Personnel and Readiness Officer: Diversity and Inclusion Critical to Mission Success. [Electronic Version]. *National Review.* Retrieved December 1, 2013, from *http://www.nationalreview.com/corner/362539/*

pentagons-chief-personnel-and-readiness-officer-diversity-and-inclusion-critical

Chapter 5: Why It Pays to Be a Cobra Pilot

1. Natops General Flight and Operating Instructions (1 March 2004). P 11-4.

Chapter 6: Diversity Training

1. Beard, S. (2013). Pentagon's Chief Personnel and Readiness Officer: Diversity and Inclusion Critical to Mission Success. [Electronic Version]. *National Review*. Retrieved December 1, 2013, from *http://www.nationalreview.com/corner/362539/pentagons-chief-personnel-and-readiness-officer-diversity-and-inclusion-critical*
2. Scarborough, R. (2013) Victims of sex assaults in the military are mostly men [Electronic Version]. *The Washington Times*. Retrieved February 14, 2014, from *http://www.washingtontimes.com/news/2013/may/20/victims-of-sex-assaults-in-military-are-mostly-sil/?page=all*
3. Scarborough, R. (2014) Doubts on military's sex assault stats as numbers far exceed those for the U.S. [Electronic Version]. *The Washington Times*. Retrieved May 30, 2014 *from http://www.washingtontimes.com/news/2014/apr/6/doubts-on-militarys-sex-assault-stats-as-numbers-f/?page=all*
4. Department of Defense (2012). *Department of Defense Annual Report on Sexual Assault in the Military.*
5. Bacevich, A.J. (2013). *Breach of Trust: How Americans Failed Their Soldiers and Their Country.* New York: Picador.

Chapter 7: Ambassador Caroline Kennedy Visits the MCAS Futenma Barracks

1. Brady, Terry. (2014, February 21). Ambassador Kennedy visits Okinawa. *Okinawa Marine*, p 5.
2. Ibid.
3. Caroline Kennedy In *Wikipedia*. Retrieved April 25, 2014, from *http://en.wikipedia.org/wiki/Caroline_Kennedy*

4. Brady, Terry. (2014, February 21). Ambassador Kennedy visits Okinawa. *Okinawa Marine*, p 5.
5. Sharp, Tim. (2012) V-22 Osprey: Controversial Dream Machine. Retrieved November 9, 2015 from http://www.space.com/16786-v-22-osprey.html

Chapter 8: Boarding the Boat and the Tactical Recovery of Aircraft and Personnel

1. The White Man's Burden in *Wikipedia*. Retrieved June 2, 2015 from *https://en.wikipedia.org/wiki/The_White_Man's_Burden*

Chapter 9: Brigadier General Mullen and Lieutenant Colonel Roesti Address the Ready Room

1. Ingersoll, G. (2014) One star: Survival is crisis response, not combat ops [Electronic version]. *The Marine Corps Times* Retrieved February 26, 2015, from *http://archive.marinecorpstimes.com/article/20140719/NEWS/307190049/One-star-Survival-crisis-response-not-combat-ops*
2. Ibid.
3. Ibid.
4. Are the Marines Procuring Their Way to Irrelevance as a Sea-Based Threat? (Magee & Duvall, 2014).
5. Roesti, G. (2014) *Getting inside the Growing Reach of A2/AD.* SIG Scouting Report.
6. Are the Marines Procuring Their Way to Irrelevance as a Sea-Based Threat? (Magee & Duvall, 2014).
7. Roesti, G. (2014) *Getting inside the Growing Reach of A2/AD.* SIG Scouting Report.
8. Are the Marines Procuring Their Way to Irrelevance as a Sea-Based Threat? (Magee & Duvall, 2014).

Chapter 10: Secretary Chucky Hagel Speaks

1. Presse, A.F., (2014) CHUCK HAGEL: Isolationism Won't Protect Us From the World's Troubles *Business Insider.* Retrieved February 26, 2015, from *http://www.businessinsider.com/chuck-hagel-isolationism-2014-5*

2. Ibid.
3. Stockman, D. A. (2013) *The Great Deformation: The Corruption of Capitalism in America.* New York: PublicAffairs. P 678.
4. Buchanan, P. J. (2011). *Suicide of a Superpower.* New York: St. Martin's Press. P 16.
5. Presse, A.F., (2014) CHUCK HAGEL: Isolationism Won't Protect Us From the World's Troubles *Business Insider.* Retrieved February 26, 2015, from *http://www.businessinsider.com/chuck-hagel-isolationism-2014-5*
6. Uhlmann, Chris. "An Interview with Chuck Hagel" *Australian Broadcasting Corporation* (Fall 2014).
7. Murray, C. (2014, September 6). *NATO-An Idea Whose Time Has Gone. http://original.antiwar.com/Craig_Murray/2014/09/05/nato-an-idea-whose-time-has-gone/*
8. Uhlmann, Chris. "An Interview with Chuck Hagel" *Australian Broadcasting Corporation* (Fall 2014).
9. *http://www.dtic.mil/doctrine/new_pubs/jp3_02.pdf.* P I-2, I-3
10. Cloud, D.S., (2010) Defense chief Gates orders review of Marines' role [Electronic Version]. *Los Angeles Times.* Retrieved December 1, 2014, from *http://articles.latimes.com/2010/aug/12/world/la-fg-gates-speech-20100813*
11. Francis, D. (2013, May 6). *Why Afghanistan Might Be the Marines' Last Fight. http://www.thefiscaltimes.com/Articles/2013/05/06/Why-Afghanistan-Might-Be-the-Marines-Last-Fight*
12. Ibid.
13. Brinkerhoff, N., Wallechinsky, D. (2010) Left and Right Unite Against Government Waste. Retrieved December 1, 2014, from *http://www.allgov.com/news/where-is-the-money-going/left-and-right-unite-against-government-waste?news=841701.*
14. Miller, K., Capaccio, A., Ivory, D. (2013, February 22). Flawed F-35 Too Big to Kill as Lockheed Hooks 45 States. Retrieved April 10, 2015 from *http://www.bloomberg.com/news/articles/2013-02-22/flawed-f-35-fighter-too-big-to-kill-as-lockheed-hooks-45-states*

15. Francis, D. (2013, May 6). *Why Afghanistan Might Be the Marines' Last Fight.* http://www.thefiscaltimes.com/Articles/2013/05/06/Why-Afghanistan-Might-Be-the-Marines-Last-Fight
16. *http://www.dtic.mil/doctrine/new_pubs/jp3_02.pdf* P I-3
17. *http://www.army-technology.com/projects/efv/*
18. Eckstein, M. (2015, March 11). Marines May Merge ACV Requirements as Industry Chases Higher Requirements. Retrieved August 27, 2015 from http://news.usni.org/2015/03/11/marines-may-merge-acv-increments-as-industry-chases-higher-requirements
19. Expeditionary Force 21 (2014) Retrieved June 2, 2015 from *http://www.mccdc.marines.mil/Portals/172/Docs/MCCDC/EF21/EF21_USMC_Capstone_Concept.pdf*
20. Ibid.
21. *http://www.ndia.org/Advocacy/LegislativeandFederalIssues Update/Documents/%20Corps%202013%20Budget%20 Update.pdf.* Retrieved August 21, 2015.
22. Jean, Grace V. (2008) Marines Question the Utility of Their New Amphibious Warship. Retrieved August 21, 2015 from *http://www.nationaldefensemagazine.org/archive/2008/September/Pages/MarinesQuestiontheUtilityof.aspx.*
23. Ibid.
24. Ibid.
25. Ibid.
26. NATOPS Flight Manual Navy Model MV-22B Tiltrotor. 15 October 2013. P 1-15.
27. NATOPS Flight Manual Navy Model CH-46E Helicopter. 1 December 2009. P 1-3.
28. *http://ingalls.huntingtoningalls.com/products/lha/class.* Retrieved 21 August, 2015.
29. Francis, D. (2013, May 6). *Why Afghanistan Might Be the Marines' Last Fight.* http://www.thefiscaltimes.com/Articles/2013/05/06/Why-Afghanistan-Might-Be-the-Marines-Last-Fight.
30. Hennigan, W.J. (2014) Pentagon unveils plan for military's response to climate change[Electronic Version]. *Los Angeles Times.* Retrieved October 13, 2014, from *http://www.*

latimes.com/world/mexico-americas/la-fg-hagel-climate-change-20141013-story.html
31. Ibid.
32. Ibid.
33. Ibid.

Chapter 11: Secretary of State Kerry Speaks

1. *http://www.defense.gov/about/*
2. Freedburg, Sydney J. Jr. (2012) Navy's Newest, LHA-6, A Dead End For Amphibious Ships? Retrieved August 21, 2015 from http://breakingdefense.com/2012/10/navys-newest-lha-6-a-dead-end-for-amphibious-ships/
3. Page, J. (2014, October 26). Deep Threat. *Wall Street Journal,* pp. C1, C2.
4. Dent, H.S. (2014). *The Demographic Cliff.* New York: Penguin Group. P 54, 67.
5. Rickards, J. (2014). *The Death of Money.* New York: Penguin Group. P 96.
6. Quinn, J. (2014, November 20) *No One Told You When to Run, You Missed the Starting Gun.* [The Burning Platform Blog] Retrieved from *http://www.theburningplatform.com/2014/11/20/no-one-told-you-when-to-run-you-missed-the-starting-gun/*
7. Meyer, A. (2014, December 10). *Food Stamp Beneficiaries Exceed 46,000,000 for 37 Straight Months.* http://www.cnsnews.com/news/article/ali-meyer/food-stamp-beneficiaries-exceed-46000000-37-straight-months
8. Rickards, J. (2014). *The Death of Money.* New York: Penguin Group. P 75-76, 155-156.
9. Griffin, G. Edward. (2010). *The Creature from Jekyll Island.* Westlake Village: American Media. P 94.
10. Waldron, Greg. (2013). South Korea to Buy 36 AH-64E Apaches. Retrieved 21 August, 2015 from http://www.flightglobal.com/news/articles/south-korea-to-buy-36-ah-64e-apaches-384810/.

Chapter 12: Hammer Speech

1. Mizokami, Kyle. (2015) It's Time for the U.S. Military to Leave South Korea [Electronic version]. *The Week* Retrieved August 13, 2015, from *http://theweek.com/articles/570764/time-military-leave-south-korea*.
2. *http://www.globalfirepower.com/countries-listing.asp* Retrieved August 23, 2015.
3. *http://www.globalfirepower.com/country-military-strength-detail.asp?country_id=north-korea* and *http://www.globalfirepower.com/country-military-strength-detail.asp?country_id=austria* Retrieved August 23, 2015.
4. Retrieved 27 August, 2015 from http://www.3rdmeb.marines.mil/Leaders/CommandingGeneral.aspx

Chapter 16: LCD Sound System and a Wardroom Poem

1. Burns, R. (2014, April 6). A Poem. *Almanac 2014: Daily News for the Sailors and Marines of the USS Bonhomme Richard (LHD 6) Volume 3, Issue 47.* Retrieved April 6, 2014.

Chapter 17: The 31st MEU's Response to a Korean Ferry Sinking

1. *http://knoema.com/nwnfkne/world-gdp-ranking-2015-data-and-charts*

Chapter 19: The Sickness of Mankind or Counter 23 Measures

1. Chivers, C.J. (2011). *The Gun.* New York: Simon and Schuster Inc.
2. Miller, D. (2002). *The Great Book of Tanks.* London: Salamander Books Ltd P 6.
3. Ibid. P. 502.
4. Ibid. P. 40.
5. Ibid. P. 45.
6. Ibid. P. 49-51.
7. Ibid. P. 27.
8. Ibid. P. 65.
9. Ibid. P. 74-75.
10. Ibid. P. 88-90.
11. Ibid. P. 92-93.

12. Ibid. P. 107.
13. Ibid. P. 503.
14. Ibid. P. 168-169, 144-145.
15. Ibid. P. 170.
16. Ibid. P. 131.
17. Ibid. P. 234.
18. Ibid. P. 277.
19. Ibid. P. 291 and 300-301.
20. Ibid. P. 317.
21. Jason Rahman (February 2008). The 17-Pounder. Avalanche Press. Retrieved October 23, 2010.
22. Miller, D. (2002). *The Great Book of Tanks*. London: Salamander Books Ltd P 15.
23. Shaped Charge in *Wikipedia*. Retrieved October 30 2014 from *http://en.wikipedia.org/wiki/Shaped_charge*
24. AH-1W Naval Aviation Technical Information Product (NATIP) 13 August 2014. P 1-56.
25. Ibid. P 1-57.
26. Shaped Charge in *Wikipedia*. Retrieved October 30 2014 from *http://en.wikipedia.org/wiki/Shaped_charge*
27. *https://str.llnl.gov/str/Baum.html*
28. Scales, R. (31 May 2010). Edward Uhl. *Time*.
29. Bazooka in *Wikipedia*. Retrieved 30 October 2014 from http://en.wikipedia.org/wiki/Bazooka.
30. Ibid.
31. "It makes the steel flow like mud." *Popular Science*. Retrieved 22 November 2014.
32. *http://www.worldwar2aces.com/panzerfaust.htm*
33. RPG-7 in *Wikipedia*. Retrieved October 30 2014 from *http://en.wikipedia.org/wiki/RP-7*.
34. RP-32 in *Wikipedia*. Retrieved October 30 2014 from *http://en.wikipedia.org/wiki/RP-32*.
35. Foss, C. (1995) *Modern Tanks*. New York: Harper Collins P 13.
36. Ibid. P 4-8.
37. RPG-7 in *Wikipedia*. Retrieved October 30 2014 from *http://en.wikipedia.org/wiki/RP-7*.

38. High-explosive anti-tank warhead in *Wikipedia*. Retrieved October 30 2014 from *https://en.wikipedia.org/wiki/High-explosive_anti-tank_warhead*
39. Meyer, T. J. (1998, May-June). Active Protective Systems: Impregnable Armor or Simply Enhanced Survivability?. *Armor.* P 7.
40. Small Arms Survey. (2011). *Man Portable Air Defense Systems*. Geneva: Graduate Institute of International and Development Studies.

Chapter 20: The Marine Net Violence Prevention Program Awareness Module and Coming Clean

1. Nick Allen, "Fort Hood Gunman Had Told U.S. Military Colleagues That Infidels Should Have Their Throats Cut," *Telegraph*, Nov. 8, 2009.

Chapter 22: Why We Fight or the Development of Heathenry

1. The White Man's Burden in *Wikipedia*. Retrieved June 2, 2015 from *https://en.wikipedia.org/wiki/The_White_Man%27s_Burden*

CPSIA information can be obtained
at www.ICGtesting.com
Printed in the USA
FFOW02n1321100718
47395146-50515FF